Republican Character

Republican Character

From Nixon to Reagan

Donald T. Critchlow

PENN

University of Pennsylvania Press
Philadelphia

A volume in the Haney Foundation Series, established in
1961 with the generous support of Dr. John Louis Haney.

Published by
University of Pennsylvania Press
Philadelphia, Pennsylvania 19104-4112
www.upenn.edu/pennpress

Printed in the United States of America on acid-free paper
10 9 8 7 6 5 4 3 2 1

Library of Congress Cataloging-in-Publication Data
Names: Critchlow, Donald T., author.
Title: Republican character : from Nixon to Reagan / Donald
    T. Critchlow.
Other titles: Haney Foundation series.
Description: 1st ed. | Philadelphia : University of
    Pennsylvania Press, [2018] | Series: Haney Foundation
    series | Includes bibliographical references and index.
Identifiers: LCCN 2017024329 | ISBN 978-0-8122-4977-4
    (hardcover : alk. paper)
Subjects: LCSH: Republican Party (U.S.: 1854–) |
    Presidential candidates—United States—Psychological
    aspects. | United States—Politics and government—20th
    century.
Classification: LCC JK2356 .C735 2018 | DDC
    973.920092/2—dc23
LC record available at https://lccn.loc.gov/2017024329

To Patricia E. Powers

Contents

Introduction. Presidential Character, Politics, and Power   1

1. Richard Nixon: The Disillusioned Idealist   13

2. Nelson Rockefeller: Ambition and Appetite   38

3. Idealism Betrayed, Opportunity Denied: Nixon and Rockefeller Compared   62

4. Barry Goldwater: Undisciplined Individualist   79

5. Ronald Reagan: Principled Pragmatist   104

6. Uneasy Allies: Goldwater and Reagan Compared   131

Epilogue. Voters and Leaders in Disarray   148

Notes   163

Index   177

Acknowledgments   181

Introduction
Presidential Character, Politics, and Power

While American politics in the early twenty-first century has become increasingly ideological for many voters, this book looks back at the careers of four leading Republican presidential contenders—Richard Nixon, Nelson Rockefeller, Barry Goldwater, and Ronald Reagan—to show that the role of political calculation, character, and temperament mattered just as much as ideology in practice. Their story revises what has become a standard narrative that emphasizes the importance of ideology over all else in politics. Each of the contenders staked out positions as ideological standard bearers that appealed to their followers. A closer look at them, however, reveals that each also showed varying degrees of ideological malleability. In the practice of politics, these rivals formed uneasy alliances among themselves, motivated by political gain and not ideological consistency. Moreover, Nixon, Rockefeller, and Goldwater possessed temperamental flaws, albeit of different kinds, that proved destructive to fulfilling their ambitions, while Ronald Reagan revealed a temperament that allowed him to gain his party's nomination, win the election, and govern successfully. Fortune, of course, played a critical factor in the careers of these men, but character and temperament proved equally decisive in their ability to convince voters they stood for principle and had the leadership qualities necessary to govern in a democratic system premised on legislative compromise. If actual politics is about power, American political history should be more than a delineation of ideology and should incorporate a deeper exploration of the interplay between principle and practice in political life.

Underlying this tension between ideological principle and the practice of politics rests a more important understanding of what makes for successful political campaigns and governance in a democracy. Discerning the balance between ideological principle and pragmatic politics, especially in governance, presents a problem for both Republicans and Democrats, one that can be traced throughout American political history. This problem was particularly acute for Republicans in the postwar years because their party was often out of power, intensely divided by ideological factions, shaped regionally, and driven by a growing and conscious right wing. As a minority party, Republicans fought among themselves about how best to win the White House and become a majority party in the electorate.

It would be naïve—and wholly incorrect—to argue that ideology plays no role in Republican politics; rather, ideological division runs throughout the party's presidential politics. This ideological divide was evident when New York governor Thomas Dewey defeated Robert Taft for the party's nomination in 1948, and then when Taft was once again defeated for the nomination by Dwight D. Eisenhower in 1952.[1] Eisenhower's election to the presidency suppressed, to a large degree, conservative opposition within the party. Nixon's foregone nomination in 1960 contained an outright factional war within the party, although when Nixon accommodated Nelson Rockefeller's demands for strong civil rights and national defense planks, conservatives were bothered to the point of breaking with Nixon. A feeble attempt to nominate Barry Goldwater at the convention in 1960 was only quelled when Goldwater declined the nomination and told convention delegates that a unified party was needed to win the election for Richard Nixon. Full-scale war within the party erupted in 1964, symbolized in the contest between Nelson Rockefeller and Barry Goldwater for the party's presidential nomination. Goldwater's loss in a landslide vote to Lyndon Johnson only exacerbated party divisions. Richard Nixon stepped back onto the presidential stage in 1968, winning the GOP nomination by appealing to conservatives as one of their own, and convincing moderate and liberal Republicans that he was not a right-wing nut job.

Once in office, Nixon distanced himself from the right in his party. His resignation from office in the midst of the Watergate scandal again opened up ideological fissures within the party. Former California governor Ronald Reagan, who had replaced Goldwater as the hero of the grassroots right, stepped forward to challenge incumbent Republican president Gerald Ford for the 1976 nomination. Reagan failed to oust Ford, but in 1980 Reagan won the nomination, running as an avowed conservative. Reagan's election to the White House marked a triumph for conservatives within the party, and after he left office, candidates running for the party's nomination had to declare themselves true to a set conservative agenda, at least until New York businessman Donald Trump won the nomination and the White House in 2016, running on a populist message.

While ideological argument was certainly apparent in presidential politics from Nixon through Reagan—and remains so today with the Republican Party—the reality of politics led each of the major contenders for the GOP presidential nomination down strange paths often inconsistent and even contradictory to ideological proclamation. The four major rivals for the presidency in the post-Eisenhower years—Nixon, Rockefeller, Goldwater, and Reagan—each found themselves confronted by the constraints of ideology and the necessity of winning election, which meant weighing principle and opportunity, ideological dogma and political practice, purity and pragmatism. Any understanding of Republican presidential politics in these years must be understood as more than just an ideological battle.

The political maneuverings of Nixon, Rockefeller, Goldwater, and Reagan to win the White House show that the struggle to become president is about, above all things, politics. Politics is about winning elections, not simply ideological consistency. As these four rivals sought the White House, they confronted the political shoals of opportunism and principle. Striking the right balance between pragmatism and ideals reveals the character and temperament of each of these presidential contenders. The importance of character and temperament should never be underestimated in judging any candidate for office, but is essential to a president in office. The fundamental character of the president determines his or her ability to govern successfully.

Students of politics, scholars, and media pundits alike can take pleasure in bringing a former or current presidential contender or former president down to size. Revelations of personal scandal and hypocrisy make for good reading, but the temperament and character of a person seeking power have practical consequences, which extend beyond superficial moral judgment. Prudent temperament and virtuous character, as this book shows, are essential ingredients for political success. Voters can ignore or misjudge the character or temperament of a presidential candidate, but ultimately the personal qualities of a politician determine his or her success or failure as a leader. Judgment as to character and temperament of a candidate will differ among the voters. Final determination about these qualities comes in a president's ability to govern and fulfill campaign promises. In this way, temperament and character matter in politics. In the highly polarized politics of the twenty-first century, a significant number of American voters judge candidates largely by their ideological stances on issues. Less attention appears to be given to character and temperament, and, indeed, such qualities will be overlooked if a candidate passes the ideological litmus test. This study posits that moral character and temperament are as important for success as political ideology. The two are intertwined and should not be separated.

Put directly, politics is about power, and, given that fact, temperament and moral character assume importance in at least two ways. First, politicians seeking office should show the temperament and moral qualities required to win office and to govern once in office, especially for the presidency. Second, voters should be concerned about the temperament, character, and principle of those elected to positions of power. Each of the men examined in this book revealed unique moral traits that proved critical to their successes and failures. Character in politics, as the ancient historian Plutarch explored in his study of Greek and Roman leaders, determines the fate of leaders and the nation.

Much of the study of post–World War II American politics has tended to focus generally on ideological alignment and realignment. This focus distorts the actuality of political practice and the chronology of American postwar politics. This is especially the case of studies looking at the conservative ascendancy during the postwar period. The focus on the ideological foundations and rise of postwar conservatism, however, often fails to see the compromises, opportunism, betrayals, and strange alliances made by conservative politicians in the postwar years that belie ideological principle. The result has been a monochromatic view of Republican politics seen as one only of ideological struggle between Northeastern liberals such as Nelson Rockefeller and Western conservatives such as Barry Goldwater and Ronald Reagan. The standard account places Richard Nixon as an opportunist, positioned between liberal Rockefeller on one end and ideological conservatives Goldwater and Reagan at the other end. The many biographies and studies of these men often gloss over their ideological flexibility, especially in the cases of Goldwater and Reagan, but a closer reading of their biographies and archival material paints a far different story.

The actual narrative of Republican postwar politics, especially in presidential campaign politics, reveals the formation of strange alignments not easily explained by simple ideological agreement. There were many twists and turns on the road to victory. The conservative ascendancy in the Republican

Party was neither direct nor linear. How can one explain that Richard Nixon offered Nelson Rockefeller a slot on the 1960 ticket as vice president and did so again in 1968? (Nixon's Democratic opponent, Hubert Humphrey, also offered Rockefeller a place on his ticket.) Can the so-called Compact of Fifth Avenue, in which Nixon accepted Rockefeller's revisions to the 1960 Republican platform, be dismissed simply as opportunism on the part of both Rockefeller and Nixon? How does a student of American postwar conservatism explain Goldwater's attempt to shift to the moderate center in his 1964 general election campaign after winning the ticket espousing strict conservative principles in the primaries? Furthermore, how is a historian to explain Goldwater's behind-the-scenes alliance with Nixon to prevent Reagan from winning the nomination in 1968? Or what should we make ideologically of Goldwater's endorsement of Gerald Ford in 1976 against the Reagan primary challenge? For that matter, what is one to make of Reagan's selection of George H. W. Bush as his running mate, or his subsequent selection of Bush's campaign manager James Baker as his chief of staff once Reagan won the 1980 election?

This is not to maintain that politics is only about the seeking of power and opportunistic gain. When Rockefeller decided to push civil rights and defense planks at the 1960 Republican convention, he realized, as warned by his advisers, that he was hurting his future presidential chances. He believed that these issues were important for the nation. Rockefeller's persistent attacks on Goldwater as an extremist after it was clear that Rockefeller had lost the party's nomination in 1964 alienated both conservative and regular Republicans at the time and four years later. Rockefeller came across as a spoiled rich man used to getting his way and as a politician less interested in party unity than in his own advancement. In his own eyes, Rockefeller saw himself as the conscience of the party. The scale weighing opportunism and principle, self-advancement and higher goals, and personal gain and collective advancement presents a delicate balance not easily discerned if viewed through the overly simple lens of ideology.

An older tradition within the study of political history understood that politics was about the acquiring and the exercising of power. Indeed, the great student of English politics Lewis Namier concluded more than fifty years ago that "considerations of principle or even of policy had only limited relevance" in the study of politics.[2] Within the Namierite perspective, professed principles provide only a facade for the otherwise naked desire for power. Namier's focus on power led him and his students to downplay, even deride, the rhetoric of principle as only an expression of sheer opportunism. Such a perspective, however, does not explain why politicians decide to campaign on one set of issues and not another, or employ a certain rhetoric and not another. Namier assumes that a politician's profession of principle is only rhetoric intended to disguise opportunism and the naked seeking of power. He dismissed the importance of principle in politics but articulated that principles, however rhetorical, can express actual political motives. Moreover, stated principles can reflect genuine beliefs that motivate a politician, while at the same time expressing both self-interest and political opportunism. In this way, professions of principle, self-interest, and opportunism are not exclusive. Principle can motivate a politician, while at the same time such a politician seizes upon an issue calculated to win power.

The founders of the American republic understood the importance of character in politics. They drew much from reading Plutarch and ancient Greek and Roman history. Well versed in eighteenth-century European political thought, the founders saw judicious temperament and moral character as necessary restraints on the misuse of power. They were imbued with a fear of unrestrained power in a tyranny, aristocracy, or democracy. Balanced governmental structure circumscribed the exercise of unrestrained power, but liberty rested ultimately on virtuous leaders and vigilant citizens mindful of their liberties. The founders sought to construct a governmental system that restrained power by dividing it among three branches of government—the presidency, Congress, and the courts. A careful balance was also constructed between a centralized federal government and the state governments. Well-ordered liberty impeded powerful interests or tyrants from exercising power at will. Just as power had been shown to corrupt leaders, so could power corrupt the *demos*. Unrestrained power of the people led, as history had shown, inevitably to tyranny. The passions of the *demos* gave way ultimately to disorder, which allowed demagogues and tyrants to gain power by playing on the emotions of the citizens.

Typical of enlightened thinkers of the day, the founders spoke often about the necessity of virtuous leadership for the preservation and growth of a republic. Virtue was a personal quality that meant self-restraint and putting the common good ahead of self-interest or self-aggrandizement. It was a commitment to courage, fairness, and the rule of law. The concept of virtue in European continental and English political thought was neither precise in definition nor uniform in practice. The insistence, however, that virtue in politics was necessary to a republican order conveyed an important insight into the rise and fall of earlier republics. Their reading of the ancients and philosophers such as Montesquieu instructed them on the importance of even temperament and stoic disposition for leaders in the new American Republic. Temperament and character were imparted to the youth through moral education. The ancient Stoic philosophers articulated this lesson. Writing in late fifth-century Athens, Antiphon in the "Art of Consolation" observed, "If a noble disposition be planted in a young mind, it will engender a flower that will endure to the end, and that no rain will destroy, nor will it be withered by drought."[3] The Greek and Roman concept of virtue was tied closely with courage, the ultimate virtue in a free man. In the classical mind, *virtus* (virtue) was integral to *libertas* (liberty) and *fides* (good faith). A moral citizen blended the proud ideal of character and conduct, which allowed restraint in temper and speech, independence of habit, and honesty and loyalty. Privilege, whether as a leader or a citizen, imposed duties to family, civil society, and the state. Mutual obligation was required for clients and dependents. The constitutional founders of the new American republic knew, however, that the rhetoric of *libertas* in ancient Athens and Rome had often been invoked in defense of the existing order by individuals and classes to maintain wealth and power.[4] American revolutionaries such as Thomas Jefferson rejected rule by a social aristocracy and spoke in favor of leadership derived from men of virtue, a natural aristocracy. A meaningful liberty within the new republic rested on popular sovereignty and representative government led by a natural aristocracy.

The founders of the American republic drew heavily on their reading of seventeenth- and eighteenth-century philosophers John Locke and Montesquieu for insights into the importance of virtue. Locke, in his *Essay Concerning Human Understanding*, observed that virtue and public happiness were integral. In espousing a doctrine of natural rights, he believed that virtue was essential to the preservation of a good society. He associated virtue closely with the upholding of rights and the rule of just law. He declared, "For God having, by an inseparable connection joined virtue and public happiness together and made the practice therefore necessary to the preservation of society, and visibly beneficial to all which who the virtuous man has to do; It is no wonder that everyone should not only allow, but recommend and magnify those rules to others . . . , which, if once trampled on and profaned, he himself cannot be safe nor secure."[5] Writing forty years later, Montesquieu insisted that imposition of virtue within the social order was even more important in a republic than within a monarchy.[6]

George Washington, Thomas Jefferson, James Madison, and Alexander Hamilton, whatever their later political differences, agreed that the rule of disinterest was a necessary quality to leadership. Disinterest meant independence from sordid, local faction and a capability for governing for the greater good. Theirs was a noble conceit that they represented what was worthy and virtuous in government. Later accused of entitled privilege by critics for their allowance of slavery and the exclusion of women and Native Americans from suffrage, these founders of the republic believed the dependence of a slave, a wife, and an unpropertied urban worker or a Native American eschewed disinterest and emboldened parochial passion. Whatever their contradictions in practice and their foibles as men, the founders held profound insights into human nature, the corrupting nature of unrestrained power, and the fragility of republics.

Luxury, greed, and ambition that were intrinsic to a commercial society threatened the subversion of liberty itself. As students of English history, the American founders witnessed such corruption by stock-market manipulators—so-called jobbers—in the wild speculation that had led to a financial collapse in the 1720s and the use of patronage for greedy clients by Robert Walpole, de facto prime minister, in this same period. British political hacks sent to the American colonies to govern too often revealed the greed and corruption in the motherland. Adam Smith and David Hume, leading Scottish philosophers, engaged in a lively debate over the subversive effects of luxury and greed within a commercial society.[7] This anxiety about the subversive effects of a commercial society on public virtue was a central theme in Alexis de Tocqueville's second volume of *Democracy in America* (1840) in which he warned of a "soft despotism" of centralized government replacing a liberty-minded republican citizenry given to greed and disappointment in the competitive marketplace.[8]

Satirized by eighteenth-century novelists and playwrights, monstrously distorted by the French revolutionaries, and relegated often to mere rhetoric by American politicians in antebellum America, former presidents John Adams and Thomas Jefferson continued to obsess over the importance of virtue in preserving republican values. Both men, now retired and renewing a friendship, believed that their revolutionary generation had done more than others in human history to foster the importance of virtue in government. Writing in late 1815, Adams reassured Jefferson that "the eighteenth century, notwithstanding all its errors and vices, has been, of all that are past, the most honorable to human nature. Knowledge and virtues were increased and diffused, arts, sciences useful to men, ameliorating their condition, were improved more than in any former equal period."[9] Jefferson remained confident in the age of expanded suffrage, growing egalitarianism in politics, and partisan discord that virtuous leaders—the natural aristocrats and virtuous citizenry—would prevail in a republic of small property holders. Imbued with a Calvinist outlook, Adams questioned Jefferson's faith in the "natural aristocrat" and improvements in human nature. He told Jefferson, "Inequalities of mind and body are so established by God Almighty in his constitution of human nature, that no art or policy can ever plane down to level." Neither man believed in human perfectibility, but Jefferson remained more optimistic about the possibilities of human improvement, virtuous leadership, and a civic-minded electorate.

In the rancor of partisan politics that ensued following the founding of the nation, language of virtue and honor was increasingly lost or made meaningless in campaign rhetoric. Late nineteenth-century reformers lamented the decline of virtue among both politicians and voters. Henry Adams, the great-grandson of John Adams, captured this sentiment of decline and corruption in American politics in his novel *Democracy* (1880). Twenty-one years later, Woodrow Wilson, a political scientist and historian at Princeton University who was soon to become governor of New Jersey and later president of the United States, echoed this dismay in mass democracy and politicians when he told readers of the *Atlantic Monthly,* "It is no longer possible to mistake the reaction against democracy." He observed, "The nineteenth century was above all others a century of democracy, and yet the world is no more convinced of the benefits of democracy as a form of government at its end than it was at the beginning."[10] Adams and Wilson spoke for a class of "better men" not corrupted by a self-interested electorate manipulated by machine politicians.

Adams and Wilson were too dismissive of voters' concerns with judging temperament and character in their leaders, especially in presidential elections. After all, voters placed Wilson, the reform-minded moralist, in the White House in 1912. While neither uniform nor consistent in their concerns with temperament or moral character in whom they elected, voters continued to judge presidential candidates and presidents on character and temperament. In 1932, Americans voted their pocketbooks, albeit many empty ones, in picking Franklin Roosevelt. He was judged to be temperamentally suited to the presidency. Character and temperament proved to be important in electing Dwight D. Eisenhower in 1952 and 1956, and other candidates were judged accordingly. Voters often misjudged character and temperament in selecting their presidents. Such was the case with Richard Nixon in 1968, but when his character was revealed in the Watergate scandals, voters turned on Nixon. In the postwar years, voters judged Rockefeller and Goldwater as not temperamentally suited for the presidency. In the 1980 presidential election, Reagan convinced the electorate that he was temperamentally suited for the presidency through debates with incumbent president Jimmy Carter.

This book presents a case study of the importance of temperament and character in presidential politics through the intertwined political careers of four Republican politicians. There are lessons to be learned today from these men of presidential ambition. Character in leadership and the balance between political aspiration and principle matter. Moreover, compromise in politics, set within a context of informed principle, is necessary to the functioning of a healthy democracy. This book maintains that *principled pragmatism*, the ability to compromise while maintaining core principles, is essential to political success. Readers will disagree over what core principles should be held; this study, however, should lead them to realize that when every issue is seen as a matter of principle, democracy does not function. The character and quality of leaders to remain steadfast in their principles, yet willing to compromise to achieve higher goals, remains essential to a functioning democratic polity.

The founders of the American republic—George Washington, James Madison, Thomas Jefferson, Alexander Hamilton, John Adams, and others—understood that good politics should be based on principled compromise, and they placed considerable weight on sound character and moderate temperament in judging the qualities of an effective leader. Adams, Jefferson, Madison, and other leaders of the new nation gave much thought to the meaning of virtue, which incorporated these qualities of judicious temperament and moral character, in politics.[11] They were students of ancient history and found in *Plutarch's Lives* historical examples of what they should look for in discerning these qualities in leaders.

Plutarch was one of the most-studied authors of the eighteenth century. He offered instruction on the fatal flaws and virtues of character that determined the fate of leaders by contrasting the parallel lives of notable Greeks and Romans. He did so by examining in each chapter the life of one Greek leader, followed in the next chapter with the life of a notable Roman; then the two men were contrasted. Plutarch's format might strike the modern reader given to continuous narrative as odd. The value of Plutarch rests in individual biography and his analytical comparison of his characters. Plutarch emphasized the importance of courage, fortitude, adherence to principle, prudence, patriotism, and disinterest in the men he found admirable. In order to capture the qualities of essential for good leadership, this book examines the personal and political biographies of each of the four presidential rivals, Nixon, Rockefeller, Goldwater, and Reagan. Unlike Plutarch, who contrasted a Greek with a Roman, this book examines the biographies of each of the men, drawing comparisons between them, to reveal their strengths and weakness as aspirants to the highest office in the United States. The lives and political careers of each man were so intertwined that their biographies are discussed in separate chapters woven together chronologically to cover the flow of presidential politics over the course of their lifetime. Absent in this short volume is pretense of great literature as found in Plutarch, but it aspires to illustrate the didactic lessons that biography offers.

The political careers of these four men reveal the interplay between ideology and principle, principle and pragmatism, foible and astute calculation in American postwar Republican politics. This relationship between pragmatism and principle suggests a larger question about presidential leadership and character of the candidates. Ultimately, decisions about politics, the balancing of principle and pragmatism, reveal the character—and political astuteness—of those aspiring to office.

This story, then, is about the gritty side of politics, but it is also about presidential leadership and character. As such, it is an exploration into the importance of character, as much informed by the aspiration to power as by the way fatal flaws and strengths of individuals influence final outcomes. In this way, the book is influenced by modern historians who understand party factionalism as well by ancient historians such as Plutarch who recognized that individual character and personality were as determinate in history as external factors for political success or failure. At a time of gridlock and ideological polarization, the importance of character and temperament in leaders, the need for principled pragmatism, and an understanding of governance remain of critical importance to the future of American democracy.

1 | Richard Nixon
The Disillusioned Idealist

Nixon's political rise proved as meteoric as Andrew Jackson's 150 years earlier, but Nixon's fall and disgrace were unequaled in American political history. He was a congressman at the age of thirty-three, senator at thirty-seven, two-term vice president at forty-three, and president at fifty-six; he experienced ignominy at sixty-one. He entered politics with the optimism of many who came of age during World War II, believing that the world could be made better. He represented the idealism of a young generation that had survived the trauma of the Depression and a global war that ended with the use of nuclear weapons, the most devastating technology ever developed by humankind. The Nixon who left the White House twenty-five years later revealed little idealism and much cynicism.

Nixon had changed from an idealistic and optimistic young man into a secretive, brooding politician by the time he entered the White House in 1969. The idealism of his youth and the optimism of an up-and-coming attorney and politician in Southern California gave way to a sense of distrust and betrayal. Nixon's idealism was tested—and later found wanting—in the blood-sport world of American domestic politics and Machiavellian international politics. His first election victories, running for Congress in 1946 and the U.S. Senate in 1950, made him into a lifelong enemy of the left. The rough-and-tumble of politics increasingly jaded Nixon's idealism. His memoir, *RN*, one of the most candid presidential memoirs next to Ulysses S. Grant's autobiography, reveals his profound sense of disappointment in his political friends not rallying to his defense when he was nearly pushed off the Republican ticket in 1952 under charges of having a "secret fund." Nixon survived with the famous "Checkers" speech. Further disappointment came when his boss, Dwight Eisenhower, suggested that he take a cabinet position instead of joining the GOP presidential ticket in 1956. Continued press attacks on him, especially *Washington Star* political cartoonist Pat Oliphant's scathing caricatures of the "diabolical Nixon" rankled him. The ostracizing of his children at school by classmates and their parents hurt both him and his wife, Pat. He thought seriously about leaving politics.

Much has been made by scholars and biographers who have traced Nixon's secretiveness, hypersensitivity to critics, and later imperial presidency to his boyhood. Nixon's flawed personality, we have been told, can be found in a dominating mother, a distant father, and status anxiety induced by growing up in a lower-middle-class family. This kind of psychologizing presumes that a person at fifty can be explained fully by looking at a boy of twelve. Childhood plays a role in shaping character and leadership abilities, but later life experiences arguably play a greater one.

Left out of this portrait, though, is the young Nixon who grew up in a tight-knit family in the Quaker-settled small town of Whittier, California. The young Nixon was bookish, highly intelligent, and well liked by his classmates through grammar school, high school, and college. What he lacked in close friends, Nixon made up for by his intelligence, energy, and spirit. He gained admission to Duke University Law School, one of the most innovative law schools in the country. He failed to get an offer from a Wall Street law firm, but he returned to Whittier a local hero and developed a successful law practice there. He married a local beauty, and in the first years of their marriage, they were wildly in love. During his time as a naval officer in the South Pacific, his men liked and respected him.

As a transport officer in the South Pacific, Nixon saw the horrors of war, coming under enemy bombardment and witnessing navy pilots who had been in crashes, one so burned he was only recognized by the wedding ring on his charred fingers. Nixon left the navy committed to creating a stable international order that could prevent the destructive global wars that had characterized the early twentieth century.

Although he had rejected the pacifism of Quakerism, Nixon drew from his war experience the need for international order to ensure peace. American leadership and international involvement were necessary to this new global world order. Nixon remained, above all else and whatever his contradictions, an internationalist. He entered politics an idealist about the future of America, its place in the world, and the role his party, the Republican Party, could play in shaping this new world.

Essential to understanding Richard Nixon was his religious background as a Quaker and evangelical Christian. He grew up in a Quaker family in a town dominated by members of this small Christian sect. His faith imbued in young Nixon a sense of public service and the notion the world could be made a better place. His mother conversed in what was called "plain speak" in which "thee" and "thou" were used. The death of his older brother brought Richard Nixon and his father to evangelical Christianity, which they combined with their Quaker faith. Although in college, Nixon rejected the literal interpretation of the Bible, he continued to attend Quaker services, a practice he maintained at Duke. As a Quaker at Duke, Nixon spoke out against racial segregation and shared with his fellow classmates stories of family dinners where they were often joined by African Americans. It is difficult to see in this young Richard Nixon the cynical, "Tricky Dick" persona ascribed to him by later political opponents, Democrats and Republicans alike. The rough-and-tumble of American politics changed Richard Nixon, revealing a character flaw that deepened over time. A more tough-minded, thick-skinned, and less sensitive man—a John F. Kennedy or Lyndon Baines Johnson—might have dismissed personal attacks and the disloyalty of political allies. Nixon did not, and in the end, history judged him lacking the character and temperament for a successful presidency.

A Boyhood in a Quaker Town

Central to Nixon's childhood was his family's devotion to the Quaker faith.[1] Nixon told his later sympathetic biographers, Earl Mazo and Jonathan Aiken, that many had overlooked the importance that the Quaker religion had played in his childhood. The Quaker branch the Nixons belonged to was especially puritanical and evangelical. The faith of the Nixon family, therefore, was not that of the quiet Quaker of lore but closer to the evangelical Protestantism of modern America.[2] Altar calls for sinners to confess and repent their sins replaced the quietism of the traditional Quakerism of its English founder George Fox and his greatest convert, William Penn, the founder of Pennsylvania.

Whittier, California, where the Nixon family moved in 1920 when Richard was nine years old, was settled by Quakers. Most of the residents and all the city leaders were Quaker, and Quakerism was the culture of the town.[3] Located a short distance southeast of Los Angeles, Whittier began as a Spanish land grant before it was sold to a group of Quaker investors with the intent of making it a religious settlement. Named after Quaker poet John Greenleaf Whittier, the small town was more a religious village than a city.

Nixon's mother, Hannah, was a student at the local Whittier College when she met Frank Nixon, a poorly educated trolley worker. He had moved to California from Ohio where he had organized fellow city trolley motormen and conductors. In Los Angeles, he became a motorman on the Pacific Electric streetcar line that ran between Los Angeles and Whittier. When Hannah and Frank announced their engagement, Hannah's family expressed reservations. Frank was loud, uneducated, and not a Quaker. He converted to Quakerism, but this did not change his argumentative personality. Hannah abhorred personal confrontation and kept out of what Nixon described in his memoirs as "tempestuous arguments with my brothers Harold and Don" in which "their shouting could be heard all through the neighborhood."[4] Whatever tumult existed in the family, the Nixons were a close-knit clan, and nobody doubted Frank Nixon's devotion to his wife or his sons.

Most of the people in Whittier were Republicans, but Frank and Hannah Nixon voted in 1916 for Democrat Woodrow Wilson because of his promise to keep America out of war. Frank was at first a hardline Republican who supported Warren G. Harding, but the Teapot Dome scandal led him to support Robert "Fighting Bob" LaFollette's Progressive Party in 1924 and later the Townsend Plan, which called for a guaranteed monthly income of two hundred dollars to anyone over the age of sixty. Although Nixon claimed that his mother exerted the greater influence on him, he learned from his father the seething anger of a working man and a small business owner—the kind of person that became the "Silent Majority" in the 1960s.

The young Richard gained from his mother a deep appreciation of history, which he continued to read throughout his life, and a love of music. Frank Nixon presented a sharp contrast to his wife. Both were deeply religious, but Hannah, who had majored in Greek and Latin in college, continued to read history and literature. She named her five sons, with only one exception, after the early kings of England: Harold, born in 1909; Richard, born in 1913; Francis Donald, born in 1914; Arthur, born in 1918; and Edward, born in 1930. She was an extremely private person. Nixon recalls in his memoirs that she took "literally the injunction from St. Matthew that praying should be done behind closed doors and went into a closet to say her prayers before going to bed at night."[5] She was soft-spoken and held in almost reverence by her family and those who knew her.[6]

The Nixon family's life revolved around church and work. Church devotionals took up Wednesday evenings, with choir on Thursday and church several times on Sunday.[7] The Nixons attended extensive religious programs of the Friends in Whittier and in the nearby town of Yorba Linda. Grandmother Almira Milhous wore a white ribbon of the Women's Christian Temperance Union and tried to instill a fundamentalist faith and a literal interpretation of the Bible into her family.[8] Even these activities did not satisfy Frank Nixon, who weekly drove the entire family to hear Los Angeles evangelist Aimee Semple McPherson at her five-thousand-seat Angelus Temple and her competitor, radio preacher Robert "Fighting Bob" Shuler at the Trinity Methodist Church. Hannah limited her involvement in these revivals because of her deep instinct for religious privacy.

Richard Nixon studied the Bible, memorized verses, and led prayers and gave witness at the East Whittier Friends Church. His faith was tested by the early deaths from tuberculosis of his brothers Arthur and Harold, especially Arthur's sudden death in 1925 at the age of seven. Young Richard hid his emotions from his parents, but in his memoirs, he admitted that for weeks afterward he cried in private. Frank, tormented by the death of his son, took it as a sign of God's displeasure in him. Afterward, he kept his country store closed on Sundays. Whatever doubts Richard had about his faith disappeared when he joined his father in a revival held by Paul Rader, head of the World Wide Gospel movement, the same year as Arthur's death. When Rader called for his listeners to "Come Forward for Christ," Richard stepped forward and rededicated his life to God.[9] The born-again Richard only rejected the literal interpretation of the Bible after he was in college.

Nixon's childhood did not instill class resentment or social anxiety. The Nixon family took pride in owning their store. Social hierarchy existed in Whittier, with a few large citrus-grove owners, land developers, lawyers, and community leaders. Whittier itself was a modest town with a Myers Department Store, a grocery store, and a few small businesses located on unpaved downtown streets. Hierarchy in a small town such as Whittier was far different from the social resentment that might have developed in a large city with its very rich and very poor, or the class resentment that might have occurred in a large corporation with highly paid bosses and relatively poorly paid employees. Whittier was a town of 7,997 people in 1920 where everyone knew everyone else.[10]

The young Nixon revealed unusual ambition for his age. In a grammar school autobiography, he wrote that he planned on attending college, doing postgraduate work at Columbia University, and traveling the world.[11] An avid reader of newspapers and magazines even at a young age, Nixon concluded that lawyers seemed to be critical players in nearly everything. After reading about the Teapot Dome scandal in Harding's administration, the young Nixon, lying on the floor with newspapers spread out in front of him, announced, "When I grow up, I'm going to be an honest lawyer so things like that can't happen."[12] The death of his younger brother when Richard was twelve deeply affected him, but the death of his tall, blue-eyed brother Harold when Nixon was in high school strengthened his desire to excel more than ever. Harold's death, after a long illness, imparted a new tenacity to Nixon's drive to be the best, as if to compensate for his parents' loss of two of their children. Nixon's ambition was not unusual for an intelligent young man. He was a bit of a dreamer, and his family saw in him something special.

Nixon attended Fullerton High School and finished at Whitter High in the late 1920s. He was well liked at both schools. The top of the hierarchy of both schools rested on athletes, student-body leaders, theater groupies, and class "brains." Richard tried to be all of these things. Thin and awkward, he made the football team, where, as a classmate at Fullerton later recalled, he took a "terrific beating. . . . He was persistent and he tried with every ounce of strength he had, but he just didn't seem to have a feel for it."[13] He won the leading role in a high-school play only to hear catcalls from the student audience. He excelled, though, at public speaking and debate. He finished third in his high-school graduating class. By the time he graduated, the character traits for later success were already in place: hard work combined with intelligence; an inner fortitude that allowed him to place himself on a public stage, even if it meant catcalls; and a young man of ambition only limited by circumstances that he sought to overcome.

His success at Whittier College came from his intelligence, hard work, and personal skills. He was not affable, but he could be gregarious, at least for him, in smaller groups. He won the respect of his classmates and became a campus leader. As Nixon noted in his memoirs, he studied hard and received high grades, but "academic pursuits were by no means the only—or the most important—part of my four years there."[14]

If academics were not high on his list of priorities, social priorities were. The first week of school, Nixon, the seventeen-year-old first-year student, joined Dean Triggs, a transfer student from Colorado College, in organizing a new social club, the Orthogonian Society (square shooters) as a counter to the one social club on campus, the Franklin Society, whose members, as Nixon described in his memoirs, had "high social status." The Franklin Society dominated social life and controlled the student-body offices on the campus of a hundred students. The mobilization against the Franklin Society targeted exclusion and elitism on campus, although Whittier College was hardly a rich man's college. Students prided themselves on having to work to pay their tuition. The Orthogonians recruited mostly athletes and men working their way through school. The club revealed the kind of sense of humor that comes from being an outsider on campus. It was devoted to what they called the Four Bs—"Beans, Brawn, Brain, and Bowels"—which translated from the college vernacular of the day to mean, "Sassiness, Muscles, Intelligence, and Guts."

Nixon fit in well with his fellow students. He won the freshman class presidency on a campaign of allowing dancing on campus. Nixon's campaign to force the administration to allow official dances might be seen as an early sign of political opportunism, especially given that he was a poor dancer himself and did not enjoy the activity. Within the political context of Whittier College and the long-standing Quaker tradition of opposing dancing, Nixon's pro-dance position took some political courage. Dancing went against Quaker culture.[15] It conjured up sexual libidinousness, physical abandonment, and youthful rebellion. Nixon in standing with his fellow students challenged established authority. He clearly was not presenting himself as a "goody two shoes" to the powers that be. As one professor who taught at the time later recalled, Nixon showed "a lot of guts and nerve and crust."[16] His negotiation of a resolution to a conflict that pitted students against the administration, conservative donors, and alumni showed surprising political skill for a first-year college student.

Nixon won respect from his classmates because of his enthusiasm and willingness to work. He was not a glad-hander, and he did not make close friends; but he won the respect of fellow students because of his willingness to do the grunt work to make sure everything functioned. He was influenced by his football coach, Wallace "Chief" Newman, a Native American, who taught him, "What really matters is not a man's background, his color, his race, or his religion, but only his character." At this point in his life, Nixon showed much character.

College education changed Nixon's fundamentalist religious views when in 1933, his senior year, he took "The Philosophy of Christian Reconstruction," taught by J. Herschel Coffin, a published author and a political liberal. This course led Nixon to reject his parents' "fundamental" Quakerism based on a literal interpretation of the Bible. Nixon concluded that a literal interpretation of the Scripture could not be reconciled with the scientific method. He maintained his faith as a Christian, however, writing in a class composition that "for the time being I shall accept the solution offered by Kant that man can go only so far in his research and explanation from that point on we must accept God. What is unknown to man, God knows."[17]

Nixon's dream of attending a Northeastern university after graduation was not realized. He was accepted to Harvard University Law School but could not afford to go there. Instead he accepted admission and a full scholarship to Duke University Law School. Under its new dean, Justin Miller, the school had lured to its faculty twelve full-time professors, many with national and international reputations. Nixon became a grind at Duke. He lived in a five-dollar-a-month rented room, but finding it difficult to study because of a group of Methodist theological students, he moved into an eight-by-twelve-foot unheated shack with just enough room for a bed and table. In his final year, he moved with three other law students into a one-room clapboard house without heat or indoor plumbing. He worked his way through Duke by taking jobs in the law library and as a researcher. Although notorious for his strenuous work habits, Nixon attended football games, and occasionally he and his friends got together for law school parties in which liquor was procured in Virginia (North Carolina was dry). He continued to attend church regularly either at the Quaker service in Raleigh or at the university chapel.

He did not hide his feelings about his opposition to racial segregation or what he considered the racial bigotry of his Southern classmates. He revealed to his fellow students that his family ancestors were Quakers who had been involved in the Underground Railroad for escaping slaves. Nixon shared that his family invited blacks to join them for lunch and that his collegiate social club at Whittier, the Orthogonians, made an African American a charter member. One Duke contemporary later recalled that Nixon was "shocked and disturbed at the prevalent North Carolina treatment of the Negro population as an inferior group. He looked upon the issue . . . as a moral issue and condemned it very strongly as such."[18] Nonetheless, Nixon was elected president of the Student Bar, a remarkable achievement given his status as a Westerner and a professed Quaker at a Southern college.

Nixon in Love

Unable to land a job with a New York law firm or the Federal Bureau of Investigation, Nixon returned to his hometown of Whittier to practice law. Whatever disappointment he might have held about not receiving a job on

Wall Street, he returned to Whittier full of energy and self-assurance. He was encouraged to join fraternal clubs and community activities necessary for a young lawyer on the rise. He became involved in a local drama group that put on plays a couple of times a year. His sense of security—combined with a kind of awkward brashness—became all too evident the first time he met a local high-school teacher, Pat Ryan, who was attending the theater group for the first time. Offering her and her friend a lift home at the end of the evening, Nixon bluntly asked Pat for a date. For Nixon, it was love at first sight of this beautiful, high-cheek-boned, auburn-haired woman.

Pat, though, stayed cool at first. Her own hard upbringing made her cautious and self-reliant. The young couple shared much in common in personality and background. Born in a miner's shack in Ely, Pat moved with her family to Artesia, California, now Cerritos, to a small ranch her father had bought. Her father was given to explosive, sometimes violent anger. Her mother died when Pat was only thirteen, leaving her to take on the roles of housewife, ranch hand, and schoolgirl. In high school, she was a rabid supporter of Al Smith. When she was eighteen, her father died after a lingering fight with tuberculosis. She enrolled in Fullerton College, but after a year moved back East to stay with two aunts, one of whom was a Catholic nun. After two years, she returned to Southern California and worked a full-time job while being a full-time student at the University of Southern California, graduating with honors in 1937 in the midst of the Depression. She had just taken a job teaching business at Whittier Union High School when she met Nixon.

The romance between the two grew slowly and then blossomed. They married in 1940. Their life was comfortable, with an active social circle in a community in which they were both respected. With the outbreak of World War II, Nixon, like many of his generation, was anxious to do his part. In 1941, he took a job working for the newly created Office of Price Administration in Washington, D.C. In April 1942, he joined the navy. As a Quaker, he could have received an exemption as a conscientious objector. His mother and aunts were upset with his decision to join the war effort. After officers' training school, he wanted a combat ship assignment. Instead he was given a post as assistant operations officer on a small airstrip in the South Pacific, in charge of enlisted men who had the task of loading and unloading combat supplies onto cargo aircraft.

In the South Pacific, Nixon showed his leadership qualities, his solid character, and his uncommon ability to relate to the common man. Nixon won the respect of his crew and fellow officers. Often, unlike other officers, he took off his shirt to join his men in the broiling sun to get the job done. They were a rough crew, city boys from New York and New Jersey, a redneck from Kentucky, a Hispanic from Los Angeles, and a Native American. They were rough, talked tough, and respected Nixon. He joined his fellow officers in camaraderie, playing poker with them and steadily putting away his earnings for a down payment on a house he and Pat wanted to buy after the war. He wrote constantly to Pat to tell her how much he missed her and loved her. He engaged in long conversations with fellow officers, relating his optimism about his own future and a better postwar world.

The Young Contender

Nixon's involvement in politics had been minimal up to this point. He had considered running for the state assembly before he joined the navy but did not receive the support of GOP leaders in his district. In 1940, he gave a few speeches for the Republican nominee Wendell Willkie. After the war, while negotiating naval contracts in Washington, D.C., and waiting for his discharge, Nixon received a telegram from Herman L. Perry, the manager of the Whittier Bank of America branch and the key player in local Republican politics. Perry asked Nixon if he would consider running for Congress against longtime Democratic incumbent, Horace Jeremiah "Jerry" Voorhis. Perry, a member of the Whittier College trustee board, had followed Nixon's career since he had been a student protest leader.

Most local Republicans believed that the seat held by Voorhis since 1936 was pretty secure. In 1946, Nixon's challenge to Voorhis was a long shot, but Nixon's backers—mostly local businessmen, including an auto dealer, a bank manager, and a furniture store owner—believed Voorhis might be vulnerable.[19] Nixon accepted the challenge. Returning from Washington with his young wife, who was pregnant with their first child, he spent the next year campaigning for Congress. Nixon had few significant financial backers and only $10,000 in personal savings. Unable to afford a place of their own, the Nixons were living with his parents when Pat gave birth to Tricia. Three weeks after giving birth, Pat began working in the campaign office. She joined her husband in keeping up a punishing schedule. Typical of this arduous pace, on September 17, his day began with a speaking engagement and a press meeting at 7:30 a.m. before traveling until late that evening to thirteen different towns in the district.[20]

The Twelfth Congressional District was staunch Democratic territory;

Jerry Voorhis had won the district, which covered five main towns: San Marino, Whittier, Pomona, Alhambra, and South Pasadena. The five-term congressman remained popular, even though his profile was not that of a person from small-town Southern California.[21] Son of the chairman of a major automobile company and Yale educated, Voorhis came from a well-to-do family. After graduating Phi Beta Kappa, he took a factory job, worked as a freight handler, toured Europe, and then worked for a while on the Ford assembly line. After he married, he opened a school for orphaned boys in Southern California. He started off as a LaFollette Progressive, became an active member of the Socialist Party, and then joined socialist Upton Sinclair's End Poverty in California (EPIC) movement in 1934, running for the state assembly. In 1936, he won his congressional seat running as a devout Franklin D. Roosevelt Democrat. After his election, he faced no serious challenger over the next decade. But the truth was that Voorhis had begun to take his voters for granted and ignored them.

Murray Chotiner, a savvy Los Angeles attorney working for the William Knowland senatorial campaign, agreed to serve as a part-time consultant to Nixon's congressional run.[22] Chotiner encouraged Nixon to link Voorhis with the left-leaning Congress of Industrial Organizations Political Action Committee (CIO-PAC) in order to portray him as more radical than his voting record in Congress suggested. The CIO-PAC was the first political action committee in modern American politics and was used by organized labor to target Republicans. Voorhis was a radical of sorts, but his legislative accomplishments were nondescript and conformed with New Deal policy. The CIO-PAC accusation blindsided Voorhis.[23] He might have been instinctually a left-leaning liberal, but he was also anti-Communist. He had launched his political career with the EPIC movement in 1934, and anyone familiar with this campaign knew that the Communist Party had denounced EPIC leader, Upton Sinclair, as a reactionary.[24]

Nixon overwhelmed Voorhis on Election Day with 57 percent of the popular vote. He won because he outworked Voorhis, who had underestimated his opponent until it was too late, and because 1946 was a GOP year in which voters demanded change in Washington, which had been ruled by Democrats since 1933. Nixon celebrated his hard-fought victory, but the fierce attacks from the opposition inflicted the first wounds on him and his wife. In the early stages of the campaign, Pat had been an integral part, but as the campaign progressed, Nixon became more distant and relied less on Pat's advice. As Julie Nixon later wrote in her biography of her mother, "politics was a harsh, even hurtful battle, a man's world," and the 1946 campaign changed her parents' relationship.[25]

Nixon went to Congress like many of the postwar generation, intent on making a better world. Here, much like John F. Kennedy, who was elected to the House the same year, Nixon found an older generation of members who, for the most part, were seat warmers, unimaginative, and in not a few cases grandstanders and media hounds. In Congress, Nixon and Kennedy, both U.S. Navy veterans of the Pacific War, although on opposite sides of the aisle, became friends. Nixon recalled that upon taking his seat in Congress that he had "the same lost feeling that I had when I first went into the military service."[26]

Nixon's opportunity to shine came when he was appointed to the Herter Committee, a select congressional committee headed by Massachusetts representative Christian Herter to prepare a report on Secretary of State George Marshall's plan to undertake a massive foreign aid program for war-devastated Europe. Appointed to the select committee by House Speaker Joe Martin, Nixon was the only freshman member. His strong internationalist views made him a natural for the committee.

Nixon's subsequent trip to Europe confirmed his commitment to an internationalist American foreign policy. He was shocked by the devastation in Europe, where he experienced for the first time what he considered the callous and cynical use of human suffering by European Communists. After meeting an Italian Communist Party leader, he wrote in his notes, "This indicates definitely then that the Communists throughout the world owe their loyalty not to the countries in which they live but to Russia."[27] In the final report, the Herter Committee strongly recommended economic aid for Europe, which placed Nixon in a political dilemma. A poll commissioned by Nixon showed that 75 percent of people in his district were "resolutely opposed to any foreign aid." He confronted, as he wrote in his memoirs, "the classic dilemma, so eloquently described by Edmund Burke [an eighteenth-century English Whig] by almost any elected official in a democracy: how much should his votes register his constituents' opinions and how much should they represent his views."[28] Nixon's dilemma was that he had aligned himself nationally with the internationalist wing of his party, but many in his home district remained Taft isolationists, not that they were going to vote for a Democrat, who might be even more internationalist, in the next election.

Signs of trouble in his home district were evident even before Nixon's trip to Europe. In a letter sent to Nixon shortly before he departed for Europe, key Republican leaders in the district denounced bipartisan foreign policy and called the Marshall Plan "dangerously unworkable and profoundly inflationary."[29] Nixon launched a public relations campaign to explain himself to his constituents. Newspaper columns were written and mail sent, and he returned home for town hall meetings. He won the day. Nixon showed principle combined with practical politics. He took a principled stand for an internationalist foreign policy, which served his interests with the national GOP, at least in one wing of the party, while convincing the right in his district that his course of action was correct.

One of the ironies of modern American political history is that Nixon would be portrayed, especially by his opponents, as a rabid anti-Communist. He was hostile to Communism abroad and at home. He was by no means a McCarthyite slinging unfounded charges of Communism. The image of Nixon as an anti-Communist firebrand was etched in his first term as a member of the House Un-American Activities Committee (HUAC). Nixon had not sought appointment to this committee. House leadership appointed him in late 1947 in all likelihood because they wanted a serious voice on a committee dominated by its chair, J. Parnell Thomas, a lightweight congressman from New Jersey.

Thomas's grandstanding appeared all too evident to Republican leadership when he called for a congressional investigation in late 1946 into alleged pro-Soviet propaganda in Hollywood movies. The nationally televised hearings in early 1947 allowed Thomas to parade before the committee an array of movie stars, studio moguls, and other Hollywood celebrities. Republican Party leaders, including Thomas Dewey and House Majority Speaker Joe Martin, tried to persuade J. Parnell Thomas to call off the circuslike hearings. They were looking at the 1948 presidential election and did not want the Republicans to be portrayed as a bunch of red-baiting loons. Thomas refused to listen; the opportunity to appear before the cameras was just too irresistible.

Yet in the Hollywood hearings, Nixon showed that he was far from an anti-Communist fanatic. He took the line that supported studio mogul claims that the Communist problem had been solved in Hollywood. At the hearings, Nixon tossed softball questions at the movie executives, allowing them to refute charges that during World War II they had been duped into producing pro-Soviet and pro-Communist movies. Nixon's approach was exactly the same as actors Ronald Reagan and George Murphy when they testified before the committee: Communism in Hollywood was a moot issue because it had already been addressed. In doing this, Nixon defended the film industry from charges of pro-Soviet propaganda. Nixon did not need to be told about the economic and political importance of the film industry in California.[30]

The Hollywood hearings showed that Nixon was not willing to play the role of a grandstander, but he sought to certify his anti-Communist credentials when he joined Karl Mundt of South Dakota in offering the first piece of legislation from HUAC in ten years, which required the registration of all members of the Communist Party in the United States. The bill passed in the House but died in the Senate. In proposing this legislation, Nixon differed from many hard-line anti-Communists, including Federal Bureau of Investigation head J. Edgar Hoover, who feared that requiring Communists to register would force them to go underground.

Nixon's image as a red baiter developed in his race against Voorhis in 1946 but was cemented on the left in his role in the Alger Hiss case that came before HUAC in 1948. Hiss, a former high-ranking State Department official, was accused by Whittaker Chambers, a former Communist Party member, of belonging to a secret Communist cell in Washington, D.C. The charges took a dramatic turn when Chambers revealed that Hiss was not just a Communist Party member but also a Soviet spy.[31]

Before the Hiss case, Nixon's political prospects were those of a congressman representing a largely agricultural, growing district in an important state dominated by a popular governor, Earl Warren, and a senator, William Knowland, both of whom had presidential aspirations. Nixon seemed to be safe in his district, but he was neither well known outside the state nor much of a player in California politics. All this changed in the summer of 1948, when Elizabeth Bentley, a former courier for a Soviet spy ring operating in Washington, D.C., came before HUAC to warn of Communist agents working in federal government. Looking for witnesses to collaborate Bentley's testimony, a HUAC investigator recommended the committee subpoena Whittaker Chambers. Nixon seized upon these accusations to pursue the investigation. In subsequent court testimony, Hiss's denials unraveled and he later went to jail for perjury.

Nixon's pursuit of the case made him a pariah on the left and, at the same time, alienated many in the Republican Eastern establishment. His opponents never forgave him for his role in bringing down Hiss and began a campaign of vilification that continued throughout his political career. For Nixon, it was an awakening. In her biography of her mother, Julie Nixon concluded that the unrelenting attacks on her father by Hiss supporters "caused an irreparable crack" in her mother's idealistic view of politics.[32] Richard Nixon's idealism also began to erode under relentless and often personally vicious attacks. The Hiss case brought Nixon to the national stage but at a high price, both politically and personally.

The Hiss case set the stage for Nixon to announce he was running for the U.S. Senate in 1950; but he was a changed man from the young, idealistic naval officer who had run for Congress only four years earlier and had easily won reelection in 1948, a disastrous election year for many Republicans.[33]

In 1950, the Republican Party in California was deeply divided, more often around personality than party principle, but Nixon won the support of former president Herbert Hoover, Senator William Knowland, and others who were considered "good government" folks in California. Earl Warren, the popular Republican governor of the state, remained a California powerhouse, even though his lackluster campaign as Dewey's running mate in 1948 had left many of the party faithful dismayed. Warren's support for a compulsory national health care system and his continued nonpartisan stance in government appointments fostered resentment in the growing ranks of the right in his state.[34] The 1948 presidential campaign had only whetted Warren's presidential ambitions, though. Anti-Warren conservatives in California saw Knowland, the wealthy publisher of the *Oakland Tribune*, as an alternative candidate. Knowland, who had been appointed to the Senate in 1945 following longtime senator Hiram Johnson's death, emerged as the voice of the right in California politics. And then Nixon threw his hat in the ring, thus declaring that he wanted to be a major player in state politics.

Nixon's timing could not have been better. International events encouraged him to run a tough anti-Communist campaign. In September 1949, President Harry Truman announced that the Soviet Union had detonated an atomic bomb. The same month, mainland China fell to Communist forces led by Mao Zedong. These events played to Nixon's advantage. At the same time, Nixon's campaign found further opportunity in exploiting divisions within the California Democratic Party. In the 1950 Democratic Senate primary, Helen Gahagan Douglas, a congresswoman from Southern California, decided to challenge Democratic incumbent Sheridan Downey for the Senate nomination. Downey had won his election to the U.S. Senate a decade earlier, in 1938, with strong left-wing credentials. He had been an activist in Upton Sinclair's EPIC gubernatorial campaign in 1934 and a supporter of the "Ham and Eggs" state movement for a guaranteed income for the elderly unemployed. Once in the Senate, however, he aligned himself with state oil interests. His health was not good in 1950, a fact that was probably known to both Douglas and Nixon as House members.

Nobody doubted Douglas's left-wing credentials after she voted against HUAC funding and aid to anti-Communist Greece, even though she had made her opposition to the Communist Party and Henry Wallace's Progressive Party clear. When Downey dropped out of the race because of ill health, Los Angeles newspaper publisher Manchester Boddy, a conservative Democrat, stepped forward to become Douglas's major challenger. The campaign was plain nasty. Boddy referred to Douglas as the "pink lady," which stuck with her after she won the nomination. His attack was vicious: "Mrs. Douglas," he claimed, "gave aid and comfort to Soviet tyranny by voting against aid to both Greece and Turkey."[35] After he lost the nomination to Douglas, Boddy threw his support to Nixon. He was not alone. Many insiders within the California Democratic Party thought Douglas was far too liberal to win the state. She was never able to unite the party behind her candidacy.

Although Democratic registration in the state outnumbered Republican registration by 58 percent to 37 percent, Douglas was at a disadvantage against the well-organized Nixon campaign. She lacked major fundraising sources, while Nixon tapped into donors anxious to defeat his opponent, including Joseph Kennedy, the father of Nixon's congressional friend John F. Kennedy.[36] Joseph Kennedy saw Douglas as a "Communist." Douglas faced other problems as well. Although she had been trained as an actress, her speeches were dull and droning. She presented herself as a New Deal–Fair Deal liberal in a state that was drifting right. Aware of this trend, she responded with one of the most bizarre attacks (of so many) in American political history. She decided to attack Nixon from the right by accusing him of being soft on Communism.

Nixon counterattacked. Picking up a theme of Douglas's Democratic primary opponent, he accused her of being "pink" on foreign and domestic politics. The Nixon campaign's most requested piece of literature, printed serendipitously on pink-toned paper, eviscerated her on national security issues. On Election Day, Nixon trampled Douglas by sweeping the entire state from the north to the south. He won more votes than any Republican running in any state in 1950, which brought him further national attention as a vote getter. For Nixon's opponents, the campaign proved to them that Nixon was a "red baiter." They labeled him "Tricky Dick," a nickname that stuck.[37] Nixon's public image was now etched in toxic acid.

Nixon's election to the Senate in 1950 did not ease divisions within the California Republican Party as the 1952 presidential election approached.[38] The liberal Warren wing of the party remained strong, and Warren supporters hoped a deadlocked convention might result in his winning the presidential nomination. California delegates elected to the convention pledged themselves to support Warren as a "favorite son" through the first round of balloting. The right in the state gave their support to Robert Taft, although some conservatives saw Dwight D. Eisenhower as a more viable and popular candidate to head the ticket. When Eisenhower won the nomination after a bitter convention fight with Taft, party leaders sought to shore up support by placing a conservative on the ticket. Nixon had aligned himself early with the Eisenhower campaign and its international foreign policy positions. Warren supporters accused Nixon of having lobbied California delegates on the train to the national convention to switch their votes to Eisenhower. Taft supporters—and Nixon's later critics—referred to Nixon's alleged lobbying as the "Great Train Robbery." This accusation took on mythic proportions as an example of Nixon's opportunism and his deceitful nature. Warren never attacked Nixon publicly, but his supporters spread the idea through innuendo that Nixon was a man without political principle, a opportunist who would do anything to gain office.

Nixon was a natural choice to join the Eisenhower ticket. He was young, a hero of the anti-Communist right, and a vigorous campaigner; and he came from a major state, California, which had voted Democratic in presidential elections since 1932. Furthermore, the Dewey Eastern wing of the party liked Nixon. In fact, Senator Henry Cabot Lodge Jr. of Massachusetts and Governor Dewey of New York recommended Nixon as a running mate. Nixon stood firmly for an internationalist foreign policy, in clear opposition to the Taft isolationists.[39] From Nixon's point of view, he confronted a choice of remaining the junior senator from California, playing second fiddle to the young, healthy Knowland, or running on the popular Eisenhower ticket. Pat Nixon loathed the idea of another tough campaign; she had grown sick of politics.[40]

However much the Republican right loved Nixon (and the Eastern wing of the party saw the need to balance the ticket), Democrats despised him. He had come into the crosshairs of an array of liberal reporters, especially Drew Pearson, whose "Washington Merry-Go-Round" column was notorious for digging up dirt on politicians. With the liberal media sniffing around for dirt on Nixon, the left-leaning *New York Post* broke a story about a secret slush fund of millionaires that had been set up by Nixon's supporters when he was in the Senate. Democrats seized on the story, demanding that Nixon be removed from the ticket. Nixon was not the only senator to have a fund to support travel and incidental expenses. Republican Party strategist and Nixon adviser Murray Chotiner noticed, however, that Democratic presidential nominee Adlai Stevenson was being noticeably quiet about Nixon's secret fund. It turned out that Stevenson himself had a secret fund of $135,000, which he had used to hire relatives and to throw his son an elaborate birthday party with a live band.[41]

While the Nixon campaign believed that the charges were easily dismissed as a cheap partisan attack, Eisenhower's ambiguous response and unwillingness to commit himself to keeping Nixon on the ticket dismayed the senator. When the Republican-leaning *Herald Tribune* joined the call for Nixon's removal from the ticket, he suddenly realized the gravity of the situation. Chotiner, who was on the train with Nixon on a whistle-stop tour of Northern California, was the first on the staff to hear about Eisenhower's trepidation about backing Nixon. When Chotiner first heard the news, he exploded: "If those damned amateurs around Eisenhower just had the sense they were born with, they would recognize that this is a purely political attack and they wouldn't pop off like this."[42]

Only a few Republicans rallied to Nixon's defense. They understood the costs of a divided Republican Party if Nixon was removed from the ticket. Herbert Hoover, Karl Mundt, and even liberal Republican George Aiken, the senator from Vermont, rose to Nixon's defense. Nixon welcomed their support, but they were minor players within the party. Nixon was especially dismayed to learn that party leaders such as Thomas Dewey, who had promoted Nixon's candidacy in the first place, had joined others in the Eisenhower camp in advising withholding support of Nixon until things sorted themselves out. Polls showed that many Americans wanted Nixon removed, which led Eisenhower to tell the press, "I am taking my time on this" and that he wanted his campaign to be "clean as a hounds tooth." Things grew worse when Dewey called Nixon to tell him that almost everyone in the Eisenhower circle wanted Nixon to offer his resignation. Eisenhower phoned Nixon a short time later to tell him that he had not made a decision, but he understood that Nixon should be given a chance to tell his side of the story in a national televised address. Nixon responded by insisting that Eisenhower make an announcement one way or the other immediately after the televised address. When Eisenhower responded that he hoped an announcement would not be necessary, Nixon lost his patience: "There comes a time in matters like this when you've got to shit or get off the pot." Still, Eisenhower remained uncommitted. The Eisenhower call left Nixon deeply upset, and, as he later wrote, "the whole episode had scarred her [Pat Nixon] deeply," suggesting he too felt scarred.[43] Nixon prepared a telegram to Eisenhower telling him he was resigning. Chotiner directed his secretary Rosemary Woods not to send it.

Nixon understood partisan attacks, but he was bewildered and angered by Eisenhower's lack of support and that many alleged friends in the party were turning their backs on him. Harold Stassen, whom Nixon had initially supported for the GOP nomination in 1948, was just one of many in the Eisenhower circle who urged Nixon to withdraw from the ticket.[44] Feeling a sense of desertion, Nixon retreated to prepare what became the "Checkers" speech. Shortly before going on national television to defend his record, Dewey phoned to tell Nixon that he should use the address to resign. Dewey intimated that he spoke for Eisenhower. Nixon's response was sheer anger, encouraged by Chotiner who told him right before the televised speech, "This is politics. The prize is the White House."[45] The results of Nixon's "Checkers" speech left no doubt, except among a few people within Eisenhower's inner circle and most of the liberal media, that Nixon should remain on the ticket. Liberal columnist Walter Lippmann thought Nixon's emotion-laden speech hit a new low in American politics. Adlai Stevenson said that Nixon's speech was a cheap political ploy. Some within Eisenhower's circle when they first watched the address thought it was too corny even for the gullible American public. But Nixon knew his audience: regular folks who did not like a man's family and children coming under attack. The response was an outpouring of public support in the form of hundreds of thousands of telegrams to the Republican National Committee, which led Eisenhower to keep Nixon on the ticket.

The episode and the failure of Republican friends to stand up for him left Nixon and Pat embittered. Pat told Mamie Eisenhower, the nominee's wife, shortly after the speech, "But you just don't realize what *we've* been through." Nixon wrote later in *Six Crises* (1962) that Eisenhower's equivocation "left a deep scar, which was never to heal completely."[46] The idealism that Nixon had brought to Congress six years earlier was dissipating quickly.

On the campaign trail in 1952, Nixon hammered Truman and the Democrats for having "lost China" and "much of Eastern Europe." His attack on Democratic presidential candidate Adlai Stevenson as a graduate of the

"Cowardly College of Communist Containment" rallied the anti-Communist Republican crowds but made him an easy target for opponents such as *Washington Post* cartoonist Herb Block, who portrayed Nixon as a sewer dweller. Nixon's fiery rhetoric came easily to him. He knew how to rally the Republican base, and the Eisenhower campaign willingly used Nixon to provide the hard-hitting rhetoric that wins elections while allowing Eisenhower to project a benign image as a president for all the people. The Eisenhower-Nixon ticket easily won in the general election.

In office, Eisenhower and Nixon enjoyed close working relations.[47] Eisenhower relied heavily on his vice president for foreign affairs advice, crafting the Civil Rights Act of 1957, and as the hard-hitting voice of the Republican Party.[48] More important, Nixon served as the liaison with the Senate and the Republican grassroots across the country. Eisenhower was highly political, but he liked to work behind the scenes, avoiding overt party politics. His relationship with the right of his party was strained to say the least. His instincts were those of a moderate, even a centrist, and he was repulsed by right-wing anti-Communist rhetoric. He found many on the right not very smart. He especially disliked William Knowland, who had replaced Taft as leader of the Senate Republicans following Taft's death shortly after Eisenhower took office. (Their relations worsened in early 1955 when Knowland announced he would not join a "draft Eisenhower" reelection movement.)[49]

Eisenhower's differences with the Republican right came early when Ohio Republican Senator John W. Bricker, a protégé of Senator Taft, decided to push forward a constitutional amendment he had first introduced in 1951 prohibiting the president from entering into agreements with foreign nations and the United Nations. Nixon's role in defeating the Bricker Amendment reveals Nixon's ideological flexibility, as well as his commitment to a strong internationalist foreign policy. The Bricker Amendment became a major cause for the anti-Communist right and found supporters in churches, the American Legion, and ad hoc committees across the country. After Nixon failed to reach a compromise with Bricker to withdraw or modify his constitutional amendment, Nixon turned to conservative Democrats in the Senate to substitute a more modified amendment, which ultimately failed to get the necessary two-thirds vote for a constitutional amendment. (Ironically, Bricker had backed Eisenhower in 1952 over his fellow Ohio senator, Taft. Politics makes for strange bedfellows). In presenting the administration's opposition to the Bricker Amendment, Nixon showed his political effectiveness.

Nixon's ideological flexibility was further evidenced in his role in censuring

Joseph McCarthy, the U.S. senator from Wisconsin who built his political career on anti-Communism. Early in the administration, Eisenhower assigned Nixon the task of trying to keep McCarthy in line. At first, Nixon appeared to succeed. For example, McCarthy agreed not to investigate the Central Intelligence Agency for Communist infiltration. The truce did not last long. McCarthy soon began to resent "the constant yack-yacking from that prick Nixon."[50] Irritated by the way a former staffer had been treated by the military, McCarthy decided instead to launch an investigation of Communist influence in the U.S. Army. If Eisenhower was going to protect any agency in government, it was the armed services. The Eisenhower administration went after McCarthy behind the scenes. For Nixon, the McCarthy issue was one of pure politics. On December 2, 1954, the Senate voted to condemn McCarthy's behavior. The Republicans split evenly on the vote, but Nixon's role in McCarthy's downfall proved critical.[51]

In September 1955, Eisenhower suffered a major heart attack in Denver, Colorado, which left him hospitalized for seven weeks. Nixon, keeping in close contact with Eisenhower, assumed running of the administration in Washington, carefully underplaying his role. In cabinet meetings, Nixon refused to take Eisenhower's chair at the head of the table. When Eisenhower returned, he profusely complimented Nixon personally and publicly for his masterful job in keeping government running during his absence. Nixon proved himself loyal to the administration, unlike some Republicans such as Goodwin "Goodie" Knight, who had succeeded Warren as governor in California in 1953, who declared shortly after Eisenhower's heart attack that he was eligible to run for the presidency.[52]

Given what Nixon had done for Eisenhower and the party, he was shocked when Eisenhower suggested to Nixon that he take himself off the Republican ticket for the approaching 1956 election in consideration of a cabinet post. In February 1955, Eisenhower announced he would seek reelection, but from Christmas until the end of April 1956, he refused to say he wanted Nixon on the ticket. This opened opportunities for Nixon's enemies, such as Stassen, to organize against him. Looking at Eisenhower's ambivalence on the ticket, historian Irwin Gellman concluded that the president's hesitation seemed "baffling."[53] Eisenhower might have been sincere in believing Nixon needed more administrative experience, but he also did not want a war with the right wing of the party if Nixon was removed from the ticket. Nonetheless, the wounds suffered by Nixon in 1956 reopened the wounds from 1952. Nixon's role once again in 1956, and subsequently in the 1958 midterm elections, furthered his reputation on the left as a vicious, unscrupulous politician.

When Nixon declared he was running for the 1960 GOP presidential nomination, he was a changed man from the one who had left the navy to run for Congress. As Eisenhower's vice president, he had played good-will ambassador abroad and political operative at home. Eisenhower disdained partisan politics and despised the right wing of his party, especially in Congress. Eisenhower used Nixon to shore up his support on the right, but politics had taken its toll on Nixon and his family. Nixon's experience with Eisenhower left him feeling unappreciated and betrayed. Reflecting later on his political life at this point, he observed, "Eisenhower tried to protect himself, but often at the expense of screwing those closest to him. Well, that's just politics." He noted that Eisenhower could also be a "pretty petty guy. He held grudges and was so protective of himself politically sometimes that he did not stand up for the people who had served him loyally."[54]

Nixon began to take the sharp and often vicious criticism from his left-wing critics personally. He confessed in his memoirs, "I resented being constantly vilified as a demagogue or a liar or the sewer dwelling denizen of the Herblock cartoons." He added, "As the attacks became more personal, I sometimes wondered where party loyalty left off and the masochism began. The girls were reaching an impressionable age, and neither Pat nor I wanted their father to be the bad guy of American politics."[55] Herblock was not alone in slamming Nixon. Drew Pearson, a widely read columnist working hand in glove with Nixon's enemies, kept up a steady stream of anti-Nixon columns full of innuendo and vituperative charges.[56]

Even before Nixon decided to run for the presidency in 1960, Pat Nixon had had enough of Washington, D.C., and politics. Her two young daughters had been ostracized at school by other children and their parents. She witnessed firsthand people coming up to her daughters in public outings, telling them their father was a disgrace and a crook. These comments left her daughters bewildered and crying. She tried to persuade her husband to leave politics and return to law, but the adrenaline of power had become addictive for her husband.

More hard lessons were to be learned by Nixon when he lost his race for the presidency in 1960, only to be defeated two years later in his 1962 campaign for governor of California. He concluded that principled ideology and moral character were less important in politics than winning. Winning became all that mattered to Richard Nixon.

Nixon in Defeat

Nixon entered the 1960 presidential context as a politician in control of his own fate, as much as any politician can control his or her fortunes. The path to the presidency had opened in 1958, when his two California rivals, William Knowland and Goodie Knight, had in effect knocked one another off politically when both lost election. Former governor Earl Warren had been appointed a chief justice of the Supreme Court. Nixon's major competition in the party remained in the Eastern liberal wing headed by Nelson Rockefeller, but this faction had dwindling influence. When Rockefeller began to explore a presidential bid in 1960, he learned that Nixon had built an impenetrable base in the party. Nixon made many mistakes in the 1960 contest, including trying to run his own campaign and unwisely deciding to uphold his pledge to campaign in every state when he should have concentrated on key battleground states. He lost the election against John F. Kennedy by only two-tenths of one percent of nearly 69 million votes cast. What especially embittered Nixon about his loss is that he knew that his opponents, John F. Kennedy and Lyndon Baines Johnson, were even more ruthless and power driven than a hostile press had portrayed Nixon.

Nixon watched as the Kennedy machine in the West Virginia Democratic primary directed Franklin D. Roosevelt Jr. to slime JFK's opponent Hubert Humphrey as a World War II draft dodger. When an angry Humphrey challenged this allegation, the Kennedy camp threw Roosevelt to the wolves by saying they had no involvement in Roosevelt's charge. (Humphrey and his wife, Muriel, were so upset by this charge that Muriel refused to shake Bobby Kennedy's hand at an inaugural ball after the election.) Furthermore, rumors were rampant that the Kennedy campaign spent thousands of dollars buying votes in West Virginia by handing out "walking around" money to precinct captains and local sheriffs. Journalist Theodore White, who covered the 1960 election, believed the Kennedy story that there was no vote buying in the West Virginia primary. Few today doubt that Kennedy bought votes before winning there.[57]

Charges of voter fraud in Mayor Daley's Chicago and Johnson's home state of Texas came out immediately after the election. The Nixon campaign in Texas filed a complaint charging widespread fraud. Johnson immediately contacted attorney Leon Jaworski, later appointed special prosecutor in the Watergate investigation, to represent the Democratic Party. The Texas courts dismissed the complaint in early December on the grounds that Texas election law did not cover voter fraud. Journalist Earl Mazo reported widely on voter fraud in both Illinois and Texas, but Nixon told him to cease his reporting. It is not clear that Nixon knew fully the extent of voter fraud in these states, but he decided not to pursue the matter before the electors met in mid-December to validate the results of the election for Kennedy.

Nixon believed he had run a clean campaign in 1960, especially compared to the Kennedy campaign in which Dick Tuck had been hired specifically to conduct dirty tricks. Critics later charged Nixon with having conducted a campaign of dirty tricks, including involvement in orchestrating a break-in into John F. Kennedy's private physician's office to steal his rival's medical records. In addition to these charges, Nixon was accused of promoting anti-Catholic prejudice in the South through evangelist Billy Graham and other Protestant ministers. Both accusations remain controversial.[58] However one interprets the historical evidence, Nixon claimed—and believed, either through conviction or self-delusion—that he had run an up-and-up campaign. In his 1962 best-seller, *Six Crises,* he devoted an entire chapter to the defense of his conduct in the 1960 campaign. Without doubt, Nixon's disappointment in losing in 1960 deepened his disillusionment with American politics.

Further disillusionment with principled ideology and party loyalty came in Nixon's failed bid for the California governor's mansion in 1962. In hindsight, Nixon's entry to the race was ill considered. Nixon had kept in close touch with California politicians, but after eight years in in the nation's capital, he was no longer well informed about state issues. More important, the California Republican Party was severely divided politically between a far-right wing and a moderate-liberal wing. This divide expressed itself in a grassroots movement on the right to challenge existing party leadership at the state level. In this regard, the struggle for control of the California Republican Party, while having ideological overtones, also involved basic power politics. The divide was further complicated by the involvement in this grassroots revolt of the John Birch Society, an anti-Communist organization organized a few years earlier by candy manufacturer Robert Welch. Many members of the society, Birchers, were given to anti-Communist conspiracy theories. They believed that the Eisenhower administration had been too soft on Communism.[59] For obvious reasons, Republican leaders sought to disassociate themselves from the extremist right.

Nixon found himself caught in a political scissors when he decided to reenter California state politics. His first challenge for the Republican gubernatorial nomination came from his longtime nemesis Goodwin Knight, who had moved left to distinguish himself within the party. Eventually Knight withdrew from the race, ostensibly for health reasons, but before doing so, he charged that Nixon had offered to appoint him the chief justice of the California Supreme Court or any other job in California he desired. Nixon exploded at the charge by entering into a bitter public exchange with Knight, which only reinforced an image of Nixon as a conniving politician without principle.[60]

Nixon's challenge from the right proved much more damaging. The California right threw their support to Los Angeles attorney Joseph Shell in the primary. The right's opposition to Nixon increased when he came out in support of a failed attempt to ban John Birch Society members in the California Republican Assembly, the largest Republican organization in the state. Nixon easily defeated Shell in the primary, but divisions within the party remained. On Election Day, the incumbent governor, Edmund "Pat" Brown, garnered 51 percent of the popular vote to Nixon's 46 percent. Nixon blamed his loss on the far right of his party. It was another lesson for Nixon that principled ideology was not the path to success in American politics.

With the loss of two elections in a two-year span, Nixon concluded that his political career was over. On the morning after the election, an unshaven, exhausted Nixon, who had stayed up much of the night sourly watching returns, came down from his hotel suite to a gathered press. At the end of his concession speech, a clearly distraught Nixon snapped, and nearly in an afterthought, told the gathering that they would not have him to "kick around anymore." Coverage of his campaign had not been universally negative, but he had become hypersensitive to any criticism.

The Nixons bid farewell to their home state to move to New York City where Richard would join a large corporate law firm. In 1964, Nixon deftly threw his support to the new hero of the Republican right, Barry Goldwater. This move won Goldwater's long-lasting support, which proved critical in Nixon's great political comeback in 1968, when he won the GOP nomination. Nixon was a far different man and politician than the one who had entered American politics twenty-two years before. He remained an internationalist in foreign policy, but his flexibility on domestic issues in 1968 and as president confused his critics on his left and right. For Richard Nixon, idealism appeared to give way to opportunism, political adroitness to self-advancement, and idealism to cynicism.

2 | Nelson Rockefeller
Ambition and Appetite

Nelson Rockefeller was a man of huge appetites, and his wealth allowed him to indulge his desires with one exception: his ambition to be president. In his quest for the White House, his wealth and ambition would be turned against him. His success as governor of New York was taken by conservatives as an indication of his liberalism being more appropriately that of a Democrat than a Republican. His divorce and remarriage were taken as a sign of appetite and lack of moral compass. He won the woman of his dreams only to find himself under siege by his enemies. His remarriage created an Iliad of misery for the rest of his political career.

Rockefeller entered American presidential politics with a sense of privilege that came from his status and immense wealth as a member of one of the richest families in the nation. He combined this sense of privilege with a sense of righteousness, derived in part from his Baptist childhood. He proclaimed that he was the "conscience" of the Republican Party. He exhorted his party to take stronger stands on civil rights and restoration of inner cities, and to distance itself from the GOP's ideological extremists. There was measured calculation in his projection of himself as the conscience of the party, but this was more than political opportunism intended to appeal to moderates and liberals within the party. Political advisers warned him that his public attacks on conservatives ensured his alienation from these growing wings of the party.

Ideologically, Rockefeller at first tried to be flexible. He won over Democrats in his home state of New York through massive spending programs. With the larger GOP, he attempted at first to declare himself a conservative only to discover that this was going to be a hard, if not impossible, sell given his record as governor. He moved to the left, but his adamant refusal to play second fiddle—accepting a slot on the ticket as a vice-presidential running mate—was testament to GOP voters that Rockefeller's loyalty was only to his own advancement. Rockefeller, for his part, simply could not believe that voters would rally to Barry Goldwater, an ideologue from a backwater state, or to an opportunist such as Nixon, the son of a small-store owner. He convinced himself that if only these misguided voters would come to their senses and see what he had to offer the country, the party and the nation would be saved. He was, after all, a Rockefeller. Unfortunately for him, voters saw him as just that—a Rockefeller.

His largest political problem lay not in his personal failings, however, but in the changes in the Republican Party, which was moving in a more conservative direction. Rockefeller, a New Yorker, for all his ability on the campaign trail, often seemed tone deaf to the mood of Republicans outside the East Coast who constituted the majority of the party. He found himself unable to outflank the right with his support for a strong national defense and unable to capture enough Republican voters with his call for the party to take a firmer pro–civil rights position. His claim to be a fiscal conservative was belied by his spendthrift policies in New York. Caught between the shoals of winnable New York State politics and a problematic national politics, as well as an ideologically and regionally divided Republican Party, Rockefeller vacillated, even when it came to declaring himself a candidate for president. When he did make a full commitment to run for the party's nomination in 1964, he could not have picked a worse year. Nixon was out of the picture, but unfortunately for Rockefeller, he found himself facing a Goldwater uprising and later, in 1968, a Nixon juggernaut. Timing just seemed a little off for a Rockefeller nomination, and for all his political skills evident in New York State politics, he always seemed a little out of step and too much caught up in his sense of privileged destiny.

For all of his urbanity, there was an odd provincialism to Rockefeller. In the late 1960s, when Governor Rockefeller grappled with the moral complexities of the abortion question, he instructed an aide to arrange a meeting with the eminent theologian Thomas Aquinas, whom he had seen quoted in an editorial. Rockefeller laughed at himself when he learned that Aquinas had died in the thirteenth century.[1] Rockefeller was not any shallower than other politicians of his age then or later. The difference was that his immense wealth allowed him to act on his hubris, and his army of experts and technocrats (some with more vision than others) encouraged Rockefeller's sense of privileged power.

A Sense of Privilege

Rockefeller's parents, John Jr. and Abigail, raised their children to assume the responsibility that comes from immense wealth, princelings groomed to be heir to a kingdom. They imbued in their children the values of frugality, hard work, and social duty. Their faith as Baptists reinforced these traditional values. The Baptist religion of the Rockefellers was a Social Gospel variety, one aimed at uplifting and serving the downtrodden, not the hard-edged Calvinism found in Southern Baptists. The Rockefellers were do-gooders, whose good works were directed by the best and brightest medical researchers, scientists, demographers, agricultural experts, and public health specialists. John Jr. took his family's faith seriously and directed his energies to fulfilling his parents' Baptist precepts to do-goodism. [2] At the age of ten, Nelson vowed to abstain from drink, tobacco, and profanity—the vows of a good Baptist boy.

Surrounded by maids, chauffeurs, gardeners, and personal secretaries, and living in numerous mansions and taking family holidays that compared to tours of Chinese emperors, inevitably imparted a sense of privilege to the Rockefeller children. Nelson grew up in a nine-story, limestone New York City townhouse on the Upper West Side. The mansion had bedrooms for each of the children, servants' quarters, a gymnasium, an infirmary, two drawing rooms, a music room, an art gallery, and a rooftop playground with a squash court. Another family mansion, even larger, was located up the Hudson River near Tarrytown, New York. A summer mansion in Seal Harbor, Maine, with almost fifty rooms, allowed the family to retreat from New York's oppressive humidity. They could escape as well to the Grand Tetons in Wyoming, where they had another home.

Nelson and his siblings could not avoid seeing the power and influence of the family exerted in innumerable ways, large and small. This influence extended well beyond knowing that the family hobnobbed with those who controlled the levers of power in politics, finance, business, and culture; realizing they went to the same schools as did the children of the family's friends; or understanding that one day they would marry into one of these families in the custom of pre–World War I European royalty. This sense of power and influence was acquired in daily life. Nelson saw family influence at work in the schools to which he was admitted, the college scholarship he won, his subsequent career, and even the impact of a modest complaint that could affect the lives of average people. Returning with his older brother, John, from a European cycling tour after high-school graduation, Nelson was met by a taxi driver at the dock from the freighter they had returned home on. Nelson wrote to his father complaining that the driver had run up a couple of dollars on the cab meter before the brothers stepped into the car. When asked about the charge, the driver replied that he had been waiting at the dock. Nelson wrote his father about the charge: "I hate to make a fuss over three dollars, but I also hate to get gypped by a taxi driver." His father took the complaint to the second deputy police commissioner, who located the cabbie and revoked his taxi license. Four months later, John Jr. was informed that the out-of-work cabbie, who was married with three children, was destitute. Rockefeller pleaded to the commissioner to reverse his decision, although the historical record is not clear what happened in the end to the poor cabbie.[3] A complaint about three dollars cost a working stiff his job. Nelson understood the power of his family and the privileges that came with being a Rockefeller.

Nelson proved especially difficult at times, although only within the high standards set by his parents. He performed poorly in school; proved unable to concentrate on anything for long, especially books; and was given to rambunctious pranks, which appear pretty harmless today. Deliberately singing off key at church, as Nelson did, was hardly the greatest sin that a youth could commit. However much his parents worried that Nelson was not going to achieve what it meant to be a Rockefeller, he was an obedient child who constantly sought the approval of his parents.

His parents enrolled young Nelson in Lincoln School, an experimental school funded by the Rockefellers. Conceived by Abraham Flexner, who worked for the Rockefeller General Board, the school imbued the progressive values of John Dewey. The curriculum was designed to encourage scientific thought, intellectual curiosity, and democratic community citizenship. His classmates liked young Nelson, electing him class chairman in eighth grade and in his senior year of high school, chairman of the athletic committee. His classmates took it as not unusual when Nelson's parents invited his entire class to a hockey match or the circus at Madison Square Garden. Classmates were invited to the Tarrytown mansion to go camping in one of the estate's cabins. Dinner guests were picked up in chauffeur-driven cars to be transported to the Rockefellers' Upper West Side townhouse.

For all of his affability and flair, Rockefeller barely graduated from Lincoln. His academic record was such that going to Princeton or Harvard University was out. Nelson decided on Dartmouth College, a less academically challenging environment. The president of the college, Ernest M. Hopkins, served as a trustee of the Rockefeller Foundation, and his family and the Rockefellers frequently socialized.

Although handicapped with dyslexia, Nelson rose to the top of his class academically and was admitted to the college honor society. There was a dilettantish quality to his academics. He majored at first in politics, then considered becoming an architect before deciding on economics as his major. Rockefeller's required undergraduate thesis was an institutional study of the Standard Oil Company, founded by his grandfather. Relying heavily on an unpublished biography of his grandfather sent to him by his father, Nelson properly footnoted the manuscript to develop a point-by-point defense of his grandfather's business practices. The final thesis was full of typos, but faculty did not ask for revision. In his junior year, Rockefeller was one of five students selected by Hopkins for the senior fellowship program. Senior fellows were given carte blanche in their projects and were allowed freedom to pursue their intellectual interests without having to attend classes, take exams, or earn grades. Graduation was automatic. This senior fellowship program was funded by a Rockefeller General Education $1.5 million grant. Fellows had been personally selected by Hopkins. Nelson spent the next year studying photographic art.

Immediately after graduation, in June 1930, Rockefeller married Mary Todhunter Clark, a daughter of a socially prominent Philadelphia family. The marriage lasted over three decades and produced five children. Over the years, however, the marriage itself became one of social convenience more akin to European nobility than American romance. Nelson went to work for his father, eventually becoming manager of the newly opened Rockefeller Center, the headquarters of the family empire. Nelson used Rockefeller business connections and a no-holds-barred approach to press corporations to lease space at the center. In business, Nelson Rockefeller combined ruthlessness and a kind of political naïveté.

This myopia was evident in commissioning left-wing Mexican artist Diego Rivera to paint a mural at the Rockefeller Center RCA Building. Rivera's pro-Soviet views were well known when Rockefeller, with the encouragement of his mother Abigail, invited Rivera to paint a mural in the entrance area of the building in 1932. Signs that Rivera's mural might present political problems were ignored, even though Rivera in accepting the RCA Building commission proposed a mural panel, showing "the Workers arriving at a true understanding of their rights regarding the means of production. . . . It will show Workers of the cities and the country inheriting the earth." Other panels were to depict workers, peasants, and the unemployed in bread lines.⁴ At the time, Rivera was completing a mural funded in part by Edsel Ford for the Detroit Museum of Art (now the Detroit Institute of Arts), which showed Ford Company Motor employees as the oppressed proletariat.

When the RCA Building mural was completed, the first panel showed a panorama of airplanes, death rays, and bayonet-wielding soldiers wearing gas masks. The second panel depicted a May Day celebration in Red Square. Next came a graphic scene of floating microbes of syphilis, gonorrhea, and tuberculosis swirling around card-playing, drinking ladies. Rivera then turned to a panel showing a soldier, a worker, and a black farmer holding hands with Lenin. Opened to the public in late April 1932, the mural caused an uproar. Finally, under public pressure, Nelson's father personally intervened, eventually ordering the mural destroyed. The entire episode embarrassed the Rockefeller family. Years of public relations work to restore the Rockefeller name in the public eye were set back by the controversy. Nelson Rockefeller should have seen this coming, but he had his mind so set on this project that he failed to see the inevitable backlash.

In 1938, bored with business, Rockefeller approached the Roosevelt administration with a proposal to head an effort to develop economic relations with South America. Franklin Roosevelt, after meeting with the thirty-two-year-old Rockefeller, gave the go-ahead for the plan and appointed Rockefeller to his administration as head of the Office of the Coordinator of Inter-American Affairs. Over the next four years, Rockefeller's agency, with a staff of 1,100 in Washington and 300 field specialists, spent $140 million. In 1944, Roosevelt appointed Rockefeller as assistant secretary of state to head the division of Latin American affairs. The State Department was notorious for byzantine in-fighting. The resignation of Cordell Hull, Roosevelt's secretary of state, in 1944, and his replacement by Edward Stettinius Jr., a businessman with little foreign affairs experience, only intensified divisions within the department. Rockefeller waded into the middle of this infighting when he convinced the ailing Roosevelt to agree to an inter-American conference to be held in Mexico City to organize a hemispheric defense alliance. The conference ran head on into opposition from State Department officials involved in planning a postwar new world organization. They correctly saw the establishment of a hemispheric defense alliance as undercutting the international ethos of the proposed new world organization.

At the Mexico City conference in 1945, Rockefeller threw his support behind the Act of Chapultepec, which called for a treaty declaring that an attack on one country in the Western Hemisphere was an attack on all. The bureaucratic warfare over the principle of regional defense alliances spilled over when forty-seven nations met in San Francisco in late spring 1945 to charter a new United Nations Organization. Against the wishes of higher State Department officials, Rockefeller chartered a private plane to bring Latin American delegates to the San Francisco conference. There, Latin American delegates joined Rockefeller, secretary general of the United Nations conference Alger Hiss, and others in the American delegation for pushing through Article 51 that allowed for regional defense alliances. Article 51 split the American delegation.[5] A year later, Nelson Rockefeller arranged to have Rockefeller property in New York City donated as the site of the new United Nations headquarters. Finally, Truman, who had stepped into the presidency after Roosevelt's death in 1945, had enough of Rockefeller's self-promotion. He forced Rockefeller out of his post.

Rockefeller returned to private life, as chairman of Rockefeller Center. His commitment to changing the world through grandiose plans and his ambition did not abate.[6] When Republican Dwight D. Eisenhower won the White House in 1952, Rockefeller saw an opportunity to reenter public life, first working with the new secretary of defense, Charles E. Wilson, a longtime Rockefeller supporter, to reorganize the Pentagon.[7]

Rockefeller then went to work for Oveta Culp Hobby, the first secretary of health, education, and welfare, a new cabinet office, as an undersecretary. The position allowed him to craft new policy proposals, develop new programs, draft legislation, and work with Congress to enact new legislation. His energy was felt throughout Washington. He proposed extending massive federal aid to education and creating an expansive national health care insurance program. He proposed new programs for vocational rehabilitation of welfare recipients, prevention of juvenile delinquency, and expansion of research into health, education, and welfare problems.

Rockefeller wanted even more. In late 1954, he called upon Eisenhower to appoint him the new special assistant to the president for Cold War planning. The enemies Rockefeller made on his climb up finally caught up with him. Secretary of State John Foster Dulles and Secretary of the Treasury George Humphrey persuaded Eisenhower that Rockefeller was a spendthrift and not a team player. Under pressure, Rockefeller resigned his government position in 1956. The forty-eight-year-old concluded that the best way to hold power was to be elected president himself.

Rocky Enters Politics

The first step to the White House ran through New York. Being elected governor of the state led to presidential nominations for Grover Cleveland, Al Smith, Franklin Roosevelt, and Tom Dewey. For Rockefeller, this meant taking on incumbent Democratic governor W. Averell Harriman, another son of a robber baron, who was seeking reelection in 1958. Guided by his chief adviser and keen political strategist Frank Jamieson, policy expert Bill Ronan, and George Hinman, a lawyer from upstate New York, Rockefeller skillfully won key Republicans throughout the state to his cause.[8] Critical to his strategy was winning upstate conservative Republicans such as William H. Hill, an influential newspaper publisher. At the same time, Rockefeller marshaled a small army of researchers to develop hundreds of studies about state problems. Deals were struck based on political interest and advancement, devoid of ideology. Rockefeller's alliances were without principle. It was old-time New York power politics.

Throughout July and August 1958, Rockefeller traveled around upstate New York, talking to large and small groups, going to dinners, stopping to hug children. His standard greeting, "Hiya, fella," imparted a common touch to the multimillionaire. He met with county Republican leaders, assuring them he could beat Harriman and once in the governor's office would open his door to them. By the time the Republican state convention met, he had enough delegates to win the nomination. Rockefeller's acceptance speech rocked the convention, and he left without making enemies, unlike Harriman at the Democratic convention who was forced by New York City Tammany politicians to endorse antireform Manhattan district attorney Frank Hogan for the Senate. Harriman's endorsement angered reform Democrats, including the influential Eleanor Roosevelt, who publicly attacked him in her syndicated newspaper column. Harriman entered the campaign with a divided party.

On the campaign trail, Rockefeller surprised people by his ability to connect with ordinary folks. He appeared easy to like. He came across as down to earth and enthusiastic, all captured in his campaign slogan, "Get Rollin' with Rock." Never a brilliant speaker in formal settings, he made up for it in meeting voters. He projected the persona of a regular guy who was genuinely interested in people. His staff found themselves time and again trying to get Rockefeller to stop talking to a voter so he could move on to the next event.

The voters found in Nelson a Rockefeller they could love. He truly enjoyed meeting the masses.

He endorsed the expansion of Social Security under the Department of Health, Education, and Welfare; federal aid to education; greater state funding to education; raising state employee salaries; a reforestation program; mass transit and the construction of new highways; more funding for agricultural research; and new investigations into organized crime. There was something for everybody in his program, except perhaps thugs on the New York waterfront and taxpayers who would have to pay for all the new programs.[9] To make sure his message got out, the campaign targeted appeals to professionals, women, the young, and every ethnic group in the city.

Rockefeller's message reached the public through an exceptionally well-organized campaign that used telephone messages, television advertising, and the press. He outspent Harriman by close to $700,000 in a $1.8 million campaign to reach independents and disaffected Democrats. Newspaper owner Dorothy Schiff of the liberal *New York Post* switched from Harriman to Rockefeller in a front-page editorial. The *New York Times* backed Rocky largely because of Harriman's ties to Tammany Hall. When Vice President Richard Nixon showed up to campaign for congressional Republicans, Rockefeller kept his distance, telling the press he was campaigning for a state office. In a Democratic year and in a Democratic state, Rockefeller did not want to be labeled an Eisenhower Republican.

Rockefeller swamped Harriman on Election Day by a margin of over 550,000 votes of the nearly six million cast. What made Rockefeller's victory all the more impressive was that nationally Republicans suffered immense losses, losing thirteen Senate seats and forty-eight House seats. Nixon, against his better instincts, had campaigned heavily for congressional seats. Many pundits saw Nixon as the loser and Rockefeller as the winner in 1958. The latter's huge victory strengthened his illusion that the presidency was within reach.

As governor of the nation's most populous state, Rockefeller would have found it difficult under any circumstances to have been a small-government Republican. New York State, in particular, was a body politic composed of special-interest groups looking to government to promote their projects: public works and expansion of education, welfare benefits, health care, community projects, the arts, and on and on. Rockefeller was not the type of ideological or practical politician to stand in the way. Indeed, he led the charge. He proposed a budget that exceeded $2 billion, the highest in state history. To support his program, he pushed through an increase in state gasoline and state income taxes. He enticed legislators with promises to support their pet projects, while other staff members warned legislators to expect to be punished if they did not get on board the governor's program. Rockefeller cajoled, threatened, and enticed legislators, labor union leaders, and power brokers. Big-government Republicanism served his political interests in New York, but as a result, the Rockefeller name became anathema to grassroots conservatives in the growing Sunbelt. There was a certain irony in this. Once despised by the left as symbolizing everything wrong with robber-baron capitalism, Rockefeller, the name and the man, became a symbol for what was wrong with liberal big-government Republicanism.

The 1960 Election

As the 1960 election approached, Rockefeller staked out two positions, one heartfelt as a champion of civil rights and the other politically calculated as a supporter of strong national defense. Few on Rockefeller's staff demurred to their boss's commitment to run for the White House, even though it was clear Nixon had a hammerlock among party leaders. The polls themselves should have told Rockefeller his chance of winning the nomination was nil. Since the GOP election debacle in 1958, Nixon had increased his support in the party to 61 percent, more than enough support to head the ticket. After just six months in the governor's office, Rockefeller's numbers had fallen to just 18 percent of Republicans who favored him for the presidential nomination.[10]

Rockefeller and his staff saw Nixon as nothing more than an opportunistic politician without vision. As a key political adviser, L. Judson Morhouse wrote Rockefeller in fall 1959, "For seven years Nixon has been doing favors for people who will be or will control delegates." He added that the central strategy of the Nixon campaign was to take advantage of Rockefeller not announcing he was declaring for the presidency. An unknown insider in the Nixon campaign reported to Morhouse that the "greatest fear" of the Nixon group was a Rockefeller candidacy. Morhouse concluded, "The warmth of the Rockefeller smile, charm and personality make the Nixon group cringe."[11] Morhouse was convinced that Nixon was a hollow candidate, who once punctured would collapse.

Rockefeller undertook exploratory trips to get a sense of his presidential chances. He discovered two discouraging facts: he had the support of neither the Republican Party leaders nor the rank and file. For example, when he traveled to Los Angeles in 1959 to cultivate party leaders in that state, he was greeted at the airport by Republican national committeeman Ed Shattuck wearing a Nixon button. Later that evening, Rockefeller addressed the Western Republican Leadership Conference underneath a huge portrait of Nixon. This experience was repeated on other trips. Even in his own backyard, upstate New York Republican leaders distanced themselves from his presidential race. Reality finally sunk in. In December 1959, Rockefeller announced he was not going to seek the presidency. The decision was debated right up to the time of the announcement.[12]

Rockefeller did not hide his disappointed feelings. Rejection came hard to him. When Richard Nixon, who was sweeping the primaries, mentioned to reporters that Rockefeller might have a place on the ticket, Rockefeller churlishly responded, "Did he say what place?"[13] Nixon worked hard at trying to improve relations with Rockefeller. Nixon inquired whether Rockefeller wanted to give a keynote address at the convention or chair the national convention. In reply, Rockefeller hinted that he might not even attend the convention, a clear slap in the face of Nixon.

Even though Rockefeller announced he was not seeking the nomination, he harbored hopes that somehow the party might turn to him. Rockefeller continued to entertain larger ambitions—the presidential nomination itself. When an American spy plane was shot down over the Soviet Union and the pilot, Gary Powers, captured on May 1, 1960, Rockefeller seized the opportunity, against the advice of his staff, to criticize Eisenhower's foreign policy. To attack Ike, the most popular politician in America, was folly. Americans had full confidence in the military judgment of the commander of the European Theater and the D-Day invasion.[14] Eisenhower was especially irate about Rockefeller's criticism. When Rockefeller privately asked Eisenhower, the president he had just criticized, whether he should make a bid for the presidency, a furious Eisenhower replied that he believed Rockefeller's remarks on the weak state of American defenses had unnecessarily alarmed the American people. He advised Rockefeller not to enter the race to avoid being ridiculed as "off again, on again, gone again Finnegan."[15]

Once again in the news, Rockefeller began calling for the federal government to enforce desegregation, for more federal funding for education, and for the establishment of a national health system for the elderly. If this was not enough to alienate grassroots conservatives, he declared that the nation-state was obsolete and urged the establishment of a North Atlantic confederation with a common trade market and a unified defense system. He confirmed to the growing right in the party that he was a big-government internationalist—a nemesis of true Republican Party values.

By July, Nixon feared a full-blown public fight at a time when delegates were just arriving at the Republican convention in Chicago. Anxious to avoid a public relations disaster, an anxious Nixon phoned Rockefeller to inform him, "I want to go all the way with you on defense and foreign policy."[16] He asked if a personal meeting might be arranged to hash out their apparent differences. In the catbird seat, Rockefeller insisted that such a meeting take place in his New York Fifth Avenue apartment and that any press release following the meeting must state that Nixon had requested the get-together. As Republican delegates gathered in Chicago, the duo met on July 22, 1960, for dinner followed by a long night of negotiation, with a telephone hookup with Charles Percy, chairman of the Platform Committee, and Rockefeller associate Emmet Hughes in Chicago.

At the dinner, Nixon offered Rockefeller the vice-presidential slot, which was turned down without hesitation. The offer was genuine. The polls showed that Rockefeller would add a couple of points in the popular vote. With Johnson on the ticket with Kennedy, Nixon knew that Northern-tier states such as New York and Pennsylvania were needed to compensate for the projected loss of key Southern states that Johnson would bring to Democrats. Nixon understood also that Rockefeller could bring financial resources to the campaign. Nixon later recalled in his memoirs, "I was not altogether sorry, because Rockefeller's independent temperament would have made him a much more difficult running mate for me to deal with than Johnson would be for Kennedy."[17] Rockefeller's rejection of the second spot led Nixon to turn to Henry Cabot Lodge Jr., a liberal Massachusetts Republican who added little to the ticket. Rockefeller's obstinacy in not wanting to play second fiddle in 1960 might have been one of his greatest political mistakes. If he had accepted Nixon's offer, Rockefeller would have shown party loyalty and introduced himself to the larger electorate under the shadow of Nixon, which would have restrained the full-scale assault he would experience four years later from conservatives.

Instead, Rockefeller—who had now decided to be the conscience of the Republican Party—pressed Nixon to agree to stronger civil rights and national security planks in the party. The fourteen-point agreement reached by Nixon and Rockefeller included seven points on foreign policy and seven on civil rights. The next morning, Rockefeller called a press conference to announce the agreement and to report that Nixon had asked for the meeting.

The announcement of the deal—branded the "Compact of Fifth Avenue"—came just as the Republican convention was opening in Chicago. In a press conference the next day, Nixon told the press he had offered the vice-presidential slot to Rockefeller, who had declined; but while there were differences in detail and emphasis, they agreed on the basic principles of foreign and domestic policy issues confronting the American people. Nixon's press conference glossed over the deep differences within the party between the liberal and conservative wings.[18]

Reports of the agreement sent shock waves through the ranks of conservatives. The conservative *Chicago Tribune* captured the dismay many delegates felt over the pact when it headlined its report "Grant Surrenders to Lee." Cornered by the press, Goldwater denounced the agreement as nothing less than the "Munich of the Republican Party." Rumors circulated that Goldwater was going to throw his hat into the ring, as many of his followers were urging him to do. Nixon persuaded delegates to accept a stronger civil rights plank, but conservative anger was only quelled when Goldwater told the entire convention on television that he would not accept the nomination. He said, "We had our chance. . . . Let's grow up, conservatives. If we want to take this party back—and I think we can someday—let's get to work."[19]

Nixon's loss to Kennedy in 1960—as close as it was—left the Republican Party deeply divided.[20] The loss of the nomination to Nixon left Rockefeller depressed, but he campaigned heavily for the Republican ticket—to little avail in New York, which went Democratic by close to a half million votes. Republican politics over the next four years became a Manichean world of the forces of light versus darkness, as both sides perceived the other as representing the twilight of the American Republic.

Rockefeller Looks to 1964

Nixon locked Rockefeller out of the 1960 nomination because Nixon was the party leadership's favorite, but the problem went deeper than this. Republican voters—those outside New York—simply thought Rockefeller was far too left-leaning politically to carry the GOP banner. Any benefits he might have gained as a Cold War hawk were negated by his liberal positions on domestic issues. Rockefeller staff claimed that their man had a broader vision than the Republican Party, which suggested that voters were myopic.

The fact of the matter is that not enough Republican voters liked Rockefeller. Whatever the problems with Rockefeller's big-government Republicanism, the greater problem rested in voters' distrust of his character and their lack of confidence in his principles. He projected ambition, political vacillation, ambiguous core principles, and lack of party loyalty.[21]

Voters were repulsed by Rockefeller's perceived lack of character and his mercurial temperament. A reporter for the *New York Post* summed up Rockefeller's problem at the time: "He cannot keep his pecker in his pants."[22] The problem with Rockefeller was that he liked to brag to reporters about his sexual prowess. This would not have been a problem in the 1950s, when journalists agreed not to talk about the sex lives of politicians unless it involved public scandal, espionage, or homosexuality. When Rockefeller announced he was getting a divorce and then a short time later announced he was marrying Happy Murphy, a recent divorcee with four children, he came across as an adulterer and a home-breaker. The Murphys' bitter divorce proceedings, closely followed by New York's tabloid press, damaged both Nelson's and Happy's public images.[23]

Rockefeller's advisers had reassured him that the press uproar would die down after a couple of months. They were wrong. The political damage proved deadly. William Rusher, publisher of the *National Review*, observed that Rockefeller was one of the few people in the world to turn motherhood into a liability. Others joked that they could not distinguish the wedding bells from death tolls. The announcement of the couple's first child in the midst of the California Republican primary in 1964 reminded voters once again how Rockefeller was a home-breaker. Rockefeller simply could not understand why voters did not accept his need for personal happiness or why he drew the wrath of voters, while many other politicians (and voters) were having extramarital affairs. After all, he had done the honorable thing and married Happy, and he had made his love public. Rockefeller's problem, though, was that he thought he could have it all—personal fulfillment and the presidency.

After Nixon's loss in 1960, Rockefeller's presidential aspirations were revived. The path to a nomination in 1964 seemed open to him. Nixon's defeat for the governor's race in California in 1962 and Rockefeller's landslide gubernatorial reelection that same year against Democrat Robert Morgenthau appeared to make Rockefeller a major contender. The only person standing in Rockefeller's way was the icon of the GOP right, Barry Goldwater, the U.S. senator from Arizona. Rockefeller advisers saw Goldwater as too far right and too personally eccentric—not to mention being from a backwater state—to receive the nomination. There was fear, though, that a deadlocked convention might lead Nixon to step into the breach. Rockefeller decided to counter the Goldwater threat by tacking to the right. This strategy was laid out in a letter Rockefeller wrote to New York liberal U.S. senator Jacob Javits, urging him to temper his attacks on conservatives. Rockefeller declared, "I do think we should be careful not to cast our campaign in the form of an issue with other Republicans and especially not to be guilty of personal aspersions that none of us mean. We are all sincere in our views, and, especially on the international issues, it has always seemed to me that our differences are mostly in the realm of semantics."[24] Rockefeller's advisers warned him that the mood in the Republican Party was against ultraliberalism. He began to eschew ideological labels by parsing his allegiance. He described himself as an "economic conservative and a human rights liberal."[25] Pursuing his new role as an economic conservative, he arranged to meet with the national leadership of Young Americans for Freedom, a recently formed conservative youth group organized by William F. Buckley Jr. and William Rusher of the *National Review*. At the meeting at his New York office, Rockefeller tried to convince the young conservatives that he, too, was a conservative. Rockefeller did not convince anyone. Young conservatives, for the most part, despised Rockefeller almost as much as Soviet Communism.[26]

Rockefeller next turned to outright gifts to win over conservatives. The Rockefeller family arranged for William Miller (later Goldwater's running mate), an upstate conservative congressman, to receive a $30,000 personal loan.[27] Rockefeller reached out to Goldwater himself by arranging a monthly dinner where Goldwater would bring five conservative friends who would meet with an equal number of Rockefeller liberals. Rockefeller and Goldwater also began to meet regularly in Washington for breakfast. Goldwater asked that these clandestine meetings remain secret.[28] Rockefeller believed he was winning Goldwater over to his cause. Later, Nelson's brother Laurance observed about the Rockefeller-Goldwater détente, "I've never seen anyone more susceptible to a pat on the back than Barry Goldwater. He responded to all manner of flattery."[29] In his memoirs, Goldwater observed that the "Nelson Rockefeller I saw in 1961 and 1962 appeared much more conservative than his public image."[30] Even when it was clear that the rapprochement had failed, Goldwater felt comfortable enough to write a "Dear Nelson" letter, with "best personal wishes," to ask him to donate money to the University of Arizona.[31]

When Rockefeller's marriage to Happy came under public attack, Rocke-feller blamed conservatives. The fact of the matter was that it was not just conservatives who were upset by Rockefeller's remarriage. Former Connecti-cut U.S. senator Prescott Bush, seen by many as a liberal Republican, blasted Rockefeller in public in 1963. "Have we come to the point in our life as a nation where the Governor of a great state, one who perhaps aspires to the nomination for President of the United States, can desert a good wife, mother of his grown children, divorce her, then persuade a young mother of four youngsters to abandon her husband and their four children and marry the Governor?"[32]

By 1963, Rockefeller had decided that the key to defeating Goldwater was to depict him as an extremist or as naïve about right-wing extremism. His staff reported that political operative F. Clifton White, who had worked ear-lier for Thomas Dewey's campaign in the 1940s, was organizing a large grass-roots effort to secure Goldwater the nomination. Goldwater supporters insisted that there were tens of millions of potential voters just waiting for a true conservative to come on the scene. Grassroots conservatives tended to believe their own heated rhetoric about Americans' sense of betrayal by liber-als on foreign and domestic policy. GOP conservatives dismissed too easily the antiextremist literature found in books, magazines, and newspapers that streamed forth in this period. The John Birch Society and other anti-Communist organizations, paramilitary and racist groups, and conservative publications, such as Buckley's *National Review*, were conflated in these at-tacks as part of the extreme right.

Conservatives failed to understand the poignancy of civil rights demands for ending racial segregation and protecting black voting rights. Nor did they understand the appeal during the postwar economic boom by liberals to ad-dress issues of poverty, health care for the elderly, and an array of urban problems through federal programs and monies. Raising taxes was less con-troversial when everyone enjoyed higher wages. Denouncing liberals as so-cialists in sheep's clothing and ranting about treason in America attracted hard-core ideological voters, and might win a few hard-core Southern white voters upset by the end of the old racist order, but it did not present a mes-sage for winning a general election. For many on the far right, Rockefeller was as much the enemy as any overt Marxist Leninist.[33]

Rockefeller presented himself as an alternative to the dark road he per-ceived the party was walking down. He viewed himself as the voice of reason and the conscience of the party. This self-anointed role was understandable:

he stood as the voice of liberal Republicanism in the country; he had won two landslide elections as governor of the nation's most populous state; he had undertaken urban reform in the country's largest city; and he stood as a leading advocate for civil rights and a strong national defense. While the New York State budget had grown exponentially under his administration, Rockefeller prided himself on having introduced workfare pilot programs for welfare recipients in the state. Indeed, the Rockefeller campaign seriously considered in 1964 promoting a "crack down on welfare abuse" as a way of countering Goldwater's conservatism.[34]

Rockefeller found Goldwater temperamentally ill-suited for the presidency, vague on foreign policy, and too linked to far-right extremism in America. Rockefeller's huge research staff began accumulating files documenting right-wing extremism. Throughout the summer of 1963, he assailed the extremist elements, Birchers, and the lunatic fringe that had gained influence within the Republican Party whose methods included "threatening letters, smear and hate literature, strong arm and goon tactics, bomb threats and bombings, infiltration and takeover of established political organizations by Communist and Nazi methods."[35] Rockefeller's assault on the far right and his attempt to associate these elements with the Goldwater campaign failed to slow Goldwater's continuing surge in the polls.

Much of the Goldwater campaign tracking came from an inside informant. In April 1962, Rockefeller's staff learned through a source close to Stephen Shadegg, an influential Arizona conservative, that Goldwater was definitely going after the nomination and planned to start rounding up delegates right after the upcoming midterm elections.[36] George Hinman told Rockefeller that he considered Shadegg a "neo-fascist."[37] The Rockefeller people understood Goldwater's vulnerabilities. His personal behavior made for good humor among the Rockefeller staff, as when Hinman noted that Barry had hired an attractive young secretary who "cannot take dictation or type and her qualifications are not visible or perhaps they are."[38] The Rockefeller campaign paid particular attention to Goldwater's efforts in California. They were especially attuned to the strength of the right wing in the state. In a confidential report to Rockefeller, Arthur M. Richardson observed, "The John Birch Society cannot be underrated in Southern California." He noted that while on a recent trip (in March 1962) he attended several Republican meetings dominated by members of the Birch Society, adding that they are "young, emotional and well-financed."[39]

Even while focused on the Goldwater campaign, Rockefeller people continued to worry about Nixon stepping into the race as a party unifier. They had followed Nixon's failed bid for the California governorship.[40] Caspar Weinberger, a moderate Republican from the state, warned Hinman that Nixon was opposed to the far right but that did not mean he would forgo a bid for the presidency in 1964.[41] Their fears were confirmed in early 1963 when they learned that Nixon told a key Republican operative that he believed George Romney could stop Rockefeller and, if this happened, Nixon thought he could win the nomination.[42] Part of the effort by the Rockefeller team to stop Nixon was to encourage anti-Nixon forces in California, including Nixon nemesis Goodwin Knight. But when Knight opened a Rockefeller campaign headquarters in Los Angeles in early 1963, Rockefeller personally ordered him to close it down until an official announcement was made that he was seeking the nomination. After that, the Rockefeller staff had little use for Knight, who they saw as trying to latch onto Rockefeller as a means of rehabilitating himself politically, spewing anti-Nixon "venom," and making money through television and radio appearances.[43]

At the same time, the Rockefeller campaign continued to release extensive policy papers for Rockefeller's own positions. For all his projection of policy know-how, Rockefeller's campaign continued to flounder. Finally, in early 1964, Rockefeller's key foreign policy adviser, Henry Kissinger, who had become increasingly involved in campaign strategy, stepped forward in an attempt to right the ship. In a lengthy and confidential memorandum sent to Rockefeller, Kissinger maintained that the campaign focused too much on "short-term-public relations considerations at the expense of fundamental moral concerns which are your primary raison d'etre. The quest for tomorrow's headline jeopardizes your capacity to lead six months from now." He bluntly told his boss that "the test of your role is not tomorrow's editorial but the one three or five years from now. Only such an attitude can reverse the collapse of values and of thought which has characterized so much of our post-war policy."[44] Kissinger urged Rockefeller to focus on Vietnam. Nonetheless, Rockefeller continued to flit from issue to issue. By the time Rockefeller spoke on Vietnam on April 26, calling for U.S. air strikes against Viet Cong supply lines in Laos and Cambodia, he had lost primaries in Illinois, New Jersey, Massachusetts, and Pennsylvania.

Rockefeller's major problem was not just the growing strength of the GOP right but his own political vulnerabilities outside of New York. Under Rockefeller, New York taxes had increased, while state expenditures had skyrocketed 61 percent over Harriman's final budget.[45] Some polls in early 1963 still gave Rockefeller a sizable lead over Goldwater, but Republican support for him crashed after his remarriage to Happy. Rockefeller began his quest for the presidency in 1963, enlisting New Hampshire governor Hugh Gregg to direct his activities in the first primary. When Henry Cabot Lodge Jr., Nixon's running mate in 1960, announced he was not going to enter the New Hampshire primary, Rockefeller saw his opening. He announced his candidacy on November 7, the first to enter the race officially. Fifteen days later on November 22, President John F. Kennedy was assassinated. His death changed the dynamics of the presidential campaign. It is doubtful that Kennedy would have lost reelection if he had lived, but his death assured the victory of his successor Lyndon B. Johnson. Johnson won a sympathy vote and could get Southern votes beyond Kennedy's reach. Nonetheless, an ambivalent Goldwater announced in January 1964 he was seeking the party's presidential nomination. Privately, he felt neither qualified nor electable for the presidency, but he felt obligated to his supporters to make a run for the White House.

Republican strategists saw the weaknesses of both candidates. Goldwater was weak in the Northeast, and his potential for winning the South against Lyndon Johnson was small. Rockefeller's strength outside the Northeast did not translate to support in the Midwest or West, let alone the South. This situation provided the opportunity for Michigan governor George Romney and Pennsylvania governor William Scranton to pose as compromise candidates.

Rockefeller entered the New Hampshire primary full blast. Goldwater believed he could win New Hampshire if moderates split their vote among Rockefeller, Scranton, and Romney. What neither campaign calculated was a write-in vote for Lodge. On March 10, Lodge surprised everyone when he won the primary with close to 36 percent of the vote compared with Goldwater's 22 percent and Rockefeller's 21 percent. Write-in votes gave Nixon 17 percent. The next major contest came in Illinois, where Rockefeller did not mount an effort. Goldwater swept the state with 61 percent against Senator Margaret Chase Smith, the first female presidential candidate to launch a major campaign. Following Illinois, Nixon and Lodge told followers to stop their write-in efforts. Nonetheless, Lodge won New Jersey with write-in votes. Rockefeller's campaign appeared to be going nowhere.

Two days before the Pennsylvania and Massachusetts primaries, Rockefeller sought to turn things around by calling for a more aggressive stance in Vietnam. Nonetheless, Lodge took his home state of Massachusetts and Scranton won his home state of Pennsylvania in their primaries. At this point, Republican voters were not lining up for either Goldwater or Rockefeller. Early May marked a turning point for Goldwater, as he swept primaries in Texas, Indiana, and Nebraska—only to come to a screeching halt when suddenly Rockefeller, after heavy campaigning, won Oregon with 33 percent of the vote, nearly double Goldwater's tally. As the month drew to a close, both campaigns (and pundits) saw that the nomination had come down to the June 2 California primary, whose winner got all the state's delegates. It was a closed primary restricted to registered Republicans in a state where Republicans were a minority.[46]

The California primary became a personality contest, one that played to Goldwater's benefit. The Rockefeller campaign assailed his rival as an "extremist." In a state with a sizable John Birch Society membership, the largest in the nation, charges of extremism did not faze these voters. Rockefeller's divorce was not so easily smoothed away, even though California had one of the highest divorce rates in the country. The issue was not just about divorce but what appeared to be Rockefeller's involvement in breaking up a happy home so he could indulge his appetite. The Rockefeller campaign hoped to overcome this issue by arranging for him to speak to undergraduates at Loyola University, a Roman Catholic college in Los Angeles. Just before Rockefeller's scheduled speech, James Francis Cardinal McIntyre, the conservative bishop of Los Angeles, called a press conference to explain that the Catholic Church was not imparting an official blessing to the candidacy of a man who had been divorced and then remarried. Matters worsened when sixteen Protestant evangelical ministers in the state issued a statement calling for Rockefeller to withdraw from the race because he could not handle his own domestic affairs, let alone the nation's. When Happy gave birth to a boy a couple of days after the ministers' plea, voters were reminded once again of Rockefeller's personal problems.[47] Kissinger recorded in his diary that an experienced journalist concluded that Rockefeller lost California partly because of Nelson Jr.'s birth and partly because the campaign lacked substance.[48]

This evaluation was somewhat unfair. The birth of Rockefeller's son in the heat of the campaign no doubt hurt him to a degree. He was already weak among Southern California voters and did not have enough strength in Northern California to compensate for his loss in the south. Nevertheless, there was substance to Rockefeller's campaign. The problem was perhaps too much substance and little focus. His New York–based staff lacked insight into what motivated California's numerous suburban Republicans. Rockefeller proved unable to articulate what he stood for, which allowed Goldwater to create a negative narrative about Rockefeller, the man and the liberal politician. Goldwater scratched by with a narrow victory of only 55,000 votes, but the death knell for Rockefeller had tolled. The massive California delegation gave Goldwater a majority at the convention. Rockefeller's bid for the presidency had effectively ended. He was of no mind, however, to slink off into the night. He was used to getting his way, even though most adults know that childish temper tantrums will not gain favor.

The Rockefeller camp now launched a full-scale attack on the prospective Republican nominee. Goldwater characterized the attack as trying to portray him as a "racist, trigger-happy warmonger, a nuclear madman, and a candidate who couldn't win."[49] They were joined in these attacks by the media and leading Republican politicians. Goldwater delegates, many of them attending the convention for the first time, were portrayed as a far right-wing mob. They played into this caricature when Rockefeller took the stage on television to protest the defeat of his attempt to insert a stronger civil rights plank in the platform. In the speech, Rockefeller deliberately taunted the delegates by speaking of "goon squads and Nazi methods," which led delegates to begin chanting, "We want Barry." In response, Rockefeller turned directly to the television camera and replied, "This is still a free country, ladies and gentleman."[50] Kissinger, attending his first political convention, watched with abhorrence the anger expressed by Goldwater supporters. He wrote shortly after the convention that whatever Goldwater's real views, as a "phenomenon his movement is similar to European fascism."[51]

Rockefeller did not come to the San Francisco Republican National Convention seeking party unity. His intent was to project his campaign as the voice of reason and himself as the prince of light standing against those voices of unreason and darkness within the party. He brought to the convention the righteousness of a Baptist, the self-assuredness of a successful governor, the arrogance of a man of wealth, and the foolishness of a Don Quixote. Any real chances of him ever winning his party's presidential nomination ended on July 14, 1964. One of the ironies of 1964 and Rockefeller's high moral stance was that it opened the door for his archenemy, Richard Nixon, to step forward in 1968 as the candidate who could reconcile the severely divided party.

Dreams Unfulfilled

Defeated in 1964 and alienated from much of the Republican Party for his lack of support for the party's nominee, Rockefeller nonetheless maintained hopes that he might become president. Immediately after the election, his staff began thinking about how to secure the party's nomination in 1968. Position papers were once again produced, campaign strategies crafted, press conferences called, and delegates counted.

Rockefeller entered the 1968 presidential campaign with full knowledge that his lack of support for the Goldwater-Miller ticket in 1964 had hurt him within the party. Political strategist Graham Molitor warned Rockefeller to avoid trying to defend his position because Nixon, who had campaigned for Goldwater, would "come out on top of any such controversy."[52] This issue alone should have given pause to Rockefeller's quixotic attempt to secure the nomination. There was a pathetic quality to his presidential ambitions in 1968, which belied political reality and self-reflection, encouraged by a campaign staff anxious to appease their master's ambitions and ego. Instead, the staff continued to boost a perspective that Nixon was disliked by most Republicans and the general electorate. They acquiesced, if not encouraged, Rockefeller to see himself as a voice of conscience for the Republican Party and the nation. They told him that his appeal went beyond partisan Republicans to the entire nation.[53]

Four months before the convention, his staff submitted to Rockefeller an eighty-page comprehensive research and intelligence strategy report on securing the party's nomination.[54] The detailed report recommended that Rockefeller start taking his message to voters in various regions and begin contacting delegates. When it became clear that this strategy had collapsed, his strategists came up with their most fanciful plan yet: a Rockefeller-Reagan ticket. In making the offer to Reagan, Rockefeller was not about to let ideological or policy differences stand between him and the nomination. The earlier report had shown irreconcilable differences between the two camps, which nonetheless did not prevent Rockefeller from offering Reagan the vice presidency. Reagan, of course, turned this offer down. Reagan knew he had a long political career ahead of him.

The convention gave Nixon the nomination on the first ballot.[55] To ensure support on his right, Nixon selected Spiro Agnew, governor of Maryland and one-time Rockefeller supporter, who had transformed himself into a darling of the conservatives for his call for law and order. One of the little ironies came a few weeks later when Hubert Humphrey, the Democratic Party presidential nominee, asked Nelson Rockefeller if he would consider being his running mate. Rockefeller declined.[56] Humphrey barely lost the election to Nixon. If Humphrey had won, Rockefeller's hopes for another presidential run in 1972 would have been reignited. But Rockefeller's presidential ambitions were never fully extinguished.

Rockefeller accommodated himself to the Nixon administration by cooperating in securing federal funding for his state. Nixon appointed Rockefeller people to posts within the administration, including Rockefeller's appointment to the President's Foreign Intelligence Advisory Board. Rockefeller's enduring influence on the administration came when Nixon appointed Henry Kissinger as national security adviser and later as secretary of state. Kissinger, who had been anti-Nixon since 1960, jumped the Rockefeller ship, certain that his advice on Vietnam and U.S. foreign relations was necessary to the Nixon presidency.

Nixon's appointment of Kissinger surprised many, including Kissinger himself. He had left the 1968 convention convinced that Nixon's nomination was a disaster. He wrote Rockefeller aides Oscar Ruebhausen and Emmet Hughes that he had "grave doubts" about Nixon, noting that "the man is, of course, a disaster. Now the Republican Party is a disaster. Fortunately, he can't be elected—or the whole country would be a disaster."[57] The fact is Nixon shared Kissinger's views on Vietnam. It was a debacle created by misconceived policies by the Kennedy and Johnson administrations that were given more to bureaucratic infighting than developing coherent foreign and defense policies. Kissinger and Nixon agreed that American postwar hegemony had ended, and in an unsafe world, the United States needed to exert leadership, not dominance, to maintain a stable international order, while realizing that the Soviet Union still posed an existential threat. If politics makes for strange bedfellows, so can foreign policy.

Appetite Insatiable

As it turned out, Rockefeller finally got a chance to enter the White House—not as the president but as vice president. Richard Nixon's fall in 1974 opened the door that had been shut to Rockefeller for more than a decade. Rockefeller had won a tough reelection campaign as governor in 1970, running as a conservative. Anxious to get conservative support, he begged Vice President Spiro Agnew, who had become the right's hero for his denunciation of liberals, to campaign for him in upstate New York. Rockefeller won reelection, but the state was headed toward financial disaster. As governor, he established a statewide low-income housing policy, regional mass-transit system, and a statewide university system, and he undertook early clean water and environmental reforms.

His liberal credentials would be tarnished when he ordered state police to retake Attica State Prison after two thousand inmates had seized control of the prison and had taken forty-two guards hostage in September 1971 following a prison riot. The ensuing assault by state police left forty-three dead, including ten guards. Reports of torture and killing of inmates and guards by the rioters failed to dissuade an outraged public that Rockefeller was without conscience.[58] Following the riot, Rockefeller pushed through mandatory sentencing legislation for drug possession in the state. Any laurels he might have received from liberals were replaced by a crown of thorns symbolizing what later critics would call the incarceration state.

Rockefeller knew this would be his last term as governor, so he welcomed Ford's invitation to become vice president. Nixon, just before resigning from office, advised Rockefeller not to get involved with the Ford administration. He warned that Ford was not up to the task of the presidency, and this could set up Rockefeller for a presidential run in 1976. He promised his support if Rockefeller were to make such a bid. Nixon, even as he fell from grace, remained as Machiavellian as ever.[59]

Rockefeller's tenure as vice president would be troubled and short.[60] The Senate confirmed his selection as vice president, but the hearings were brutal. Once in office, Rockefeller found himself being undercut by bureaucratic rivals led by Ford's chief of staff Donald Rumsfeld and his deputy, Dick Cheney. Rockefeller discovered his former adviser, Secretary of State Henry Kissinger, too busy protecting his own turf to help a bleeding Rockefeller.[61] As the 1976 election approached, Ford told Rockefeller that he did not want him on the ticket. This was Rockefeller's last political hurrah. He returned to private life. He died in January 1979 in a New York hotel room in coitus with a female staff member, his political ambitions perhaps abated but his carnal appetite unquenched. His ambitions were constrained neither by personal nor by ideological fidelity to core principles. He, like a Greek mythological figure, found that wealth, a golden fleece, cost him a kingship. Hubris inevitably gave way to tragedy in Rockefeller's life, which might have been avoided in a person with a more carefully calibrated moral compass.

3 | Idealism Betrayed, Opportunity Denied
Nixon and Rockefeller Compared

Henry Kissinger observed that everything that could be said about Nixon was both true and yet somehow wrong: "He was politically astute and highly intelligent, yet prone to self-destructive acts; exceptionally analytical, yet done in by yielding to ill-considered impulse; deeply patriotic, yet wont to hazard his achievements on tawdry practices; possessed of a considerable capacity to feel guilt coupled with an instinct to gravitate toward actions guaranteed to evoke these very feelings; an outstanding judge of people, except of those whose actions could affect his own interest; successful in the gregarious profession of politics, although introverted, almost reclusive." Kissinger found in Nixon the self-destructive flaws of a character in a tragedy.[1] Indeed, the rise and fall of Nixon has a Faustian cast:

> Till swollen with cunning of self-content,
> His waxen wings did mount about his reach
> And, melting heavens conspir'd his overthrow.[2]

Nelson Rockefeller, whom Kissinger had worked for as well, presents a less complicated personality. Rockefeller exhibited flaws of character and temperament as well: intelligent, yet not intellectual; gregarious in public, yet cautious, nearly diffident in private; patriotic and public spirited, yet always to his own advancement; honorable in general principle, yet malleable in politics and his personal life. Although exceptionally astute when it came to New York politics, Rockefeller proved unwilling, perhaps incapable, of graciously accepting defeat and repairing battered bridges. Too often, he gathered around him sycophants too feeble in their dependency to tell him the need to accept defeat. Rockefeller carried into politics an attitude of a princeling. Sent to the best schools, surrounded by the political and policy advisers considered the best in the nation, endowed with family wealth and the connections necessary to advance a political career, Rockefeller lacked the one ingredient necessary for a successful politician with presidential ambitions: common sense. Common sense might have told him that he should have accepted Nixon's offer to place him on the ticket as a running mate in 1960; a touch of common sense would have told him that he needed to accept Barry Goldwater as the Republican presidential nominee in 1964; and common sense might have told him that it was a wasted effort to challenge Nixon for the nomination in 1968. One is reminded of William Shakespeare's characterization of Henry IV: "I would you had but the wit; 'twere better than your dukedom."[3]

Richard Nixon and Nelson Rockefeller represent political rivals driven more by ambition and the desire for power than by principle, although this is not to say they lacked totally in principle. Nixon remained consistently an internationalist; Rockefeller stayed consistent in his belief in expanding civil rights. Nonetheless, both proved highly flexible in their ideological views, even though they proclaimed themselves opposites: Rockefeller, the Northeastern liberal, and Nixon, the moderate seeking conservative votes. Both were Cold Warriors. Rockefeller as governor accommodated himself to New York liberalism and the special interests and unions in his state. He pivoted to law and order and fiscal conservatism in the 1970s, however. Nixon claimed to be a rock-hard conservative, and he convinced many conservatives he was such; but once in the White House, he expanded the regulatory and welfare state and pursued détente with the Soviet Union and China, much in the same way Rockefeller would have if he had become president.

Both Nixon and Rockefeller brought to postwar American politics personalities that elicited genuine enthusiasm from their followers and deep hostility from their opponents. They were political leaders in their respective states, California and New York, both of which were controlled by the Democratic Party. As a result, Nixon and Rockefeller were politicians able to reach beyond their Republican base of support. At the same time, they were leaders in building the Republican parties in their states. Their skills as politicians should not be judged solely on the races they won or lost. Nixon appealed to the strong anti-Communist base within the Republican Party; Rockefeller's appeal was to Northeastern moderate and liberal Republicans.

Nixon and Rockefeller came of age in World War II and the Cold War. From their experiences in World War II, they concluded that the Republican Party could no longer stand as a party of isolationism. They declared themselves internationalists who believed that America, now the dominant nation in the world, needed to assume responsibility in crafting a new world order. They rejected the isolationist wing of the party represented by Robert Taft. They called for a strong military to confront Soviet expansionism and Communist threats in other countries. They saw foreign aid as a necessary tool to bolster American allies, and both concluded that regional defense alliances in Europe, Asia, and Latin America should be formed as defense strategies against Communist expansion.

As Cold Warriors in the late 1960s, they confronted a failed Vietnam War policy and the disintegration of bipartisan foreign policy. The breakup of the Cold War consensus was evident in the divide in the Democratic Party between antiwar and prowar factions. On the public stage, Nixon and Rockefeller continued to support American involvement in Vietnam, but both realized that the Vietnam War was a foreign policy disaster with larger implications for American power in the world. They sought to extricate the United States from the war as quickly as possible without totally destroying American credibility altogether. Along the way, Henry Kissinger, a key adviser to Rockefeller on foreign policy, emerged as a principal figure in the Nixon administration, negotiating an end to the Vietnam War and recrafting a new American foreign policy for a post–Vietnam War era. Nixon accommodated himself and American foreign policy to this new world order by opening relations with mainland China and pursuing trade agreements and arms-control treaties with the Soviet Union. It is doubtful that Rockefeller, if he had been president at the time, could have won Republican congressional or grassroots support for a radical shift in American foreign policy that came with the recognition of mainland China or the Strategic Arms Limitation Treaty (SALT I) with the Soviet Union.

If Nixon and Rockefeller agreed much on general domestic and foreign policy positions, their base of support within the Republican Party required them to adjust their rhetoric and campaign strategies accordingly. They emerged as national politicians at an especially tumultuous time in American history, characterized by growing urban poverty, a civil rights movement, and racial tensions. They each were strong supporters of civil rights and ardent opponents of racial segregation. As vice president under Eisenhower, Nixon played a critical role in crafting the Civil Rights Act of 1957, the first major civil rights legislation since Reconstruction. The final legislation was modified in significant ways to undercut federal enforcement by the Democratic-controlled Senate, under Majority Leader Lyndon Baines Johnson.[4] As a presidential candidate, especially in 1968, Nixon often carefully parsed his political rhetoric and policy proposals to ensure his support among grassroots conservatives—white working-class and white suburban voters: he supported civil rights, urban renewal, expansion of the welfare state, and corporate regulation. Rockefeller appeared more adamant in his liberalism, but much of his difference with Nixon was often a matter of tone and not deep substance, although this was not apparent at the time.

As Republicans, they confronted a rising tide of grassroots conservativism within the GOP, revealed fully in Goldwater's nomination in 1964 to head the Republican ticket. That nomination represented the shift in the party to Sunbelt conservatism. This shift culminated in Ronald Reagan's election to the White House in 1980, but it was clear by the mid-1960s that Northeastern moderate and liberal Republicans were already on a downward slide. Rockefeller became a symbol of Northeastern Republicanism, which represented the values of the urban East Coast. In order to win election, these Republicans needed to win urban votes by presenting themselves as moderates willing to expand government programs and to address the problems of deteriorating cities, growing social inequality, and racial injustice. Sunbelt conservatism was based on the suburban values and the new urban West and South found in Atlanta, Dallas, Los Angeles, and Phoenix. Fundamental to this shift in population to the Sunbelt was a profound economic transformation from an industrial economy to a new postindustrial economy based on advanced technologies in electronics and aerospace, highly skilled workers, and innovative research.

The New Deal political order, which Rockefeller and other Eastern Republicans tried to accommodate to in order to win election, was based on an industrial order that was collapsing with deindustrialization and a population shift to the Sunbelt.[5] The New Deal political coalition rested with urban voters in the North, labor unions, ethnic and racial minorities, and poor Southern whites. New Deal liberalism, which continued to be reflected in the Democratic Party through the late 1960s, was premised on an industrial order composed of a unionized workforce earning high wages and benefits in a regulated corporate economy based on mass-production manufacturing. Progressives crafted a welfare state to care for those people who found themselves unable to work, either temporarily or permanently, in industrial America. Widows, the laid-off, the injured, the aged, and the disabled all became beneficiaries of a prosperous America. Farmers were given subsidies and price supports to address the problems of crop surplus induced by new agricultural technology in the Midwest and to ensure that the cotton-producing South remained a Democratic stronghold. The reliance of the racially segregated South as a Democratic bulwark in this New Deal political stronghold restrained liberalism from advancing fully the welfare state, government expansion, and civil rights until the 1960s.

The New Deal vision of a good society was undermined by the shift to a postwar economy, as the workforce became more white collar and less unionized and companies left cities in the East and Midwest for friendlier—and less unionized—business environments in Sunbelt states. Economic growth in Sunbelt states coincided with a population shift from the industrial East and Midwest to Southern and Western states. Population growth in the Sunbelt occurred in the suburbs, as people moved to better jobs, cheaper housing, safer neighborhoods, and better schools. There was a racial undertone to the flock to the suburbs as people sought to escape the problems of inner cities, but the fundamental motivation of people moving to suburbs was better lives for themselves and their families, not racial prejudice per se.

Traditional Republican values of low taxes, antiunionism, small government, pro–business growth policies, traditional family values, and a strong defense found natural appeal in the Sunbelt. Postindustrial cultural values challenged older traditional values of religion, family structure, and gender roles, which led to a backlash that Republicans captured in the late 1960s. In this changing postindustrial economy, family structure was changed, as more women went to college and developed professional careers. During this time, marriage ages increased, family size decreased, and the divorce rate went up. Secularization of the culture challenged the role of mainstream churches and the place of religion in American society. These cultural changes were already apparent in the decade of the 1950s but became fully visible by the 1960s.[6] The cultural war and the rise of the religious right emerged in the 1970s, but already in the 1950s, Republicans sought to proclaim themselves as the party of God, country, and family—as well as the party of progrowth, even though the new postindustrial economy fostered the erosion of traditional values.

The political transformation of the Sunbelt into the core of the Republican Party came gradually and was never fully completed. The strength of organized labor and a sizable black and Hispanic population in California, for instance, gave a fragile status to the Republican Party there. Goldwater's home state of Arizona remained disproportionately Democratic well into the 1960s. The Republican shift in the South first appeared in the 1950s on the presidential election level, only inching into state and local elections in the

1970s; it was not completed until Reagan's election in the 1980s. Republican strength in the South rested in the suburbs, not in rural areas, which remained Democratic even as late as 1980.

Nixon adjusted to the reality of the rightward shift in the GOP. He represented within the party middle-class, suburban America, while Rockefeller represented, at least in the eyes of most Republican voters, New York City. New York could not be written off electorally by any Republican seeking the White House in the early postwar years, and Rockefeller's prominence in the state and his family's wealth meant he could not be ignored in Republican politics. Yet for all of Rockefeller's down-home campaign style, he did not play well in the rest of country. His political base rested in New York City, and to win election as governor in the state meant that he had to run as a candidate willing to expand government. His proclamations of being a fiscal conservative were inevitably belied by his expansive building, urban renewal, and welfare programs as governor.

There was a certain parochialism to Rockefeller, the politician, in his political arrogance. After first trying to accommodate himself to GOP conservatism as the 1964 presidential election approached, he decided that the path to the White House lay in attacking the right as extremist. Rockefeller's assault on the right, however, ensured there could be no conciliation between the two wings of the party. He came across as a party divider. Nixon agreed with Rockefeller that the Goldwater campaign was a lost cause in 1964, and he had little respect for Goldwater as a presidential candidate who often shot from his hip. Yet Nixon campaigned heavily for Goldwater in 1964, thereby laying the foundation for his own comeback in 1968 and endearing himself to Goldwater.

Nixon's and Rockefeller's responses to the 1964 campaign reveal a difference in temperament. Nixon's temperament—one of cool calculation—enabled him to win the White House, while Rockefeller's temperament—one of hubris—and his persistence in denouncing the Goldwater right as extremist, even after Goldwater had won the nomination, ensured he would never win the Republican presidential nomination. Rockefeller despised Nixon, but his insistence on declaring himself the conscience of the party opened the path to Nixon's comeback in 1968. If political power is achieved in a democracy by winning election, Nixon proved a better politician than Rockefeller.

Unlike Nixon, Rockefeller was an effusive personality not given to brooding. His temperament reflected a sense of assured privilege. He could tolerate personal slights, but when it came to party rejection by conservatives, he could not restrain his anger, even though it was to his long-term detriment. In the end, temperament, not ideology or ambition, proved both Rockefeller's and Nixon's greatest vulnerability.

Rockefeller Hubris

Humility did not come naturally to Nelson Rockefeller. Born to wealth and privilege, Rockefeller assumed he had a natural right to power. He expected deference and believed that his willingness to serve the public should be recognized by presidents and voters alike. After all, he could have been leading a life of leisure; or pursuing philanthropy like his older brother, John D. Rockefeller 3rd; or building the family fortune in banking like his younger brother, David. Nelson, like his brothers and his father and grandfather before him, was a builder. He brought to his public service, as did his grandfather and father, a Social Gospel Baptist belief in doing good and bettering the world. Religious faith for a Social Gospel Baptist was expressed in good works. He pledged early not to smoke tobacco or drink alcohol, and for most of his adult life, he avoided hard liquor, profanity, and smoking.[7] The Rockefeller family, grandfather, father, and brothers, John D. 3rd and Laurance, sought to uplift the downtrodden through moral reform and medical and scientific advancement. His grandfather and father were active in temperance and antiprostitution causes in New York. His father, John D. Jr. and his brother John D. 3rd, became leading advocates and financial supporters of family planning and population control. Younger brother Laurance became a leading figure in the postwar environmental conservation movement. Nelson Rockefeller committed himself to fighting poverty, disease, and urban blight, and fighting for civil rights and family planning. As governor, he signed the most liberal abortion law in the country at that time.[8] His commitment to building was in full evidence during his long reign as governor of New York. He built highways, a state university system, state capitol buildings, and housing projects.

As a young boy, Rockefeller showed a unique ability to shrug off insults. He did not take slights or insults personally. By nature and social class, Rockefeller was a social animal, not given to deep introspection. As he grew into adulthood, this temperament seemed to give way to an unrestrained appetite for power and dominance. His sister-in-law Blanchette Hooker Rockefeller observed of him, "One of those men who is full of power and excitement and who could not get along without women. In many ways he was the jewel of the family, in other ways always remained a naughty boy. He was just a little out of hand all the time."[9] Nelson relished his role as the naughty boy in the family, one given to tricks and fun. He realized that he often did not live up to the expectations of his parents and apologized profusely to them with promises that he would do better in the future. This behavior continued into college. As he found his own place in public service and politics, he became less apologetic about his behavior—bragging to the press and friends of his sexual conquests. When there was a public backlash to his marriage to Happy, he simply could not understand the complaint. From his perspective, it was a personal matter; he was serving the public and did not believe anyone should be concerned with his private life. He felt insulted and reacted angrily.

Divorce was unacceptable for most Republican voters in the 1960s. Rockefeller's problem was not just that he divorced his wife, but he also appeared to have broken up the home of a mother with four children. Rockefeller came across as the villain and Happy a kind of passive instrument without a will of her own. The divorce tapped into a lurking feeling on the part of the Republican base and the general public that saw Rockefeller as a typical model of the rich who thought he was morally above the rest of the people. This view of the rich playboy had been conveyed throughout the 1930s and 1940s in films and novels. Rockefeller evoked these images. His political opponents exploited his divorce as a matter of character, but even the patrician class, men such as Senator Prescott Bush of Connecticut, was disgusted by Rockefeller's actions. Rockefeller believed his actions in marrying Happy were honorable and voters should instead look at his record of public service to the nation.

His public service in the war years of the Roosevelt-Truman administration, and later in the Eisenhower administration, revealed a temperament inclined to barge ahead, get things done, and not worry about stepping on toes. His courtier skills were evident in his ability to cultivate Franklin Roosevelt, who appointed him coordinator of Latin American affairs in 1938. Rockefeller's reach extended into every aspect of U.S.–Latin American relations: commercial, political, economic, and cultural. He created a powerful organization not afraid of pushing out other U.S. agencies, and he made enemies along the way. He clashed with intelligence head Colonel William Donovan, folks at the Latin American desk at the State Department, and the Office of War Information. Rockefeller built a bureaucratic empire and skillfully outmaneuvered opponents. Nor did he seem to give a second thought to the enemies he made along the way. He drove himself to physical exhaustion in pushing forward.

Under Truman's secretary of state Edward Stettinius, Rockefeller became assistant secretary of state for Latin America, giving him nearly unassailable authority over Latin American policy. The old guard at the State Department cringed when Rockefeller's appointment was announced. Rockefeller proceeded to put friends and allies into ambassadorships and build relations with Latin American leaders. He was determined to empower Latin America in regional affairs. Through his efforts, Latin American leaders met in Mexico City in 1945 to cement inter-American economic, security, and diplomatic cooperation. The full ramifications of this conference were not fully recognized until the United Nations Conference in San Francisco two years later. Rockefeller was conspicuously absent from the list of official American delegates, but this did not stop him from attending the conference. He flew with the Latin American delegation to San Francisco. There he pushed the conference against the wishes of the State Department to accept an amendment proposed by the Latin American delegates to allow regional defense alliances. The result was that Rockefeller became a pariah for many within the State Department. He was a force unto himself.

In 1947, Rockefeller schemed to create an economic development agency to oversee all U.S. foreign aid and economic development programs. His proposal ran head-on into opposition from W. Averell Harriman, former ambassador to the Soviet Union and Truman's secretary of commerce. In the end, insiders in the State Department quashed Rockefeller's project. He left the administration to bide his time, which came when Dwight D. Eisenhower entered the White House in 1953.

As Eisenhower's undersecretary to the new Department of Health, Education, and Welfare, which Rockefeller had been instrumental in proposing, and later as special assistant to the president for foreign affairs, Rockefeller showed once again his skills at bureaucratic infighting. Eisenhower grew to dislike Rockefeller, whom he felt was not a team player. Rockefeller clashed with fiscal conservatives within the administration with his schemes to promote programs without concern for costs. Eventually, Rockefeller was forced out.

In 1958, when Rockefeller decided that the road to the presidency ran through Albany, he decided to challenge Harriman, who had left the Truman administration to win the governorship of New York. Rockefeller's challenge pitted two millionaires against one another. After winning the election, Rockefeller came to represent New York at its best—and also at its worst, where principle was no substitute for money and power. He crushed those who opposed him while winning over those who might have been his enemies, New York Tammany Hall Democrats and organized labor, both of which welcomed Rockefeller's expansionist vision of government. Expanded government meant contracts and money.

The fortunes of Rockefeller in national politics conversely mirrored Richard Nixon's. Nixon's presidential nomination in 1960 thwarted Rockefeller's hope for the nomination; Nixon's loss to Kennedy in the general election allowed Rockefeller to make a serious presidential bid in 1964; Nixon's comeback four years later again blocked Rockefeller's ambitions; and finally Nixon's fall from grace in 1973 opened the door for Rockefeller to enter the White House, albeit through a side door. Once in the White House, he discovered old Nixon allies, including Gerald Ford's chief of staff Donald Rumsfeld, waiting to ambush him. Rockefeller's admirable tenacity in politics was combined with a willful obstinacy to retreat when retreat was called for. Did he have to brag in front of the press that he had pushed Nixon in 1960 to accept the Fifth Avenue pact over the party platform? Would his presidential prospects have been better if he had accepted Nixon's offer to put him on the ticket in 1960? Did he have to continue his relentless attacks on Goldwater as an extremist when it was evident that his rival had won the nomination in 1964? Rockefeller, a man of wealth and privilege, brought to his political career a sense of privilege. He brought to his personal life and politics a sense of entitlement, which deafened him to his critics. He was a patrician with an appetite for power and personal gratification. He was a builder, a doer, and a man convinced he had a vision for the nation and the world. He felt party leaders and voters should recognize this. Republican voters concluded that Rockefeller was not a man of character they wanted representing their party.

It was more than just wealth that differentiated Rockefeller and Nixon, but everything that came from wealth—education, social circles, lifestyles, and acquaintance with power itself—made Rockefeller different. American novelist F. Scott Fitzgerald, the child of affluent Minneapolis parents, observed of the rich in his 1926 short story "The Rich Boy," "Let me tell you about the very rich. They are different from you and me. They possess and enjoy early, and it does something to them, makes them soft where we are hard, and cynical where we are trustful, in a way that, unless you were born rich, it is very difficult to understand." He added, "They think, deep in their hearts, that they are better than we are because we had to discover the compensations and refuges of life for ourselves. Even when they enter deep into our world or sink below us, they still think that they are better than we are. They are different."

Fitzgerald's assessment that the rich were soft and more cynical than those below them might be debatable. But Rockefeller's background and temperament prevented him from seeing either Goldwater or Nixon as equals. The two men represented, Rockefeller believed, the worst aspects of the Republican Party. He remained convinced that they and their followers lacked the big ideas to move the country forward. Both tapped into the small-mindedness of hinterland Republicans who were obsessed with anti-Communism, were given to simplistic answers about confronting the Soviet Union, proposed narrow-minded fiscal and social policy, and willfully ignored the major issues of the day: civil rights, health care for the elderly, and the urban crisis. What did Nixon, who came from California, or Goldwater, the pretend cowboy from Arizona, really know about the urban poor, housing shortages, and racial conflict? What did either know about the real power structure of America, the Eastern financiers, bankers, and social elite that Rockefeller had grown up with and of which his family was an integral part? Rockefeller believed without hesitancy that he deserved to head the Republican Party and Richard Nixon did not.

Nixon's Scars

In reality, Nixon's own background, political skills, and years of campaigning imparted an understanding of the average American that Rockefeller lacked. Average Republican voters and their local party leaders did not need much convincing that Richard Nixon was really one of them. Nixon spoke to their dreams and fears.

His upbringing as a Quaker and evangelical Christian imbued the young Nixon with a sense of social equality. Religious faith lay at the core of the Nixon family. Their faith dictated family and social life in the small town of Whittier. Their faith brought them through financial hard times and the death of two of the Nixon boys. Although Nixon later rejected the fundamentalism of his mother while an undergraduate at Whittier College, he continued to go to Quaker services through his college and law school years. Quakers prided themselves on their egalitarianism and their treatment of others as equals. Later, in law school in the South, Nixon was shocked by racial segregation and spoke out against it. Quaker principles remained central to young Nixon at least as he entered the navy in World War II. His war experience reinforced his idealism that peace could be achieved in his life-time. His own abiding principle, which he never departed from, was interna-tionalism and world peace through a balance of power. As president, he made it a point to give televised addresses on foreign policy behind Woodrow Wil-son's desk. His Wilsonian outlook followed from his upbringing as a Quaker and his having witnessed the tragedy of war firsthand.

The social egalitarianism of his religious upbringing was reinforced by his father, a laborer turned small-business owner. At the heart of Frank Nixon's politics was a severe antielitism and a defense of the little guy against the special interests. Richard Nixon's own politics were never those of a populist, but he related to and understood average Americans as well as any national politician of his day. And they related to him. He projected this understand-ing on the political stump and on television. He could deliver a powerful speech to Republican crowds by striking just the right chords and hitting on the right words. He could be aggressive in tone, which rallied the Republican base and repulsed his opponents, especially on the left, who saw him as a demagogue and a political attack dog. Nixon could not rely on a naturally effusive personality like Rockefeller's or the charm of his 1960 Democratic opponent, John F. Kennedy. Instead, Nixon projected himself as a candidate who represented average Americans, the white middle class. His greatest ap-peal as a politician was less about tapping into the resentment or paranoid fears of average Americans and more about being a candidate who understood their aspirations for a better and safer world and who shared a patriotic belief that America was a land of opportunity.[10]

In high school and college, Nixon was well liked by his fellow students. But he was also socially awkward, given to an inner privacy that tempered any projection of effusive affability. He compensated for his awkwardness through hard work, a projection of school spirit, and a willingness to get his hands dirty doing tasks nobody else wanted to do. He won the respect of his classmates. He conveyed a strong sense of antielitism. This was evident in college when he organized a social club that welcomed all comers, including African Americans. His club took pride in its antielitism, refusing to wear tuxedos for their class picture in the yearbook. There was a satiric humor to the club's activities that appealed to Whittier students in the Depression years of the 1930s.

Nixon conveyed in his early years a steady stability. Through hard work and natural intelligence, he took advantage of the opportunities presented to him to advance his career. In these years, he was not the brooding man haunted by deep resentments who came later, but a young man who took pride in his rise as a small-town boy who made good. His first years of marriage to Pat were ones of fun and exploring the world around them through weekend trips and dreams of larger travels. World War II interrupted their romance only briefly, but their commitment to one another was conveyed through frequent letters.

As a navy officer in the South Pacific, Nixon was able to further extend his understanding of the common man. He won the respect of enlisted men in his unit through his willingness to take off his shirt and throw himself into the work his men were doing. He learned to gamble and swear like any good sailor. From reminiscences of fellow officers stationed with him, it is evident that Nixon gave much thought to what the postwar world was going to look like and America's place in the world. Like many World War II veterans, the experience left Nixon with a firm conviction that another global war must be prevented. Further, like most American veterans, Nixon was optimistic about America's future. He was anxious to return home, start a family, enter civilian life, and renew his career. Unlike many of those who had entered the military during the war, he had a set career ahead of him as a practicing lawyer.

His entrance into politics was serendipitous, although inevitable given his disposition for the pursuit. In their separate memoirs, Richard and Pat Nixon remember fondly their excitement of driving as a young couple across the country from Washington, D.C., to return to their hometown of Whittier to begin a political campaign that would change both of their lives forever. With a young, pregnant wife expecting their first child, Nixon moved into his parent's home where he took up his new role as a congressional candidate, a David against a Goliath, a first-time Republican candidate, a novice in the world of politics standing against a popular incumbent in a heavily Democratic district. As soon as their child was born, Pat joined the campaign. The Nixons made a team; Dick and Pat were joined at the hip. By the end of the campaign, Nixon had taken the first steps to becoming a professional politician, and he would never rely on Pat again so heavily as he did in this campaign.

Politics is as natural for a lawyer as a stinger is to a bee. Political campaigning brings out the natural competitiveness of the lawyer, trained in preparing and strategizing a case to win before a jury, in this case, the electorate. Nixon knew from his involvement in Whittier before the war that trying to climb the political ladder from local office to state office to Congress became a dead end for most people. He jumped at the opportunity to skip the political rite of passage and present himself as a candidate for Congress. Once Nixon made that decision, he began a pattern he was to follow throughout the rest of his life: study the issues and his opponent; work overtime during the campaign; present himself as a candidate who understood the average guy and gal—and play hardball to win. Most politicians follow these practices, but Nixon's intensity was unmatched.

Before entering Congress, Nixon was not any more anti-Communist than most average Americans. He did not stand to the right of his party on the Communist issue. Nonetheless, Nixon became the symbol for the left of anti-Communist hysteria in America. His victory over Helen Gahagan Douglas in 1950 solidified Nixon's reputation as a fervent anti-Communist. The stereotype of Nixon the anti-Communist warrior stayed with him throughout most of his political career and facilitated détente with the Soviet Union and China when he was president.

Given the emotions of the early Cold War, the left's hatred of Nixon is not surprising. Perhaps a less sensitive man might have ignored the viciousness of these attacks. Being made into a national monster would have been difficult for any person, but the attacks on Nixon from his enemies spilled over to his family in public and personal ways. Nixon might have lived with the left-wing press attacks on him, but seeing caricatures like the one in 1954, where he was portrayed as a rat coming out of a sewer by Herb Block, *Washington Post* cartoonist, upset him.[11] He worried about his daughters opening the paper and seeing their father depicted as a rat.

Nixon personalized the left's attacks, and he lost faith in supposed Republican friends who deserted him at critical moments. The idealism of his youth died with a thousand cuts sustained along each step of the way: the desertion of early supporters when he ran into trouble in 1952 when he was accused of having a secret fund; Eisenhower's initial hesitancy to declare him his running mate in 1956; the common gossip in Republican circles that Nixon was tricky and an opportunist without conviction or depth; and the good riddance many Republicans gave him after he lost the 1962 California governor's race. Those who met Nixon personally at social events or in politics found him likable, even at times charming in his own way. Those who worked closest to him understood he had wounds.

To describe Nixon or Rockefeller as ambitious or ideologically malleable tells us little more than what is a truism for all presidential candidates. Nixon's life in politics was that of being taught humility. He expected attacks by liberal critics who would never forgive him after Alger Hiss was sentenced to prison for perjury. What he could not forgive or forget was the betrayal by allies who deserted him, Eisenhower's treatment in the 1956 election, and his servile apprenticeship under Eisenhower during his eight years as vice president. He suffered humiliating losses, for the presidency in 1960 and for governor of his home state of California in 1962. These lessons in humility damaged Nixon's inner character and his moral outlook on the world. In the presidency, no longer constrained by the humility that comes with lesser offices, Nixon's character flaws were revealed. Seeing the world—domestic politics—as one of us versus them, suspicious that his enemies would use anything to bring him down, too anxious to protect himself from his critics, Nixon sealed himself off within a bubble of a small group of advisers. When his reelection campaign was discovered to have undertaken dirty and illegal tricks, Nixon's first instinct was to defend his team. In doing so, he entered into an illegal conspiracy to obstruct justice. He saw his actions as principled. He did not desert his friends. This proved not only to be a political miscalculation of incalculable consequence for his presidency and the nation; it revealed a serious flaw in Nixon's character as a man.

The Irony of Presidential Politics

Of course, the great irony in 1968 was that GOP party leaders along with the grassroots judged Nixon as the candidate who was more trustworthy. Nixon's many critics, then and later, described him as secretive, vengeful, and consumed by ambition. His fall from the presidency appeared to affirm this view of the man. In 1968, however, contrary to later critics who explained Nixon's voter appeal as tapping into the worst instincts of the American electorate, Nixon appealed to many voters not because he was cynical or Machiavellian. Instead, Nixon's appeal was that many average Americans saw in Nixon the realization of their dreams. He personified their hopes for themselves and their children. Nixon's story was compelling: a boy from a modest background who had worked his way through college, gone to a prestigious law school (although not Harvard or Yale), served his country during World War II, and then returned to gain national attention for taking on the Communists in Washington as seen in the Alger Hiss case. He endured the persistent assaults of the media and the liberal elite. For voters, Nixon stood as a man of courage. After losing two elections, Nixon once again came back.

Many Americans related to a story of a man who suffered defeat only to rise again. Nixon's appeal was not to the cynicism of the American people but to their idealism and their belief in individual courage, inner fortitude, and redemption.

Nixon's supporters misjudged his temperament and character, however. Once an idealist, Nixon had become an embittered realist, a shift that appeared to serve him well in foreign policy. Working with Henry Kissinger, another realist who understood the importance of moral good and the possible, Nixon forced a withdrawal from Vietnam and a balance of power through détente and arms control with the Soviet Union. This world order through the balance of power was never fully accepted by the Republican base, however, and would be rejected by conservatives led by Ronald Reagan who called for American military and nuclear superiority in foreign policy. In domestic policy, Nixon showed opportunism unrestrained by conservative principles of fiscal restraint and limited government. Nixon's expansion of the New Deal entitlement and regulatory state would also be rejected by Reagan Republicans.

By the time Nixon won the presidency in 1968, little of his earlier idealism was left. The tendencies to a sensitive and secretive temperament appeared, and in the end, his character, necessary for any successful presidency, was affected for the worse. In this regard, the GOP voters had misjudged him with serious consequences for the health of their party and nation.

Rockefeller was judged by the voters on his character and found wanting. He represented big-government Republicanism, but many voters projected what they saw as Eastern Republican liberalism as a reflection of moral turpitude. Few doubted Rockefeller's affable temperament to be president. Indeed, his ability to work across the political aisles was seen as a character flaw.

In the end, history appeared to prove voters wrong. Nixon lacked the character to be a fully successful president. Rockefeller, whatever his limitations in his personal moral conduct, showed by his willingness to become Ford's vice president an eagerness to serve the public good. By temperament, a Rockefeller presidency, if somehow he had won the nomination and general election, would have meant the further expansion of the welfare and regulatory state, so despised by the GOP right. By temperament, Rockefeller was a builder and an expansionist. At the same time, assured of his own righteousness and sense of privilege, he found it impossible to restrain his vituperative and ultimately self-defeating criticisms of the GOP right and to accept a lesser role, such as a second spot on any presidential ticket, thus preventing his election to the presidency. Whatever his flaws in his personal life, Rockefeller proved to be a man of character.

By 1968, Nixon's political life appears much like a character in Harriet Beecher Stowe's novel *Oldtown Folks,* a more nuanced book than her famous *Uncle Tom's Cabin.* In *Oldtown Folks,* she presents the character of Ellery Davenport, whose youthful idealism turns to complete opportunism when he loses his Christian faith. Stowe modeled the character on Aaron Burr, the New York politician who was charged with treason by the Jefferson administration and who killed his political rival Alexander Hamilton in a duel. Burr was the grandson of Puritan divine Jonathan Edwards, and Stowe saw in him the consequences of a hard Calvinist faith that easily gave way to a secular sense of self-anointment and standing above the law. Nixon was not a traitor, but he was a politician who betrayed himself personally and betrayed the principles of his party, which proclaimed itself as the protector of the Constitution and the rule of law.

4 Barry Goldwater
Undisciplined Individualist

Following the death of Senator Robert Taft in 1953 and the censure of Senator Joseph McCarthy the following year, Barry Goldwater, a senator from Arizona, emerged as the leading voice of conservatism in America. Tall, ruggedly good looking, blunt spoken, Goldwater rode onto the national scene out of the desert, as a kind of Western movie hero coming to clean up the town after a takeover by bandidos. For conservatives, the bandits were New Deal liberals who were robbing taxpayers to pay for a welfare state that was undermining American individualism and who had a perceived lack of resolve to confront the Soviet enemy bent on world conquest. Goldwater, the Westerner, stood tall against the Eastern wing of the GOP represented by Nelson Rockefeller, who was seen as what later would be called a RINO, a "Republican in name only." For the GOP grassroots right, these Eastern, Wall Street Republicans were too anxious to collaborate with the socialist outlaws in order to protect their own interests.

Goldwater came to personify conservatism within the Republican Party, at least until Ronald Reagan came on the scene. To followers, Goldwater projected ideological purity. As a politician, however, he proved remarkably flexible in adjusting principle to the reality of politics. The litmus test for him was winning elections, for his party and himself. This is not to say he was an opportunist or not a true believer; it is to maintain that at critical junctures in his career, party was placed over principle. Goldwater supporters overlooked inconsistencies in their man. They loved that he called for adherence to the founders' Constitution, spoke of the benefits of free enterprise, and warned of centralized federal government as a threat to liberty. He was direct, spoke from the heart, and "told it like it is." If he was raw, given to angry outbursts or misspoken words, or seemed to have a poor temperament for the presidency, they overlooked his flaws and translated his eccentricities into virtues.

Goldwater was above all else a loyal party man. The Republican Party came first for him. Within the confines of conservative Republican politics, he showed he was a wily, astute, and flexible politician. He was fiercely conservative, delicately balancing his loyalty to the party with conservative principles. These two—partisan gain and ideological principle—created a tension within Goldwater. As a senator during the Eisenhower years, he complained that the administration was not doing enough to roll back the New Deal or confront the Soviet threat; yet his criticism of Eisenhower was generally muted. He might have led a revolt at the convention of 1960 after many conservatives were enraged when the party's presidential nominee, Richard Nixon, struck a deal over civil rights with Nelson Rockefeller. Goldwater did not dissent; instead he told conservatives to "grow up." He won the presidential nomination in 1964, running as an avowed conservative; yet, in the general election, his campaign tried to move to the center to such a degree that it was hesitant to put Ronald Reagan, co-chair of California Citizens for Goldwater, on television lest he appear too radical to the voters.

After he lost his presidential race, Goldwater supported the least conservative candidate in the GOP field in 1968, 1976, and almost in 1980.[1] Goldwater's support for Nixon and Ford pitted him against Ronald Reagan who had emerged as the hero of the GOP right. By the time Goldwater stepped down from the Senate in 1986, having barely won in 1980, the conservative movement, which he had helped inspire, seemed to have passed him by. He had become a vociferous critic of the party's religious right. A longtime supporter of reproductive rights, although he had downplayed this in the early 1980s, he believed the Republican Party had gone too far right for his tastes. Goldwater's political beliefs were deeply held; his loyalty to the party was sincere; he was a natural leader and an adept politician in Congress. Nonetheless, there was an eccentricity and self-indulgence to the man and politician that belies ideological firmness, disciplined political leadership, and deep moral conviction based on traditional values, which conservatives so prided themselves on espousing.

Frontier Imagination

Goldwater played on the theme of being a Westerner. It was not a false role. Born in territorial days to a pioneer family, he loved his home state of Arizona, with its desert expanse and rugged mountains. He began collecting Navajo kachina figures as a teenager, and his photographs of Native Americans and Arizona landscapes found publication in professional magazines. He rode horses, traversed the rapids of the Colorado River, and traveled throughout the state, flying his own plane. He was a World War II veteran, a jet pilot, and a reserve U.S. Air Force major general.

Although he grew up in one of Phoenix's most socially prominent families, Barry was never accused of being genteel. As one relative later observed, Barry "drunk his share of whisky, cussed like a mule-team driver, associated with gamblers, befriended madams, and raised considerable hell along the way."[2] Many saw in the young Barry his grandfather Mike, a Jewish immigrant from Poland, who found fortune in the copper camps of Arizona. Michael Goldwater arrived in America in 1852 with his young brother, seeking fortune in the gold fields of California. Venture after venture failed, but eventually Mike found success in a store in Prescott, Arizona. The romance of the frontier, and Mike Goldwater's eventual success, framed Barry's worldview of rugged individualism and equal opportunity.

Equally important in his life was his uncle Morris Goldwater. Morris was the voice of the conservative wing of the Democratic Party, the dominant party in Arizona.[3] Morris was conservative personally, politically, and in the family business. Not until 1895, pushed by his brother Baron who had joined the family enterprise, did Morris agree to expand from Prescott and enter the Phoenix market with a new department store. Phoenix had become the capital of the territory but was little more than a village of two thousand residents at that point. The Goldwaters staked out the high end of this market and became *the* place where the wealthy Phoenicians and the growing tourist crowd visited. Under Baron Goldwater, Barry's father, the Goldwater Department Store flourished and became the premier, high-end store in the state.

Charming, always dapper, and wearing the latest fashion, Baron became a leading merchant and citizen in Phoenix. He was a member of the Elks Lodge and Chamber of Commerce board, and an active volunteer in an array of charities and civic groups. Unlike many in Phoenix, he was not given to real-estate speculation and even rented his house. He met his future wife, Josephine Williams, when she was shopping in Goldwater's. Josephine, a trained nurse, came to Phoenix from the Midwest when she was diagnosed with tuberculosis. She was a bouncy, independent woman who loved the outdoors. Her family traced its roots back to freethinker and religious dissenter Roger Williams of Rhode Island. She was given to cussing and blunt talk. Down to earth, she set a sharp contrast to Baron, who while liking good food, card playing, and sharing drinks with friends, hated the outdoors, and was proper in his appearance and suave in his demeanor. They were married on New Year's Day 1907 in an Episcopal church. Two years later to the day, in 1909, their first son, Barry, was born, three years before Arizona became a state. The couple later had two other children, Bob, born in 1910, and Carolyn, born in 1912. The children were raised in an indulgent house, staffed by a cook, maid, and chauffeur.[4] Religion played little role in their lives. Barry, with adolescent humor, described himself as a "Piscopalian."

The Goldwater children grew up in a large, Victorian-style, three-story home in north central Phoenix. The grounds of the house were spacious, with a large barn in back, landscaped with ash trees and a large green lawn. Baron was a distant father, often at work or socializing. When he was home, he liked peace and quiet. Jo and Baron were socially prominent in a town of then about 11,000 residents. They went to the Phoenix Country Club, entertained often, and threw large parties. They were part of the upper crust of a growing city—not fabulously wealthy by Eastern or San Francisco standards, but part of the city's elite. Baron's downtown store, the first building in Phoenix constructed with reinforced concrete, became a place where the wealthy shopped.

Jo Goldwater raised her children to be independent and carefree, and to explore life in their own ways. The Goldwater children present a sharp contrast to the Rockefeller children growing up at the same time. John D. Rockefeller Jr. and his wife, Laura, kept close watch over their children, imposing a strict Baptist discipline. Jo Goldwater was about as far from a Baptist as an Arizona cowboy from an Eastern city slicker. As a mother, she was extremely permissive, imposing minimal rules on her children. The children were indulged with clothes, toys, and free movie passes. Barry never carried cash; when he wanted something, he simply charged it to his father. Baron built a garage in the back of the house that provided room for the two family cars and two trucks used by the store. The space above the garage provided hangout space for Barry and his gang of friends, many of whom became his political confidants, including Harry and Newton Rosenzweig, Bob Lewis, and others. Barry was tall, athletic, and a continual prankster, with his tricks sometimes bordering on mean. In one prank, he placed a microphone (he liked electronics) in the basement bathroom of a friend's house so the sounds could be heard throughout the house. He got in trouble for shooting a cannonball over a Methodist church and photographing people in compromising situations at parties. He was decidedly nonintellectual. His sister claimed she never saw him reading a book.

When he entered public high school, Barry Goldwater was, as described by a sympathetic family historian, "spoiled and self-centered." He won election as freshman class president only to spend the rest of the year not opening a single book, getting bad grades, and disrupting class. At the end of the year, the principal suggested to his father that Barry not return to school. Baron immediately enrolled him in Staunton Military Academy in Virginia. Here, Barry became a nationally ranked diver and leading cadet. He did not excel in the classroom but passed his courses. Following graduation, he enrolled at the University of Arizona, showing up in a Chrysler roadster. He became first-string center on the freshman football team, pledged Sigma Chi fraternity, and was elected class president. Never academically inclined, he was probably on his way out of college when the death of his father in 1929 forced Barry to withdraw from school and return home to take over the family business. The Goldwater store in Phoenix had fifty employees and revenue of $400,000 a year. Shortly afterward, Barry was joined by his younger brother, Bob, who had graduated from Stanford University.

The two made an excellent team: Barry provided marketing and advertising skills, and his brother provided the financial talent. Barry Goldwater's promotion of branding-iron dresses in the 1930s and underwear imprinted with ants ("Antsy Pants") after World War II illustrated his talent for marketing and design. In the midst of an economic depression, the store did not downsize and actually developed an employee benefit plan. By 1941, the Goldwater stores were doing an annual business of a million dollars a year.[5] By this time, Barry spent less and less time at the store and could often be found at the Phoenix Country Club or his second home in La Jolla, California. He was given to heavy drinking and bouts of depression that continued throughout his life.

In 1934, Barry Goldwater gained further social prominence when he married Peggy Johnson, daughter of the president of Warner Gear Company, based in Muncie, Indiana. Peggy was a well-known socialite in Phoenix, where her parents wintered. Both Barry and his new wife were active in Phoenix social and civic circles. Peggy, although naturally shy, was especially active in the growing Phoenix community. In 1937, she became involved with the city's first birth-control clinic, initially called the Mother's Health Clinic and later Planned Parenthood of Phoenix. Barry Goldwater never hid his support of Planned Parenthood, although his wife's founding role in the clinic was not touted.

Peggy Goldwater's involvement with the organization was more than just casual. She was part of a small group of women who sponsored Margaret Sanger, founder of the modern birth-control movement in America. The Phoenix birth-control clinic, located at Seventh Street and Adams in the downtown area, provided free diaphragms and contraceptive spermicides. The clinic consciously targeted poor women, African Americans, and the larger Hispanic population.[6] As a charter board member, Peggy was a leader in the organization, and as president of the board from 1941 to 1942, she orchestrated the group's affiliation with the newly formed Planned Parenthood Federation of America.[7] She continued to be involved in fundraising for Arizona and national Planned Parenthood throughout her life.

Following World War II, Planned Parenthood gained the support of several prominent Phoenicians, many associated with Goldwater politically, including his closest advisers, Harry Rosenzweig and Denison Kitchel, and former governor J. Howard Pyle. They were listed as sponsors of the organization along with Barry.[8] By the 1960s and early 1970s, Planned Parenthood of Phoenix had opened other clinics in the adjoining cities of Tempe, Glendale, and Chandler. Posters and Planned Parenthood literature could be found in local libraries and were distributed to schools and universities. Special efforts were made to target Mexican migrant workers. The primary focus of the organization was to reduce poverty and overpopulation through family planning. Following national Planned Parenthood guidelines, particular attention was given to publicly funded abortion, the relationship between unwanted births and dependency, and childrearing among the poor with large families.[9] Peggy Goldwater summarized the organization's activities in the 1965 fundraising campaign, where she served as honorary cochair: "Most women who come for attention are from the lowest economic strata, depending on Public Health for medical care." By not providing family planning to the indigent, she wrote, we see all around us "suffering, poverty, delinquency, unemployment, crime."[10]

This work to control the indigent population drew strong Republican support from liberals and conservatives alike. In 1967, the Illinois Republican U.S. senator, Charles Percy, a moderate aligned with the Rockefeller wing of the party, wrote Peggy Goldwater congratulating her on a piece she had written. Titled "Why I Believe in Planned Families," the essay was inserted in the *Congressional Record* by Paul Fannin, a Goldwater Republican colleague. Percy gleefully told Peggy that he had been participating in initiating family-planning classes in the Twenty-Ninth Ward of Chicago, which he described as "an area of high density, public aid families, mainly AFDC [Aid to Families with Dependent Children]." He added, "I must admit that I felt somewhat hypocritical entering the course as the father of five children, but somehow I explained this away."[11] Percy need not have added that his concern for global overpopulation and America's poor having too many children did not mean that the right sort of people should not have children. Support for family planning was further evidenced when Jack Williams, the conservative Republican governor of Arizona, proclaimed "Population Awareness Week" in the state in 1974.[12]

Although Barry Goldwater, a politician in a conservative state, tried to distance himself from his wife's activities in Planned Parenthood, the organization's support for legalized abortion placed him in a difficult situation. In 1969, four years before the Supreme Court in *Roe v. Wade* declared abortion a constitutional right, Planned Parenthood in Arizona opposed provisions in the state criminal codes criminalizing abortion. The resolution declared that because "abortion is a medical procedure, it should be governed by the same rules as apply to other medical procedures in general when performed by properly qualified physicians with reasonable medical safeguards."[13]

Planned Parenthood was just one of the many civic activities the Goldwaters were involved in before the outbreak of World War II. Boosterism came easily to Goldwater. He had grown up in the state; his mother imparted to him her love of the natural beauty of the desert; he had begun collecting native Navajo kachina dolls as a young man; and in the 1930s, he had become an experienced pilot, which enabled him to learn even more about the state. He developed his talents as a photographer and began taking hundreds of pictures of Arizona landscapes and its native people.

In 1941, Goldwater saw war coming. A few months before Pearl Harbor and America's official entry into the war, the thirty-two-year-old Goldwater signed up for a year's active duty with the Army Air Corps. He was assigned to teach aerial gunnery, even though he wanted to fly military planes. He finally talked his way into being assigned to the Ferry Division, flying planes and equipment to the front lines. He ended the war as a lieutenant colonel and became a reserve officer in the Arizona Air National Guard, which he helped organize after the war. He was not home much during this time, and even before the outbreak of war, he had begun to lose interest in the store. When he returned home, like other veterans, he began to set his sights on something larger.

It Began with a Breakfast: Goldwater's Sudden Rise in Politics

The political landscape in Arizona after the war was a one-party state controlled by Democrats. The party drew its strength from the farming and mining industries, which gave Democrats a strong progressive ethos. The dominance of the progressives enabled George W. Hunt to win election as governor six times throughout the 1920s and into the 1930s. Carl Hayden, a Democrat from Maricopa County, served in the House as the state's single representative for fifteen years before winning election to the Senate in 1926, an office he held for the next fifty-seven years. The state voted Democratic in every presidential year, with the exception of the 1920s decade.[14] Republican successes were few and far between. The party won the gubernatorial contest in 1916, playing on an antilabor backlash. The Depression years in the 1930s further secured Democratic control of the state. From 1933 to 1951, Republicans failed to win a single state Senate seat and reached a high of only eleven of the seventy-two seats in the state House. Party registration fell from 39,000 in 1928 to approximately 21,000 in 1940. In the first thirty-eight years of statehood, only one Republican had been elected attorney general; one Republican, secretary of state; one Republican, superintendent of public instruction; and one Republican, state auditor. No Republican had ever become state treasurer.[15] In 1942, Arizona received a second congressional seat, giving the state two Democrats in the House.

In this situation, Republicans found themselves sharply divided into conservative and liberal wings, but neither faction was effective in mobilizing voters. Conservatives—the so-called Standpatters—did not want to rock the political boat and were content with holding party offices and the occasional patronage that came their way. Liberals, the "Insurgents," sought to accept progressive experimentation offered by the New Deal. The postwar period offered the first opportunity for Republicans to reconfigure the political environment. The three Cs—copper, cattle, and cotton—which had dominated the state economy in the prewar years had begun to give way to tourism. Along with this, Maricopa County, the location of the state capital and the state's largest city, Phoenix, became the most populated county in the state after the war. This growth coincided with an increase in Republican registration, from 12 percent to 25 percent from 1940 to 1952, which was attributed to Midwesterners moving to the state.

The change toward a tourist economy fostered business boosterism in Phoenix. Copper interests in the state, led by the Phelps Dodge Corporation, had dominated state politics. Although Phelps Dodge was antilabor, the company exerted a powerful influence on the Democratic Party. Arizona State Democrats worked well with large corporate copper and agribusiness companies, contrary to what has been stated by some historians and later left-wing activists who portrayed the rise of the Republican Party as simply a procapitalist takeover of state politics.[16] Politics has a dynamics of its own that cannot be fit snugly into neat ideological categories.

The first signs of political change came on the local level in Phoenix when voters came out in support of a state right-to-work bill, making it illegal to require a company employee to join a labor union as a condition of employment. During the 1930s, organized labor had made some inroads in the state by organizing agricultural workers, miners, and government employees. Goldwater's involvement in the campaign was minimal. The right-to-work movement began with a group of veterans upset with closed-shop requirements in union-controlled industry. There was also a religious dimension to this campaign. Baptists were one of the largest Protestant denominations in Phoenix. Indeed, the Phoenix First Baptist Church claimed the largest congregation in the country.[17] Baptists were opposed to pledging to any organization other than their church. At the same time, Phoenix business was not unanimous in its support of the right-to-work legislation. Organized labor did not have much of a presence in the city itself, but the campaign expressed a general postwar backlash against organized labor. City boosters sought to bring new businesses to the state, especially defense and electronics companies.[18] Until this point, Goldwater himself had not paid much attention to organized-labor issues.

The Goldwater brothers took pride in their employee relations, but forced unionization went against their business interests and their Western libertarian instincts. The importance of the right-to-work campaign for Barry Goldwater is that it enabled him to confirm and extend his growing reputation as an articulate business leader. The campaign attracted young Mesa attorney John Rhodes and Harvard Law School–educated Phoenix attorney Denison Kitchel, who later headed Goldwater's 1964 presidential campaign.

Although a registered Republican since 1928 (largely a business decision), Goldwater stayed out of partisan politics. He was a civic leader and a spokesman for Arizona growth. His hometown of Phoenix had grown during the war. For many businessmen, city government was a barrier to further growth. Its executive manager-council form of government—an outgrowth of early progressives' desire to keep politics out of government—had proved to be a disaster. Between 1915, the year of the city council's inception, and 1946, the council had replaced the city manager thirty-one times. Furthermore, the city was running huge deficits. Cronyism was rampant. In 1947, pressured by business and civic leaders, the city's Democratic mayor appointed a committee of forty prominent people to review the situation. They proposed a new charter to establish a strong and qualified city manager, free from the whims of the city council, which was to be increased from five to seven at-large members. Although the charter was approved the following year, the council refused to act on the changes. In response, another citizens' commission composed of more than a hundred prominent people called for the election of a council to live up to the new city charter. They put together a slate of candidates to run for election in 1948. They charged that not only had the current city council members ignored the new charter, but they had allowed gambling and prostitution operations to flourish. The extent of gambling and prostitution in the city at the time was perhaps questionable, but it made for good reform politics.

The reformers approached Barry Goldwater to run for a seat on the council, which he declined at first but finally agreed to. On Election Day, Goldwater won more votes than any candidate on the reform slate that swept into office. He was appointed vice chairman of the City Council, and two years later, he handily won reelection. The city's deficit was turned to a surplus in two years; modern budgeting practices were instituted; and contracts were placed on a competitive bidding basis. The new charter government did not reflect a "capitalist" takeover of government. Businessmen had headed the effort, but they represented small business interested in good government to boost city growth. They saw good government and boosterism going hand in hand. Goldwater represented this sentiment. Goldwater had become a politician, but the city council remained nonpartisan. The fact remained, however, that the Republican Party in the state was weak, disorganized, and without a strong voter base.

The awakening of the Republican Party in Arizona came about rather serendipitously, as often happens in politics. Discussions about revitalizing the state party began with a small group of World War II veterans, mostly lawyers who met regularly at the Saratoga Restaurant in downtown Phoenix for breakfast.[19] Concerned with the one-party state controlled by the Democrats, they decided on a strategy of putting young conservatives into key positions in the state Republican Party. Over the next few years, they elected more than forty young Republicans to precinct posts and key party positions.

By 1950, the insurgents had enough strength in these young politicians to call for a small state convention. They asked J. Howard Pyle, a local radio celebrity, to provide the keynote speech. Pyle was already well known in the state before he became a radio war correspondent during World War II. Pyle, as a dedicated Republican, delivered a rousing speech at the convention calling for young Republicans to dedicate themselves to building the party. When he was approached afterward to run for governor, he was in a position where he could hardly refuse. This was an off-year election in 1950, and most senior party members did not believe Republicans had much of a chance anyway; so why not let the young Republicans take the gamble on a statewide celebrity?[20]

Pyle brought a popular appeal and political experience to the campaign. He picked Barry Goldwater to manage it. The two made a good combination, the radio-personality candidate and the good-looking, young campaign manager. Goldwater flew Pyle around the state in his plane. Fortune was on their side. Democrats nominated long-standing government official Ana Frohmiller. Pyle won the election by a mere three thousand votes. Democrats whispered that Frohmiller lost the election because she was a woman, but she was also an exceptionally poor speaker and ran a lackluster campaign.[21]

Goldwater Wins the Senate, 1952

When the forty-year-old Goldwater decided to run for the U.S. Senate in 1952, the odds were heavily against him. The incumbent senator, Ernest McFarland, was popular and held the prestigious post of majority leader in the U.S. Senate. Having been elected to the Senate in 1940, he looked unbeatable. What Goldwater had going for him, however, was a changing political climate nationally and in the state. The GOP had nominated Dwight D. Eisenhower to head the presidential ticket in 1952, and demographics were shifting toward the Republican Party in Arizona.

Goldwater focused much of his campaign on attacking McFarland's support of Truman's Fair Deal. In his announcement speech on the steps of the Yavapai County Courthouse in Prescott, Goldwater declared that the principal issue of the race was simple: "The Truman Fair Deal, after seven years of expanding government" has brought a "pyramiding confusion of crisis, and crisis of confusion." He spoke in favor of small government, state rights, and a strong foreign policy. At the same time, he showed he was not a reactionary by affirming his support of the Social Security System, unemployment insurance, and aid to families with dependent children (AFDC). He approved of the Federal Housing Administration. He told voters that these programs were created by Congress and that "no responsible Republican has any intention or any desire to abolish any one of them."[22]

McFarland, albeit a supporter of the Fair Deal, was hardly the liberal that Goldwater painted him. In the Senate, he aligned himself closely with Southern Democrats and refused to oppose a right-to-work amendment to the state constitution that banned the closed union shop.[23] Nonetheless, organized labor in the state rallied behind his candidacy. The biggest mistake in the campaign, however, was that McFarland underestimated his opponent and the emergence of a well-organized state Republican Party. When he called the Korean War a "cheap" war, he was pilloried by his energetic young opponent.

Goldwater turned to Stephen C. Shadegg to manage his campaign. Shadegg brought to the campaign a wily, tough-minded approach to politics. In a small state without a large class of professional campaign consultants, Shadegg stood out. He had worked primarily in Democratic campaigns—understandable in a one-party state. Shadegg was deeply conservative and fervently anti-Communist. In 1950, he wrote to his friend Senator Carl Hayden, warning that "here in Arizona we have active communists, servants of a foreign power," who were worming their way into positions of power.[24] Still, Shadegg was not about ideology but about winning elections any way he could. He demanded one thing of Goldwater: to follow instructions. Shadegg was to direct the campaign and wanted the candidate to do as he was told.

Shadegg's strategy targeted the heavily populated Phoenix and Tucson metropolitan areas. From 1940 to 1950, Arizona's population increased 50 percent, with much of the growth in Phoenix, which had over a hundred thousand people. Shadegg drew support from professional, white-collar, and female voters in these areas. The campaign got a boost when Republican presidential candidate Dwight Eisenhower campaigned in Phoenix. Maricopa County had been Taft country, and the Republican delegation had lined up behind Taft in the primaries, with two notable exceptions: Barry Goldwater and Howard Pyle were Eisenhower supporters. Further energy was added when Wisconsin senator Joseph McCarthy came to Tucson. Goldwater's heavy campaign schedule traversed the state, with Goldwater piloting his plane to remote areas.

His campaign was well financed, outspending McFarland two to one, with half of Goldwater's donations coming from out of state, including from

Texas oil baron H. L. Hunt, who contributed four thousand dollars. Phoenix's two leading newspapers, the *Arizona Republic* and the *Phoenix Gazette,* recently purchased by conservative Eugene C. Pulliam, provided extensive coverage of the Goldwater candidacy. Goldwater campaign staff consisted of one speech writer, a volunteer press officer, a treasurer, and campaign manager Shadegg, the mastermind. Shadegg understood the changing nature of politics. The campaign used television and radio advertising to promote their candidate. Phoenix at the time had only one television station.

On Election Day, Goldwater won a narrow victory by 6,725 votes of the more than quarter million cast. Eisenhower won the state by more than 44,000 votes, an indication that Arizona voters had split their ballots. Goldwater would not have won without riding on Eisenhower's coattails. Howard Pyle, the incumbent governor, won reelection by 53,000 votes.[25] In addition, John Rhodes, the Mesa attorney, won election to Congress. For the first time, Arizona had a Republican U.S. senator and governor.

Freshman Senator Goldwater Draws Organized Labor's Wrath

Goldwater entered the Senate in 1953 hoping to get an appointment to the important Armed Services Committee. Instead, Senate Majority Leader Robert Taft assigned him to the Labor Relations Committee because he said the party wanted a businessman there. Goldwater claimed not to know much about organized labor, but this assignment turned out to give him the national attention that made him into a star in the party. It also earned him the enmity of organized labor. On the Senate Select Committee on Improper Activities in Labor and Management, chaired by Senator John McClellan of Arkansas, Goldwater openly attacked Walter Reuther and the United Automobile Workers for violent tactics during a strike at the Kohler Manufacturing Company in Wisconsin. In a radio address, Goldwater described Reuther as America's number-one enemy of freedom, a remark he immediately apologized for making, but the damage had been done. Goldwater became organized labor's number-one enemy.

In the Senate, Goldwater gained a reputation for being charming but too blunt spoken to be effective in the legislative process. Goldwater deferred the heavy lifting of legislation to Arizona's senior senator, Carl Hayden, a long-time family friend.[26] Goldwater emerged as a national voice for conservative causes: opposition to the recognition of mainland China, criticism of the United Nations, and demands for congressional investigation into Communist infiltration into government and organized labor. He cosponsored the Bricker Amendment, which called for constitutional restriction of presidential war powers. Opposed by the Eisenhower administration, the Bricker Amendment failed. He gained further national attention for denouncing Eisenhower's first budget as a "dime store New Deal." Eisenhower did not like the remark but remained friendly with Goldwater, one of the few conservative Republicans in the Senate Ike did not despise.[27]

Goldwater's strong views on what he considered the international and domestic threat Communism posed placed him in the anti-Communist camp in the Senate. He was friends with McCarthy, although he believed McCarthy often overstated claims of Communist subversion.[28] He had gotten to know McCarthy in the 1940s when the future Wisconsin senator visited Arizona for health reasons. McCarthy campaigned for Goldwater against McFarland, and the two became drinking buddies once Goldwater moved to Washington. In early 1954, when McCarthy faced an impending censure by the Senate, Goldwater arranged through McCarthy's lawyer Edward Bennett Williams to sneak into the Bethesda Naval Hospital where McCarthy was recovering from elbow surgery. They pleaded with McCarthy to sign a letter stating that he regretted having shown discourtesy to fellow senators and thereby avoid a likely censure vote. A drunken McCarthy refused. On December 2, 1954, sixty-seven senators voted to condemn him. Behind the scenes, the Eisenhower administration supported the censure as part of an effort to overcome what Eisenhower described as a "reactionary and recalcitrant splinter group"—far-right conservatives—in the GOP.[29]

In 1958, Goldwater came up for reelection. He had barely won his first race and, as the junior senator, was vulnerable to defeat. Meanwhile, McFarland had carefully positioned himself to regain his Senate seat.[30] His first step in his comeback was to defeat incumbent Howard Pyle for the governorship in 1954. Pyle had garnered bad publicity when he ordered a raid on polygamous Mormons in northern Arizona. McFarland thumped Pyle in the governor's race in 1954. As governor, McFarland pursued prolabor, prowelfare, and generally liberal policies. At the same time, his administration sought to lure high-tech defense industries to the state, and he called for lower corporate taxes.

Goldwater's role in the gubernatorial race reveals that politics is often more than ideology: it is also political calculation. Behind the scenes, the Goldwater camp decided not to throw its full support behind Pyle, even though Goldwater had served as his campaign manager in 1950. Goldwater feared that if Pyle won reelection as governor, he would challenge the long-standing incumbent senior senator Carl Hayden for reelection. The Goldwater family and the Hayden family went way back. Uncle Morris Goldwater was a close friend of Hayden's father. Goldwater looked up to Carl Hayden, who as senior senator pushed for federal water development for the state and was fairly conservative in his politics. Boosterism—the push for water necessary for Arizona's growth—proved more important than political party.

Behind-the-scenes maneuvering to defeat Pyle for reelection as governor began in the Goldwater camp in early 1953 with a letter from Shadegg to Carl Hayden warning that Pyle was thinking of running for his seat. Shadegg, who had served as Hayden's campaign manager in 1950, told Hayden that Goldwater was not pushing Pyle to run for Hayden's seat in 1956. "To prevent this," Shadegg wrote, "I think we must defeat him in 1954 with a good Democrat candidate, that his difficulty in the next two years should be exploited, and that ways must be found to permit the voters to discover a great deal more than they now know about Howard Pyle." Shadegg added that during Goldwater's campaign to defeat McFarland, "Howard [Pyle] was very little help to Barry and actually ran more as a non-partisan than as a Republican. There is considerable resentment among the working Republicans here over this, and I intend to keep that resentment alive. And I shall make it my special purpose to see to it that when Carl Hayden runs for Senate in 1956, he is the successful candidate."[31] There is little reason to doubt that Goldwater was informed of this strategy to defeat Pyle. In fact, Goldwater wrote President Eisenhower a confidential letter two years later in spring 1956 urging him to try to dissuade Pyle from attempting a run against Hayden that year. Goldwater added that he was willing to do what it took to ensure Republican political success, "even though I know it would be against the wishes of one of my best friends, Howard Pyle."[32] Goldwater and other Republican Party leaders continued to support Hayden through his last election in 1962.[33] Hayden had seniority in the Senate and promoted federal water projects for the state.

The 1958 Senate race in Arizona proved especially nasty. Organized labor targeted Goldwater as a major enemy, and its political action committee, COPE, poured money into defeating him. Labor went beyond funding Goldwater's opponent. Shadegg later reported that the Goldwater campaign offices were bugged and that labor sent operatives into the state to follow the candidates. This latter charge was especially damaging to organized labor's effort to oust Goldwater. Shortly before the election, with evidence provided by

Shadegg and an investigative reporter, the October 19, 1958, issue of *Arizona Republic* ran a front-page story with the headline "Arizona Democrats Resent Invasion—COPE Agents Muscle In." These revelations turned the campaign into an issue of outside influence in state politics.

From the outset, McFarland found himself on the ropes, and he failed to exploit the information that the Goldwater campaign had received heavy financing from Texas oilman H. L. Hunt and Massachusetts candy manufacturer Robert Welch, who was to found the far-right anti-Communist John Birch Society.[34] McFarland was further damaged when organized-labor operatives were caught distributing leaflets supposedly representing the Communist Party, declaring that Stalin had endorsed Goldwater. Attacking Goldwater from the right seems quite absurd, but labor was desperate to defeat him. The Republicans use of television, personalizing Goldwater the family man and independent-minded conservative further benefited the campaign.[35]

In the end, Goldwater won the election handily, with over 164,000 votes to McFarland's 120,000 votes. This victory was especially impressive because the 1958 midterm election proved to be a Democratic year on the national level. Democrats picked up thirteen Senate seats. William Knowland, the former Senate majority leader, was defeated in his bid to win the governor's mansion in California; he lost largely owing to his support of a state right-to-work initiative. Knowland's loss made Goldwater the leading voice for conservative Republicanism in the Senate. The national press had followed the Arizona Senate race closely, further making Goldwater into a well-known name in American households.

Preparing for a Presidential Run

In the late 1950s, the conservative movement was incipient and ideologically incoherent. It was composed of serious intellectuals around William F. Buckley's *National Review,* founded in 1955; a few elected Republican officials; some free market and anti–organized labor businessmen; internationalists and anti-internationalists; antisegregationists in the North and segregationist states-rights types in the South; and some genuinely unbalanced conspiracy-theory nuts.[36] What united the right in the 1950s was its opposition to the New Deal regulatory and welfare state, anti-Communism, and a belief that the founding principles of the American Republic were not being adhered to by those running the country. The Republican Party itself was divided among the Eastern Rockefeller wing, the Midwest, and the

Sunbelt South and West. Furthermore, many on the grassroots right placed ideological principle above party loyalty. This anti-GOP sentiment manifested itself in an early Draft Goldwater Committee that emerged to secure Goldwater the GOP nomination in 1960 and, if this failed, to organize a new third party. Clarence Manion, a former dean of the University of Notre Dame Law School and prominent conservative radio host, organized the committee.[37]

For most political observers within and outside the Republican Party, Richard Nixon had the Republican presidential nomination for 1960 sewn up. On the whole, conservatives were not excited by Nixon's nomination, but they feared the alternative, Nelson Rockefeller, who typified for them the Eastern, internationalist-minded party establishment. For conservatives, the choice between Nixon and Rockefeller was no choice at all, and so they turned to a grassroots effort to draft Goldwater for the nomination. If these pro-Goldwater activists could not win the nomination for him at the convention, they hoped to form a new conservative third party uniting conservative Republicans and Democrats. From the start, the movement was quixotic. For one thing, Goldwater had publicly endorsed Nixon. Goldwater was a loyal Republican who believed that talk of a new third party was cockamamie. Furthermore, Goldwater privately worried about even having his name placed in nomination at the 1960 convention because he feared it might look as if he was trying to undermine Nixon.

The Draft Goldwater Committee's greatest accomplishment was to get Goldwater to allow a book to be written in his name laying out the principles of modern-day conservatism. Manion commissioned Brent Bozell, William F. Buckley's brother-in-law, to write the book. When published in March 1960, *Conscience of a Conservative* became a runaway best-seller. Manion arranged for bulk orders of the book. Whether Goldwater read the manuscript remains unclear, but the text aligned with his views. The 127-page book, written in a simple-to-read style, presented conservatism as based on the principles of individualism. It resonated with the followers of Ayn Rand, whose novels were also best-sellers at the time. The book detailed the philosophical foundations of conservatism and policies that followed from the principles of individualism: anticollectivism, whether it be Soviet Communism, fascism, or the New Deal regulatory state. The book called for winning the Cold War through a strong national defense; ending the New Deal welfare state, including consideration of privatizing Social Security; opposing national health insurance; ending agricultural subsidies; privatizing the

Tennessee Valley Authority (TVA); supporting voluntary racial integration; and returning power to the states.

The book encouraged the growth of Draft Goldwater Committees throughout the country but, more important, brought Goldwater conservativism to a larger public. Goldwater found a further platform for his views when the *Los Angeles Times* in 1960 invited him to write a syndicated column, "How Do You Stand, Sir?" Goldwater used Stephen Shadegg as a ghost writer for the column, which by 1962 appeared in nearly 150 newspapers.[38] By the time of the 1960 Republican Party primaries, Goldwater for President clubs had been organized in thirty-one states. Goldwater encouraged this grassroots movement by keeping track of it through his close friends Frank Brophy, Eugene Pulliam, and Stephen Shadegg. Pulliam, publisher of the *Indianapolis Star* as well as Phoenix newspapers, was close to Manion. Goldwater, through his extensive travels as Senate Republican campaign chair, knew that the rank and file and state leaders of the Republican Party supported Nixon for the nomination—a fact that had been slowly learned by Nelson Rockefeller. Goldwater had a better sense of where the party stood; so whatever thoughts he had about his limitations as a presidential nominee (including his Jewish name and lack of education), he knew that this was not his time.

He sought to push the Republican Party and its favored candidate, Nixon, to the right. Meanwhile, Rockefeller forces sought to move the party to the left. Rockefeller knew early that Nixon had enough pledged delegates to win the nomination at the convention. He did not enter the primaries to challenge Nixon and appeared to be out of the running, when suddenly in early June, after a failed Eisenhower–Khrushchev summit and the shooting down of an American U-2 spy plane over the Soviet Union, Rockefeller spoke out. He was driven both by his own conscience about the future of the party and by political ambition. Rockefeller declared that the time had come for "plain talk" and warned that Nixon was misleading the party.

Goldwater countered Rockefeller by calling for a statement by the party that it stood for conservative principles. He appeared before the GOP National Platform Committee to offer his "Suggested Declaration of Republican Principles" in which he proposed that the party platform adopt general principles rather than lengthy policy positions. These principles presented what became the theme of his 1964 presidential campaign. He argued for victory in the Cold War, a condemnation of deficit financing, confirmation of a "sound and balanced" budget, and "voluntary unionism." He proclaimed, "We believe any society that proposes to relieve its citizens of all responsibility—and thus condemns them to a state of perpetual childhood—is acting contrary to the best purposes of mankind."[39]

The battle between Goldwater conservatives and Rockefeller liberals was symbolized in the fight over civil rights and defense planks in the party platform. Nixon feared that if Rockefeller further pursued his critique of the Republican platform, it would damage the party in the general election. Not only was Rockefeller attacking the right in the party; he was openly criticizing the Eisenhower administration on civil rights and defense. Like any presidential candidate running after his party had held the presidency for two terms, Nixon was in the delicate position of having to defend the previous administration while offering something new. Nixon decided that the best way to stop Rockefeller from damaging the party in the general election was to incorporate him. In an arranged meeting, Rockefeller and Nixon hammered out the "Fifth Avenue" agreement for a party platform containing strong national defense and civil rights positions. When announced, the Rockefeller–Nixon agreement was immediately denounced by conservative delegates at the convention as the "Fifth Avenue sellout." Shooting from the hip when asked by the press about the accord, an angry Goldwater called the agreement "a Munich," an overt attempt by Nixon to "appease the Republican left."[40] Nixon needed New York's forty-three electoral votes more than he needed Arizona's four, and then there was Rockefeller's money. Conservative delegates rebelled and wanted to push Goldwater's nomination then and there.

Goldwater's initial outburst gave way to calculation. When his name was placed in nomination by Texan Bruce Alger, South Carolina's Greg Shorey, South Dakota's L. R. Houck, and his friend Representative John J. Rhodes— a nomination he hesitated over in the first place—Goldwater withdrew his name by declaring himself for Nixon.[41] He told convention delegates, "I think conservatives have made a splendid showing at this convention. We've had our chance. We've fought our battle. Now let's put our shoulders to the wheel for Dick Nixon and push him across the line." He added, "This country is too important for anyone's feelings."[42] Goldwater preferred the Republican candidate who had the best chance of winning the White House for the party. In 1960, Goldwater believed this candidate was Richard Nixon.

Even with Goldwater's endorsement, many conservatives remained tepid about Nixon. They were not reassured when Nixon selected Henry Cabot Lodge Jr. as a running mate. Lodge represented the Eastern establishment as much as did Rockefeller. Nonetheless, Goldwater went all out for the Republican ticket by making 126 speeches in twenty-six states during the campaign. He proved a more adept campaigner than Lodge, who was especially lethargic on the campaign trail.

Goldwater Loses the White House

When Nixon lost the close 1960 contest to the youthful and vigorous John F. Kennedy, and then lost his bid to win the California governorship against the less than politically adroit Edmund "Pat" Brown in 1962, the path to the Republican presidential nomination for Goldwater was cleared. The only roadblock he faced was Nelson Rockefeller. The primary contest between Goldwater and Rockefeller was fought over the soul of the party. In many ways, the differences between the two were not as sharp as either of them suggested or their followers believed. Rockefeller was a Cold Warrior who believed in a strong national defense. Both men feared a global overpopulation crisis and supported family planning. Whatever they had in common, Goldwater was a Western conservative who sought to scale back the federal government. Rockefeller, when all is said and done, was a big-government liberal Republican. If both candidates stood in favor of racial integration, Goldwater maintained that full racial justice could not be imposed by the federal government without threatening basic constitutional principles.

Shortly before the Republican National Convention, still in the heat of the primaries, Goldwater cast his vote against the Civil Rights Act of 1964, introduced by the Johnson administration. Republican leadership in both the Senate and the House backed the measure. Nonetheless, Goldwater, an early member of Phoenix's branch of the National Association for the Advancement of Colored People, broke party ranks to vote against the bill. The majority of Senate Republicans supported the bill, which had a higher percentage of Republican support than Democratic support. Goldwater opposed the bill on constitutional grounds that federal regulation of public accommodations and employment, found in Title II and VII, overstepped the proper role of government. He concluded, "If my vote is misconstrued, let it be, and let me suffer the consequences."[43] Goldwater's vote continued to haunt him throughout the 1964 campaign. Although the bill would not have become law without Republican votes, Democrats became the party of pro–civil rights, and Republicans were seen by many, especially black voters, as the party of states' rights.

The battle between Goldwater and Rockefeller for the nomination became increasingly personal. At first, Rockefeller made a bid to win the right by attacking Kennedy's proposal for a new federal department on urban affairs and then denouncing the nuclear test ban treaty. Realizing that he was not going to win the right, Rockefeller focused his primary campaign on warning of a takeover of the party by the extreme right. Both Rockefeller and Goldwater took a blow when Henry Cabot Lodge won a surprising write-in victory in the New Hampshire primary. This opened the door for other Republican candidates to throw their hats in the ring, but by June, the race had come down to Goldwater and Rockefeller in the California primary. California played to Goldwater's strength. Rockefeller's only hope was to win overwhelmingly in the northern part of the state, the stronghold of liberals in the party, while cutting into Goldwater's natural appeal in the southern region. Rockefeller relied upon George Christopher, the former mayor of San Francisco, who had helped carry the city for Eisenhower in 1956. Rockefeller assailed Goldwater as a candidate representing the extreme right. When Rockefeller's second wife, Happy, gave birth to their child, voters were reminded of charges that Rockefeller had broken up a happy home. Orange County, just south of Los Angeles, played a big role in getting out the Goldwater vote. Rockefeller depended on television, which was less effective. Goldwater effectively mobilized Southern California conservatives to win the primary, 52 percent to 48 percent. By doing so, he won the nomination.

For his opponents, Goldwater might as well have come before them as an Israelite prophet before the feast of Baal. A defeated Rockefeller continued to lash out at extremists within the GOP. He was joined by other leading Republicans who depicted Goldwater as a warmonger, racial bigot, and extremist. Eastern sophisticates saw Goldwater as a yahoo senator from a podunk backwater state. They were joined by the established press, organized-labor leaders, and civil rights activists. Magazines such as *Life* and the *Reporter*, both part of the establishment, warned of the "tide of zealotry" sweeping over the convention. Goldwater arrived at the National Republican Convention in San Francisco greeted by forty thousand civil rights demonstrators denouncing him as America's next Adolf Hitler. This association with Hitler was reinforced when CBS reporter Daniel Schorr broke a false story that Goldwater was planning after the convention to travel to Bavaria to pay homage to Hitler.[44]

The attacks were taken personally by Goldwater, much like Nixon had taken Republican attacks against him twelve years earlier in 1952. Goldwater expected venom from liberal columnists such as Joseph Alsop of the liberal Republican *New York Herald,* who transferred obsessive hatred of Nixon to Goldwater, or Walter Lippmann who described Goldwater as "trigger happy." What pained Goldwater were attacks from Republican leaders such as Pennsylvania's governor Bill Scranton, whom had earlier, in 1964, urged Goldwater to run for the presidency. On Sunday evening, just as the convention was getting started, Scranton released a public letter calling for Goldwater to step down from the nomination. Among other charges, the letter declared that Goldwater "too often casually prescribed nuclear war as a solution to a troubled world."[45] Goldwater, who had been considering Scranton as a possible running mate, reacted with an ill temper that matched Rockefeller's. His decision to place an obscure Catholic and conservative, anti-Rockefeller congressman from upstate New York, William E. Miller, on the ticket confirmed that Goldwater was not going to mend fences.

An irate Goldwater instructed his speech writers, Karl Hess and Harry Jaffa, to take the gloves off and answer critics charging him with extremism. His televised acceptance speech would not be the typical call for party unity and to let bygones be bygones. "Extremism in the defense of liberty is no vice," they wrote. The quotation was reputedly from Cicero, and in his memoirs, Goldwater recalled that he had come across the phrase from reading novelist Taylor Caldwell, although he did not mention that she was a Bircher.[46]

Goldwater's intemperate defense of extremism in his defiant acceptance speech sent shock waves through the party leadership; they understood that their nominee had little chance of winning the election, but feared that he threatened to bring down the entire slate and that the damage might even extend into the 1968 election cycle. Eisenhower was especially irritated by Goldwater's intemperate speech. At Nixon's urging, Eisenhower arranged for Goldwater to attend a summit meeting of party leaders in August in Gettysburg, Pennsylvania, Eisenhower's hometown. The purpose of the meeting was to convince Goldwater to stop "shooting from the hip." The meeting brought Nelson Rockefeller, George Romney, William Scranton, and Nixon together to call for a united party. At the meeting, Goldwater appeared to accept their conciliatory advice. A press conference had been called following the closed-door meeting to present the "new" Goldwater, a serious presidential candidate. Any hope that Goldwater had gotten the message was smashed at the press conference, when he took the bait of a reporter's loaded question asking whether he would consider giving military commanders in the field control over the use of nuclear weapons. Goldwater replied yes, and then refused to back away from his position or to agree that he had reconciled with his former Republican challengers. An infuriated Eisenhower concluded, "You know, before we had this meeting I thought that Goldwater was just stubborn. Now I am convinced that he is just plain dumb."[47]

Goldwater accepted the presidential draft because of his loyalty to the conservative movement and his followers. It was an act of principle. He came before the electorate as a physician of old attempting to cure the humors of an ill republic. During the election, his campaign—managed by Denison Kitchel, who had never run a national campaign, and American Enterprise Institute president William Baroody—tried to move to the political center by staying away from issues such as privatization of Social Security, the war in Vietnam, and civil rights. When Goldwater met with his Democratic challenger, incumbent president Lyndon Johnson, in the White House in late July, Goldwater assured Johnson that during the campaign he would not bring up the issues of racial riots and Vietnam.[48] So concerned was the Goldwater campaign to distance themselves from charges of extremism, it initially refused to let Ronald Reagan appear on television for a half-hour speech promoting the campaign. Only when major California funders Walter Knott and Henry Salvatori threatened to cut off funding did the Goldwater campaign relent and let Reagan appear. Reagan's televised address won wide praise and brought new cash to the campaign, but the speech came too late, even if Goldwater had had a chance of winning. Even as the campaign tried to moderate the candidate's image, Goldwater's message remained undisciplined. Goldwater still continued to shoot from the hip. He talked about his opposition to Social Security to a crowd in St. Petersburg, Florida, and his opposition to the TVA in Nashville, Tennessee, even while he tried to reassure voters that as president he would not end Social Security or sell the TVA.[49]

By November, it was clear that Goldwater would lose the election. The questions were by how much and how many Republicans would go down with him. The results were brutal. Johnson won a landslide victory, taking all but six Southern states. Democrats picked up thirty-six seats in the House. Both houses of Congress had liberal majorities. The way was paved for Johnson's domestic Great Society and his expansion of the war in Vietnam. Conservatives rejoiced that their candidate had won twenty-seven million votes. This devastating loss, however, cleared the path to Nixon's nomination in 1968.

An Echo, Not a Choice

Goldwater stepped down from the Senate to run for president in 1964, and so in 1968 he campaigned and won the Senate seat once held by his longtime friend Carl Hayden, who finally retired after first entering Congress in 1912. Goldwater was reelected in 1974 and then barely maintained his seat in 1980 by only a couple thousand votes. He retired in 1986. By this time, the conservative movement seemed to have passed him by. He was at a loss to explain why.[50]

For Goldwater, the rise of Reagan Republicanism was frustrating and not what he envisioned as genuine conservatism. He despised the religious right, denouncing the influence of preachers such as Jerry Falwell, leader of the Moral Majority. He believed that injecting religious issues into the bedroom by regulating abortion subverted the conservative principles of small government. He remained loyal to the Republican Party, but his politics were increasingly driven by partisanship and not ideology. He supported Richard Nixon in 1968 and Gerald Ford in 1976. He distanced himself from Ronald Reagan, who had once looked upon the Arizona senator as his mentor. After Goldwater left the Senate, he became increasingly hostile to the religious right, endorsing a Democrat running for Congress in 1994 against a Republican candidate he thought too evangelical and too socially conservative. He endorsed and contributed to Democrats Dennis DeConcini and Morris Udall. His support after his retirement for abortion and gay rights alienated many conservatives. In the end, as his sympathetic biographer Lee Edwards concludes, there were two Goldwaters: the uncompromising conservative of 1957 to 1964 and the politician whose sails were set by party loyalty and his own eccentricities, who would describe Rockefeller as a great American who would have made a great president.[51]

Goldwater consistently supported a strong military. He remained deeply patriotic, and whatever the inconsistency in his views about social issues, his campaign in 1964 revealed the growing strength of the conservative movement within the Republican Party. It came by fits and starts, and sixteen years later, the man now considered the quintessential conservative, Ronald Reagan, won the White House. The nation in 1964 was not ready for a Goldwater presidency. Conservatives rejoiced in winning twenty-seven million votes for their candidate in 1964, but few stopped to ask what a Goldwater presidency might have looked like. There would not have been a Great

Society under Goldwater, but as president, he would have faced a Democratic-controlled Congress intent on pursuing a liberal agenda.

Goldwater's personality reflected a Western individualist ethos and the eccentricities of the region and his own upbringing. He increasingly fired from the hip, taking stubborn pride in speaking bluntly. Stephen Shadegg enforced discipline in Goldwater's first two campaigns for the Senate, but in 1964, without his former campaign manager at his side, Goldwater revealed his temperamental weaknesses, dismaying both Eisenhower and Nixon. The assaults on Goldwater's character during the campaign were vicious. So were the assaults on Rockefeller. Both men were quick to anger. They set a sharp contrast to Reagan, whose temperament, character, and consistency of principle better suited the presidency.

5 | Ronald Reagan
Principled Pragmatist

Ideologues, whether reactionaries or revolutionaries, maintain a moral certainty that the world can be made perfect. They remain certain that moral order can be created. Reactionaries seek to restore an imagined previous moral order, while revolutionaries envision the creation of a new moral order that breaks from history. Both reactionary and revolutionary ideologues welcome chaos in the existing social and political order. Chaos confirms their sense of moral superiority and provides them with an expectation of opportunity for radical change. Gradualists within their ranks are denounced as opportunists and grouped with actual self-aggrandizing opportunists who pervade politics as usual. As to deciding what the perfect world will be, reactionaries and revolutionaries fall into factional sectarianism, which only becomes more pronounced when radical change does not come. Histories of right-wing and left-wing ideological movements are ones of purist doctrinal divides. The tragedy of ideologues, even when radical change occurs, is that perfection is never achieved in an imperfect world and history never ends.

American conservatism and the Republican Party in 1968 encapsulate these tensions between ideological purists who demanded purity of principle and gradualists who believed that change could occur within the existing system, even at the expense of principle. Ideologues abounded within the American conservative movement and were found in an array of organizations and individuals with varying degrees of influence. These ideologues shared a common belief that the Republican Party had been corrupted by special interests and careerist Republican-in-name-only (RINO) politicians. Their hopes for a resurrected Republican Party based on conservative principles had not been completely dashed even after the Goldwater debacle in 1964. Following Goldwater's defeat, the ever-astute and ever-calculating Richard Nixon saw his opportunity for political redemption. By 1966, he had created a presidential campaign organization carefully staffed without ideological rhyme or reason by liberals, centrists, and conservatives. Nixon wanted a staff that could craft political responses to whatever situation might arise. His presidential run in 1968 was not issue oriented or principled, but designed only to ensure his nomination and election. The ever-ambivalent Nelson Rockefeller sensed an opportunity for his national resurrection, too. As the 1968 presidential session began, Rockefeller initially backed Michigan governor George Romney, and when Romney's efforts collapsed, Rockefeller made his own clandestine bid. By that time, however, Nixon had the primaries sewn up, and so Rockefeller was forced to make a last-ditch effort at the Republican convention to stop Nixon. It was at this point when things got bizarre. Rockefeller, in an effort to stop a Nixon nomination, proposed forming an alliance with Ronald Reagan. Reagan was not interested in a vice-presidential slot on any ticket, least of all with Rockefeller, and he rejected the offer outright.

Reagan's refusal reflected his pragmatism and principled politics. He knew that any alliance with Rockefeller would alienate his own conservative base; moreover, he rejected on principle any alliance with Rockefeller. Reagan brought to American politics a rare combination of core principles, natural political talent, and strategic understanding of what could be achieved to further a conservative agenda. His natural political talents were apparent as president of the Screen Actors Guild in the 1940s. In this role, Reagan further developed negotiating skills, which served him well as governor of California and later as president of the United States. In office, Reagan learned to govern. He was elected to the governorship in 1966 without his having much understanding of the constraints of elected office. It was one thing on the campaign trail to call for an across-the-board 10 percent cut in government spending and a reduction in taxes—promises he made to voters in his 1966 governor's race—and then to fulfill these promises once in office. As governor, he learned the practicalities of governing while maintaining his core principles. He balanced ideology with pragmatic governance while remaining popular among voters. This was a remarkable achievement of leadership at a time of increasing and deepening polarization within the electorate. As ideological polarization intensified, conservatives made Reagan into an icon, the great communicator who translated high ideological principles into a language understood by average Americans. Progressives constructed an image of Reagan the snake-oil salesman who accomplished little as president. Both constructions neglected Reagan's ability to compromise in pursuit of larger goals. Reagan embodied idealism with a realistic understanding that the world could not be made perfect but could be made better.

Reagan: The Early Years

Reagan's character, temperament, and core political principles were shaped in his childhood and his subsequent career in Hollywood.

His persona of the small-town Middle American was belied by a childhood that was far from idyllic. His father's severe alcoholism and inability to keep a job or find success as a businessman meant that the family moved frequently and struggled to make ends meet. Jack Reagan had a glib tongue and dashing good looks.[1] At the age of sixteen, he took a job at a dry-goods store in Fulton, Illinois, where he learned to sell shoes, which became his specialty. He had already developed a drinking problem when he married seventeen-year-old Nelle Wilson, who traced her family back to the American Revolution. After the birth of their first son, Neil, Nelle convinced her husband to leave Fulton (mostly to escape the influence of Jack's rowdy brother) and move twenty-six miles away to Tampico, a small town of a little over a thousand residents. Shortly after their move, Nelle became a member of the Disciples of Christ, an offshoot of the Presbyterian Church. The Disciples of Christ, also known as the Christian Church, espoused unity of all Christians through salvation. In 1911, their second son, Ronald, was born. Jack nicknamed him "Dutch" because of his robust appearance. Nelle raised her two sons to be Christians, taking both children with her to Wednesday Bible study classes and two services on Sunday. When Jack was fired from the store where he was working, the family began a series of moves around the region before finally landing in the little town of Dixon, Illinois. Here, Jack became part owner in a shoe store, but the store never quite made it, barely surviving.

Ronald Reagan's life mostly revolved around his mother. He attended church services with her. His mother imparted ambition and the importance of education, while his father passed on his gift for gab and his liberal politics. Jack despised the Republicans, whom he saw as the party of the rich. He stood with the common man, which meant he also detested the Ku Klux Klan. He told his son, "The Klan's the Klan, and a sheet's a sheet, and any man who wears one over his head is a bum."[2] This belief was reinforced by his mother's Christian Church, which preached equality of color and had black parishioners and ministers.

His mother insisted that her sons go to college, even though the family was atruggling financially. Ron, although younger, entered college first, later joined by his hard-drinking and less ambitious brother. Through his mother's efforts, Ron was admitted to a small church-affiliated school, Eureka College, in 1928, a year before the country entered the worse economic depression in its history. One of Ron's first acts as a student was to become a spokesman for a student strike against the college's ban on dancing. The protest drew national attention. Students elected Reagan their spokesperson because of his skills as a public orator. Reagan did not excel academically or on the athletic field: his poor eyesight hurt him in both. He got by on his remarkable memory and his enthusiasm. He was popular without being a heavy partier and active in his fraternity, the drama club, and the school newspaper. Graduating at the height of the Depression, Reagan set his sights on becoming a radio sports broadcaster. Through sheer good fortune and an active job search, Reagan landed a job at a small station in Davenport, Iowa, which was a stepping-stone to his becoming chief sports announcer for WHO in Des Moines. By this time, WHO had become a major station in the Midwest, bringing Reagan some celebrity. At this point, he was a strong Democrat, but he remained open to discussion with colleagues and the station's top brass, who were anti–New Deal.

In 1937, as the Depression continued and Reagan enjoyed local success, he arranged to travel to California to cover the Chicago Cubs spring training practice on Santa Catalina Island. His good looks and all-American persona landed him a seven-year contract at Warner Brothers studio starting at two hundred dollars a week. Only six years out of college, the poor kid from Dixon had hit it big. Reagan was given roles playing the all-American. He remained loyal to the studio run by autocrat Jack Warner. The four Warner brothers, all Roosevelt New Deal supporters, were seen as running the most liberal studio in Hollywood. Unlike other studios, they produced anti-Nazi films in the 1930s that got all their films banned in Germany. In 1943, as Reagan's career began to take off, his reserve unit was called up for service in World War II. Although his contribution to the war effort was in an entertainment unit in and around Los Angeles for the most part, the three-year stint had a damaging effect on his movie career.

In Hollywood, Reagan became active in Democratic politics, which was not exceptional at that time. Republicans claimed a few big stars—Gary Cooper, Clark Gable, Jimmy Stewart, and later John Wayne—but Hollywood remained mostly a liberal town.[3] Reagan and his movie-star wife, Jane Wyman, became active in Hollywood Democratic circles and in the Screen Actors Guild (SAG). In 1941, Reagan became an alternate on the union's executive board, and a year later Jane Wyman was also elected to the board. In 1946, he was elected third vice president of the board and the following year became the president of SAG.

Reagan's transformation from a liberal to a conservative began with a single issue: Communism. His anti-Communist views developed while fighting a sizable Communist faction in the union. Following World War II, Hollywood found itself in its own war with Communist-controlled unions and labor strikes. The first major strike occurred in 1945, when the Conference of Studio Unions (CSU), an umbrella union for technical workers, called out its ten thousand members in a jurisdictional dispute with its rival union the International Alliance of Theatrical Stage Employees (IATSE). Opponents accused the CSU of being Communist-controlled.[4] The strike embroiled forty-two craft unions and pitted the unions against the major studios. The strike ended when IATSE workers crossed the picket lines. During the strike, Reagan received personal threats for having crossed the picket line as a member of SAG. Fearing for his life, he took out a gun permit.

In September 1946, CSU went out again on strike. The thirteen-month strike was characterized by violence, car bombings, mass arrests, death threats, and riots. The most bitter and violent strike in Hollywood's history came to an end only when fourteen union leaders were indicted for inciting violence. Although SAG refused to support the strike, the union tried to mediate an end to the strike by leading a delegation headed by Reagan to meet with CSU officials to bring peace to Hollywood. When these negotiations failed, progressives within SAG accused Reagan of being a strike breaker. Taking these critics head-on, Reagan called for a mass meeting of all SAG members to be held in the Hollywood American Legion Stadium in October 1947. More than 1,800 actors showed up, many of them angry at SAG's antistrike stand and its failure in negotiations with CSU. At the rally, Reagan took the podium. Speaking without notes for nearly an hour, Reagan presented a clear and persuasive account of SAG's failure to mediate the strike. He did not talk about what many saw as Communist influence in CSU. Instead, he spoke as a union negotiator facing another union that did not want to negotiate. His performance won over the audience, many of whom had not known just how bright and articulate Ronald Reagan was off the screen.

Following the strike, Reagan emerged as one of the strongest anti-Communist voices in Hollywood, but he was by no means rabid in his stance compared to many within the industry. He joined James Roosevelt, Franklin Roosevelt's eldest son; composer Johnny Green; and actors Olivia de Havilland and Melvyn Douglas in resigning from the former Hollywood Democratic Committee when it refused to pass a resolution against Communism. He remained a Democrat, however, and would not change his official registration to Republican until the early 1960s. His liberalism was evident in 1946 when he joined left-wing Democrats in a radio program "Operation Terror," which was part of a series about the growing threat of fascism in the United States. The project had been initiated by Robert Kenny, California's attorney general, who received reports of Ku Klux Klan violence in his state. In 1946, the left expressed deep anxiety that fascism was on the rise in the United States. In his radio address in early September, Reagan alleged that there was a conspiracy afoot, "a capably organized systematic campaign of fascist violence and intimidation and horror," to bring fascism to America. This was typical talk on the left in 1946, and it continued even when local California authorities dismissed the alleged violence as little more than the work of juvenile "pranksters."[5]

In 1948, Reagan campaigned for Truman and flew out to Minnesota to help Hubert Humphrey's campaign. He made a radio ad for the International Ladies Garment Workers Union denouncing Republicans and big business for setting back progress for "liberal government in America." Reagan's strong left leanings expressed themselves as well when he offered to support Helen Gahagan Douglas in her race for the U.S. Senate in 1950 against Richard Nixon. His offer was turned down by Douglas because she thought his reputation as a leftist liberal might hurt her.[6]

Whatever his progressive leanings in these years, Reagan also expressed strong but tempered anti-Communist views. When first approached by members of the House Un-American Activities Committee (HUAC) in 1947 to testify at its hearings investigating Soviet propaganda in Hollywood films, Reagan expressed great reticence. He informed the HUAC staff that he vehemently disagreed with many within the anti-Communist right in Hollywood and did not want to be associated with them. He said that the Communist issue in Hollywood had been addressed and there was no need for a congressional investigation.[7] When he finally testified in 1947, he joined studio heads and former presidents of SAG, George Murphy and Robert Montgomery, in their testimony that the small Communist problem in the industry had been fully addressed by the studios and was no longer a concern.[8] He articulated an anti-Communist position from a civil libertarian point of view. In his testimony before HUAC, he declared, "I detest, I abhor their [Communist Party] philosophy," but warned that our country's ideals of civil liberties should not be compromised in a witch hunt.[9]

Becoming a Conservative

Reagan's marriage to his second wife, Nancy Davis, facilitated, indeed was instrumental to, his shift from the left to the right. The breakup of his marriage to Jane Wyman in 1947 hit Reagan harder than did his declining movie career. As a young actor in Hollywood, he had made a career playing the all-American boy. At the end of World War II, Reagan was only thirty-four years old, but the movie industry was in transition. Movie ticket sales began to decline as the public stayed home to watch television. The movie industry responded by targeting the youth audience with science-fiction, horror, and teenage romance films. All-American-type actors began to be replaced by a new breed of darker actors, such as Marlon Brando and Paul Newman. Reagan found roles in comedies, westerns, and war movies, films such as *The Voice of the Turtle, John Loves Mary, The Hasty Heart, Bedtime for Bonzo, Cattle Queen of Montana, Tennessee Partner,* and *Hellcats of the Navy*. (Critics never let him forget his playing second fiddle to a chimpanzee in *Bedtime for Bonzo,* which actually did pretty well at the box office.)

Wyman said that the marriage broke up because of her husband's political ambitions and his involvement in SAG, which kept him increasingly away from home and their three children. Actually, Wyman appeared to be growing distant from Reagan long before the divorce was announced. There was a ponderous side to her husband that could be annoying. She later observed that if you asked Ronnie the time, he would tell you how the clock works.[10] In 1945, however, Wyman's acting career was just taking off, while Reagan found himself playing in second-rate movies. She had received critical notice for her serious dramatic roles in *The Lost Weekend, The Yearling,* and *Johnny Belinda*. While on the set of *Johnny Belinda,* she was rumored to have an affair with actor Lew Ayres.

After his divorce, Reagan seemed like a lost soul in Hollywood until he met Nancy Davis, an aspiring actress. A stepdaughter of a Chicago surgeon and outspoken conservative, she loved politics and loved hearing Reagan talk. She encouraged his political ambitions. Their best friends in Hollywood, including actor William Holden and his wife, were conservatives. These friends helped convince Reagan that he was no longer a liberal or a Democrat.

Initially, Reagan remained a registered Democrat, but at heart, he had already become a Republican. He publicly supported Eisenhower in 1952 and 1956, and Nixon in 1960, although he disliked Nixon in 1952. Reagan's speeches as a paid spokesperson for General Electric, which took him around the country, expressed his pro-business and free-market beliefs.[11] He was a favored speaker for anti-Communist organizations and rallies throughout the country. He became active in the growing conservative movement by becoming a board member of the Young Americans for Freedom, a student group organized by William Buckley Jr. By 1964, he had developed a strong following among Republicans in California. The more they heard Reagan, the more they liked him for his denunciations of Communism, his enunciation of free-market principles, and his ability to communicate the problems of big government.

His eloquent speech on behalf of Goldwater, "A Time for Choosing," inspired grassroots conservatives. Reagan traveled up and down California giving the speech. Still, some longtime Hollywood Republicans, such as actors Jimmy Stewart and Robert Taylor, as well as hard-core conservatives within the state party, such as Joe Shell, resented Reagan's popularity. Suspicions of Reagan became evident at a mass meeting of California Citizens for Goldwater in Orange County in August 1964, a month after the national convention, when Reagan came under attack for being appointed head of the committee. Many in the audience favored Phil Davis, a right-wing Beverly Hills businessman, to head the committee. Reagan was seated next to Goldwater organizer F. Clifton White when Davis launched a full-throated attack on Reagan. White started to rise to defend Reagan when Reagan grabbed White and whispered, "No Cliff. This is my fight and I will handle it." Reagan came to the podium to defuse the situation by declaring, "Folks, I'm the new boy on the block. I have been less involved in a campaign like this in the past. But I can see that there's trouble here, and there ought not to be trouble here." By stating this, Reagan showed modesty and ability to compliment an audience. He then launched into a rousing speech on behalf of Goldwater and what he represented to America's future. He ended by recommending that Phil Davis be elected cochair of the committee. Reagan's natural political instincts carried the day.[12]

Reagan's stump speech for Goldwater caught the attention of Henry Salvatori and Holmes Tuttle, two wealthy Southern California businessmen who headed the state campaign's finance committee. Both had known Reagan for more than a decade. They liked his fundraising skills and his affable manner.

They invited Reagan to keynote a thousand-dollar-a-plate fundraising event for Goldwater. Afterward, Tuttle approached Reagan to ask if he would be willing to give the speech on television. Reagan replied, "Sure, if you think it would do any good."[13]

The proposal for Reagan to appear on television divided the Goldwater camp. Denison Kitchel, Goldwater's campaign manager, and William Baroody Sr., the campaign's chief strategist, thought Reagan's speech too controversial. They were worried that Reagan might come across as too extremist and call for privatization of Social Security, even though Goldwater had made the same suggestion in *Conscience of a Conservative*. Under pressure from his Southern California donors, Goldwater finally relented after meeting with Reagan. After watching the speech, Goldwater turned to an aide and asked, "What the hell is wrong with that?"[14] The Goldwater campaign, however, insisted that private money needed to be raised to put it on the air. Tuttle, Salvatori, and right-wing businessman Walter Knott tapped their extensive financial sources to finance the speech. Actor John Wayne reached out to his fraternity brothers from Sigma Chi at the University of Southern California to contribute to the cause. Activists began writing the Goldwater campaign demanding the speech be televised. Once aired, "A Time for Choosing" electrified Goldwater conservatives across the country, raised an estimated $8 million, and set the stage for Reagan's own entry into politics.

Two months after the Goldwater defeat, the soft-spoken Southern California auto dealer Holmes P. Tuttle called a meeting in his home to discuss running Reagan for governor in 1966.[15] Those who gathered in Tuttle's home were mostly self-made men. A. C. Rubel, chairman of the board of Union Oil Company, was the notable exception. The others who gathered included Henry Salvatori, founder of the Western Geophysical Company who had made a fortune in oil exploration. He hated both "big oil" and Communism. William French Smith, Reagan's lawyer; Taft Schreiber, Hollywood agent; millionaire Leonard Firestone; Leland Kaiser, retired investment banker; Arch Monson Jr., western manager of Autocall Company; and Jaquelin Hume, president of Basic Vegetable Products, joined the meeting. Not everyone at the meeting had been a Goldwater supporter early on. Firestone had backed Nelson Rockefeller in the California primary. These men considered themselves conservatives and supporters of the free market, but they liked winners. They told Reagan they wanted him to run for governor. Tuttle suggested that the key to a victory lay in bringing in the political management firm Spencer-Roberts, which had run the Rockefeller primary campaign in California in 1964.

Stuart Spencer and Bill Roberts were moderate Republicans who had started out working for the Los Angeles County Central Committee before branching out to win thirty-four of forty congressional races with Republican candidates. Approached by Tuttle to run the Reagan campaign, Spencer-Roberts made a political calculation. The front-runner for the Republican nomination to challenge incumbent governor Pat Brown was the moderate former San Francisco mayor George Christopher, another Rockefeller Republican. Most believed Pat Brown was a shoo-in for reelection. The Spencer-Roberts team was less certain of Brown's chances but concluded that Christopher would not play well on television or in Southern California. Politics in the state was about media, and here Reagan had a natural advantage. Their only hesitations were that Reagan might be too right wing and that he had a reputation for being difficult to work with. After an evening in Reagan's home, they decided neither was the case. They signed on to run the campaign. Reagan's willingness to have the firm direct his campaign revealed his political pragmatism. He wanted the best people around him, even if they were not ideological purists. He manifested this trait throughout his next twenty-two years in politics. Reagan remained a hard-core conservative, but he also remained remarkably flexible in choosing his staff and achieving his larger political goals.

When Reagan entered the governor's race, he faced a divided state party.[16] His major challenger for the Republican nomination was Christopher, who underestimated Reagan as an amateur and a right winger. Reagan countered this image by declaring himself a "citizen politician" and distancing himself from extremists within the party. When confronted by the press on his support from the John Birch Society, Reagan responded simply by saying, "Any member of the society who supports me will be buying my philosophy. I won't be buying theirs."[17] This was far different than Nixon's attempt in 1962 to ban the Birchers. After Reagan won the nomination, Pat Brown's campaign pursued Christopher's strategy of attacking Reagan as an extremist and an actor. The Brown campaign underestimated Reagan and had been convinced that Christopher was going to win the GOP nomination. They had brought out negative stories about Christopher during the primary, and one result was that Christopher, who might have endorsed Brown after he lost the primary, threw his support to Reagan and unified the party.

Brown's attacks on Reagan backfired. After the Watts riot in Los Angeles in 1965, Brown's poor handling of the event, and campus protests at the University of California, Berkeley, most voters were not worried about right-wing extremism but by what they saw as left-wing extremism. Brown's inept attacks on Reagan as just being an actor did not play well either in Hollywood or Southern California, the home of the movie industry. Reagan appeared down to earth, related well to average citizens, disarmed a generally hostile press with his charm, and did not make gaffes that could not be overcome. He conveyed a conservative message without coming across as a right-wing nut job. He proved adroit, and, most of all, he played well on television. He captured the anxiety of voters while remaining optimistic that the problems could be solved. He won the general election by more than one million votes.[18]

On the campaign trail, Reagan presented himself as a "citizen-politician" who could bring common sense to government. His tone was moderate, but his message was solidly conservative and would be taken by his opponents as hard right and playing to the racist prejudices of white voters. One of the problems of being a citizen-politician for Reagan revealed itself immediately when he came into office: He and his campaign staff were not prepared to govern. Reagan's faith, as expressed in "A Time for Choosing," and his campaign that "the truth is there are simple answers—they're just are not easy ones" did not provide a policy agenda or an understanding of the complexities of governing. Most on the campaign staff did not know much about state government and the legislative process. As Lyn Nofziger later told Reagan's biographer, journalist Lou Cannon, "We were not only amateurs, we were novice amateurs."[19]

The first steps in governing proved difficult for Reagan and his staff. They could not even find a suitable budget director, and when Caspar Weinberger, an experienced California legislator, was proposed, he was shot down by Tuttle because he was seen as a liberal Republican. Reagan and his staff proved to be quick learners. Reagan deferred to his experts, but at executive meetings, he zeroed in on the critical issues, kept to his core principles, and showed he was a masterful negotiator. Lou Cannon, who watched the administration firsthand, concluded that "Reagan was simultaneously conservative and pragmatic."[20] Reagan clung to his principles without allowing them to undermine his governance.

Reagan developed a working relationship with the legislature, especially the upper house. He did not try to pretend he was one of the boys. He liked to keep regular office hours, working intensively and then enjoying evenings at home with Nancy. Instead of relying on personal relationships with legislators, he developed a strong legislative affairs office—a pattern followed when he became president. Left with a huge state budget deficit by the Brown administration, Reagan agreed to the largest tax hike in state history—"a breathtaking display of pragmatism," as Cannon put it.[21] In negotiating the tax bill with Democratic Assembly Speaker Jesse Unruh, Reagan pushed for a property tax rebate, but he lost on other issues. As Reagan said, he took what he could get. After raising taxes, Reagan might have been in deep political trouble with voters, but he adroitly deflected the issue by saying with just cause that the previous administration had left the state with a major deficit problem and at least he had pushed through a property tax rebate in the bill. Inflation and a prospering state economy provided budget surpluses for the Reagan administration over the course of the next seven years.

For most of his two terms in office, Reagan faced a Democratic-controlled legislature. One consequence was that he found himself having to sign legislation he did not necessarily agree with, including budget cuts in mental health and an extremely liberal abortion bill. Reagan wanted to veto the abortion bill; but Republican legislators had voted for the bill, and he did not want to leave them out on a political limb. Later critics—both left and right—attacked him for signing these pieces of legislation. His greatest accomplishment, however, came in his second term with welfare reform. Reagan won reelection in 1970 against Democratic challenger Jesse Unruh. During the reelection campaign, Reagan promised to reform the welfare system. Winning a decisive second term, Reagan made this a high priority.

Reagan opposed Nixon's proposed Family Assistance Plan, which would have provided, in effect, a guaranteed income for the poor. In a television debate, Reagan declared, "I believe that the government is supposed to promote the general welfare. I don't believe it's supposed to provide it."[22] Instead, working with Assembly Speaker Bob Moretti, an ultraliberal from Northern California, Reagan and his team entered into tough negotiations to undertake welfare reform. Negotiations often lasted from morning through night to craft what became at the time a model for welfare reform. The California Welfare Reform Act raised benefits, decreased eligibility, and established a demonstration workfare program. Within three years, welfare rolls had dropped by nearly 300,000 people.

Testing the Presidential Waters: 1968

Two years after winning election to the governor's mansion, Reagan tepidly tested a presidential run. He remained ambivalent about whether he was prepared for a serious presidential race, let alone the presidency itself. This ambivalence was shared by his staff. Goldwater's crushing loss in 1964 set the stage for Richard Nixon's political comeback and made Reagan into the nation's leading conservative politician. Goldwater proved critical to both Nixon's and Reagan's political careers. Goldwater, the politician who claimed to be "Mr. Conservative," backed Nixon for the presidency in 1968 and not Reagan, who clearly had taken up the banner for conservatives. So appreciative of Nixon's support in 1964, Goldwater pledged his support to Nixon if Nixon was to ever run for the presidency again. Everyone knew that Nixon was going to run in 1968, making Goldwater's pledge more than just an idle promise.[23]

Reagan made no overt bid for the nomination. Acting on the advice of political consultant Cliff White, who had been instrumental in the grassroots Goldwater movement four years earlier, Reagan believed his path to the nomination lay in a brokered convention. White's strategy was ill conceived because delegates were locked into place for a candidate well before the convention convened. Furthermore, Reagan did not have the ground organization or stature at this point to pull off a national campaign in the primary states. This proved true especially against the well-organized and carefully crafted Nixon campaign organization. Initially, Reagan and most around him believed that the clear Republican front-runner in 1967 was George Romney, underestimating—at least in the beginning—Nixon's appeal to the Republican base.

The Republican establishment anxiously sought to repudiate the Goldwater wing of the party. Immediately after the 1964 election, the Republican National Committee replaced Goldwater loyalist Dean Burch with the proudly self-proclaimed technocrat Ray Bliss from Ohio as chair of the party. Bliss was a "nuts and bolts" party builder who enlisted twenty thousand Republican Party professionals and activists who were trained in seminars and workshops in campaign basics. Bliss set the stage for a Republican comeback in the 1966 midterm elections. Leading the way was Richard Nixon, who undertook hundreds of speeches on behalf of Republican candidates. He endorsed Rockefeller for reelection as New York governor in hopes that Rocky would endorse him in 1968.

Nixon's reading of the political situation in 1968 was astute. He saw that Reagan had a base in the grassroots right, but he lacked organization and the experience to run a national presidential campaign. Rockefeller and Romney won their gubernational reelection bids, but Nixon understood correctly that Rockefeller had been damaged by his remarriage and Romney was an empty shirt. Rockefeller spent over $5 million to defeat a weak Democratic challenger.[24] Nixon adroitly played to the conservative anger engendered by Romney's and Rockefeller's refusal to back Goldwater. After Goldwater's nomination, Romney wrote Goldwater, "Dogmatic ideological parties tend to splinter the political and social fabric of a nation, lead to government crises and deadlocks, and stymie the compromises so often necessary to preserve freedom and achieve progress."[25] Romney's presidential campaign collapsed when he declared in a television interview in Detroit that he had been "brainwashed" about Vietnam by Lyndon Johnson's State Department.

Shortly after the midterms in 1966, Nixon carefully assembled a national campaign staff and began projecting a new, friendlier image to the voters—the New Nixon—relaxed, smiling, and nonacerbic. The campaign staff offered balance between conservatives such as Patrick Buchanan, a Goldwater supporter and former St. Louis newspaper columnist; William Safire, a centrist; and Raymond Price, a liberal Republican. Roger Ailes, the producer of the popular syndicated *Mike Douglas Show*, was brought on to provide media skills. Many liberals on the New Nixon team did not like their candidate's courting of conservatives. In July 1967, columnist Robert Novak reported that liberal insiders within the Nixon camp were writing off doctrinaire conservatives and reaching out to Rockefeller liberals. As one insider told Novak, "Let Ronnie have the kooks."[26]

After declaring that he was not going to seek the GOP presidential nomination in 1968, Rockefeller began to have second thoughts when Johnson declared in a televised address in March 1967 that he would not seek reelection. Rockefeller began telling party leaders that he was the best candidate to challenge the Democrats in a general campaign. The assassination of civil rights activist Martin Luther King Jr. gave Rockefeller the opportunity to declare that he was the most experienced candidate to deal with the nation's problems. For his part, Nixon responded to the racial riots following King's assassination, calling for stronger anticrime policies.

Rockefeller disliked Nixon personally, politically, and ideologically, although ideology played less of a role than he claimed publicly. Rockefeller saw Nixon as a rival who had not won an election on his own since 1950 and a man who had lost the last two elections he had entered. Rockefeller had won election twice as governor in the most populous state in the Union. Rockefeller's strategy to knock Nixon out of the race in 1968 rested on a heavy media campaign without a strong ground game. He bombarded television with spot ads on a hundred stations in thirty cities and full-page ads in fifty-four newspapers in forty cities. He promoted himself as the president who could address urban problems through new spending programs, while staying away from Vietnam. After announcing he was running for president on April 30, shortly before the Nebraska primary, Rockefeller traveled to forty-five states and spoke to numerous Republican leaders and groups. He spent $8 million on his campaign, donated by his family and his own fortune. He hoped to upset Nixon in the Nebraska primary but to little avail. He received less than 5 percent of the vote. When Mark Hatfield, a moderate Republican senator from Oregon, endorsed Nixon, Rockefeller's campaign collapsed in that state. Rockefeller tried to stay the course, hoping beyond hope that somehow he might get the nomination through a brokered convention by lining up with Reagan supporters.

Reagan's bid for the nomination did not fare any better. His supporters put him on the ballot for the Nebraska and Oregon primaries. They ran ads for Reagan—a candidate who claimed he was not running for the nomination. He won a surprising 20 percent of the vote in Nebraska, considered by most Nixon country, but this proved a shallow victory. A short time later, Nixon swept the Wisconsin primary with 79.7 percent of the vote, in contrast to Reagan's 11 percent. In Oregon, Reagan supporters made their biggest effort, spending $200,000 on television. Nixon responded by campaigning heavily in the state. He won the primary with 65 percent of the vote, leaving Reagan a disappointed second again with only 20 percent of the vote. The following week Nixon won the California primary. The problem Reagan faced in 1968 was that he was still an unknown political leader, and neither the party nor the nation was ready for an avowed conservative. Furthermore, even many conservatives were not behind a Reagan run. William Buckley's *National Review* came out early for Nixon and supported him over Reagan throughout the campaign. Other conservatives joined the Nixon bandwagon, including Phyllis Schlafly, whose best-selling 1964 book, *A Choice Not an Echo,* had played an important role in exciting Goldwater supporters. She endorsed Nixon over Reagan. Many on the right were disgusted with Johnson's Great Society, the Vietnam War, and campus and urban riots, but this did not translate into support for Reagan. Behind the scenes, Nixon people subtly badmouthed Reagan to the press in 1966, suggesting he needed to distance himself from "extremists" and Birchers. Nixon described to insiders both Goldwater and Reagan as "bomb throwers" when it came to foreign policy toward the Soviet Union.[27]

In 1966, Goldwater, the "bomb thrower," was fully in the Nixon camp. Goldwater began meeting with Nixon in late 1966 about the upcoming presidential election. Goldwater warned Nixon that Reagan might prove a real threat in 1968 if he were to enter the primaries. Goldwater told Nixon that if Reagan won election to the governor's mansion in California that "the great bulk of conservatives, if you want to call them the Goldwater people, will cry out" for Reagan to run for president.[28] Two years later, Goldwater was urging Nixon to meet with Reagan to offer him the vice-presidential slot on the ticket, even though Reagan had told Goldwater he was not interested in the position. As the convention approached, Goldwater asked Reagan to release his candidates to Nixon in order to put a final lid on Rockefeller.[29] He insisted that Reagan drop the pretense of being California's favorite-son candidate and endorse Nixon.[30] Reagan did not take kindly to Goldwater's advice and felt that Goldwater was trying to push him around.

Having failed to get traction in the primaries, Reagan and Rockefeller were left hoping for a deadlocked convention, with vague hopes that delegates might suddenly shift from Nixon to either Reagan or Rockefeller. Rockefeller realized that neither the Reagan camp nor his camp had enough strength to win the nomination outright for its candidate. As a consequence, Rockefeller agents approached the Reagan staff about forming a Rockefeller-Reagan ticket to stop Nixon. This strategy was an act of desperation. Reagan rebuffed Rockefeller's ploy. He knew a formal alliance with Rockefeller would permanently tarnish his image with his base. Reagan allowed the California state delegation to place his name in nomination as a "favorite son." He feigned surprise at the nomination, which few insiders accepted at face value. As New Mexican governor David Cargo told the press, "It's like a woman who's eight and a half months pregnant announcing she's going to have a baby."[31]

Although a Reagan threat for the nomination was about as serious as the Prohibition Party winning the White House in 1968, Southern delegates, sensing an opportunity to bargain with the Nixon camp, began suggesting that they were on the verge of deserting Nixon for Reagan. It was a clever strategy to win concessions from Nixon. Clarke Reed of Mississippi bluntly said, "The harder Nixon had to fight, the more the South stood to gain. So we wanted a nice open convention."[32] Nixon, who had until then believed he had the Southern delegates locked up, reacted immediately. He called a meeting with influential Southern senator Strom Thurmond and other Southern delegates to promise them he would place a Southerner on the Supreme Court and he would accept their suggestions for a running mate.

Behind the scenes, Goldwater continued to push Reagan for the vice-presidential slot. Within the Nixon staff, Patrick Buchanan also pressed for Reagan to be on the ticket, but he was a minority voice in the camp. Nixon played along, but privately he could not abide Reagan for having played a cat-and-mouse game in seeking the nomination in the first place. Furthermore, many conservative movement leaders did not support Reagan on the ticket either. In fact, when William F. Buckley was consulted by the Nixon camp for vice-presidential suggestions, he recommended Democrat John Gardner, Johnson's former secretary of health, education, and welfare—a choice that astounded even the politically malleable Richard Nixon.[33] For all his commitment to further conservative ideology, Buckley too wanted a winning ticket.

Any hopes that somehow Nixon could be defeated for the nomination ended when he won easily on the first ballot. Many commentators thought this marked the end of Reagan's shot at the presidency. Television commentator Walter Cronkite summed up the feelings of the pundits when he told viewers watching the convention that Reagan's chances for the presidency were pretty much over given Reagan's age (fifty-seven years old). Reagan graciously accepted Nixon's victory. Rockefeller was less temperate. When asked by the press why he lost, the ill-tempered Rockefeller, who never took losing well, replied, "You ever been to a Republican convention?"[34]

Nixon selected Maryland governor Spiro Agnew as his running mate. Agnew was Nixon's kind of guy. His career had been one of opportunism without much principle. He had worked his way up the Maryland political chain as a Rockefeller Republican, finally winning the governorship in 1966. After Rockefeller's off-and-on dance as to whether he was running, Agnew endorsed Nixon. Agnew gained national press when he openly berated local civil rights leaders for not denouncing a Baltimore race riot. Nixon saw Agnew as a tough Greek who stood for law and order, and he came from a border state. The Nixon campaign had written off some of the Southern states to George Wallace's independent run for the presidency, which made border states critical to a Republican victory. In the end, Agnew proved to be a bit of a weight during the campaign because he was such a poor speaker; and once in the White House, the Nixon administration saw him as a liability. Nonetheless, in 1968, the two seemed made for one another.

The Nixon-Agnew campaign faced a country that was mostly Democratic, but after the initial shock of the violence surrounding the Democratic National Convention in Chicago, Nixon jumped up in the polls. After he won the nomination, Hubert Humphrey invited Nelson Rockefeller to be his running mate, but Rockefeller refused. Democrats finally unified behind Humphrey in late September when he broke with the administration over the Vietnam War. By the time of the election, Humphrey had closed a fifteen-point gap in the polls. At the same time, columnist Drew Pearson recorded in his diaries that Johnson was secretly supporting Nixon. Of course, Johnson did not support Nixon, and he took pride in putting Texas in the Humphrey column on Election Day. Yet it says much about the chaos of 1968 that such rumors circulated in the first place, revealing just how convoluted ideology and party loyalty had become.

Until Humphrey's jump in the polls, Nixon had played it safe by running a platitudinous campaign—reminiscent of Thomas Dewey's campaign in 1948. With Humphrey on the upswing, the Nixon campaign took the gloves off and began hammering Humphrey on the "law and order" issue. The Humphrey campaign found itself on the defensive. At the same time, the Nixon campaign could not swing too far to the right without looking like Republicans were pandering to segregationist Independent candidate George Wallace. To counter Wallace, Nixon mobilized his conservative and Southern backers to follow a strategy of not directly attacking Wallace but telling voters a vote for Wallace was a wasted vote.[35]

Nixon won election in an exceedingly close vote. He won a few states in every region, although in the South he received fifty-eight electoral votes to Wallace's forty-five. Nixon was strongest in the Midwest. He won Illinois and Ohio, along with his home state of California. Overall he won 43.56 percent to Humphrey's 42.96 percent, the lowest percentage spread since Wilson was elected to the presidency in 1912, when the Republican Party split. A shift of 112,000 votes from Nixon to Humphrey in California would have left Nixon nine votes short of an electoral victory and thrown the election into the House. He stepped into the White House with the Democrats controlling Congress. Nixon was the first presidential candidate since Zachary Taylor in 1848 who did not control at least one house of Congress at the start of his first term.

A Turn of Fortune: 1976

Reagan left the governor's office in 1975, living up to his term-limit pledge. In all likelihood, he would have won a third term. His standing in the polls remained strong. He had tested the presidential waters in 1968, but as a successful governor in the second most-populous state in the nation, he now had the credentials to claim he was presidential material. His syndicated newspaper column kept him in the public's eye while he began to educate himself on foreign policy and national domestic politics. He kept up a heavy correspondence with Republican leaders and activists throughout the country.

The political situation changed dramatically when Nixon was forced to resign from the presidency in 1974 because of the Watergate scandal. Any chance that Nixon might have escaped impeachment became nil when Vice President Agnew was forced to resign over charges of corruption when he was governor of Maryland. Goldwater urged Nixon to appoint Reagan as his new vice president, but Nixon could not forgive Reagan for his challenge, albeit as weak as it was, in 1968. It is doubtful that a Democratic Congress would have confirmed Reagan. Nixon wanted John Connally, the former Democratic governor of Texas and the secretary of the treasury, to replace Agnew, but he was convinced by staff that congressional Republicans would not confirm him. Nixon selected Gerald Ford to replace Agnew as vice president. Nonetheless, Reagan stuck with Nixon to the bitter end. Only when he learned that Nixon was preparing his resignation speech did Reagan break with him.

Reagan's loyalty to the standing Republican president and to party unity did not continue into the Ford presidency. Reagan had been planning a presidential run as early as 1974, but Nixon's resignation forced Reagan and his team to reconsider. Ford made the decision easier by the way he treated Reagan. Ford's appointment of Nelson Rockefeller as his vice president upset Reagan and most conservatives in the party. Further insult came when it became public that Reagan had not even been placed on the list for consideration for the vice presidency. Word began to leak out that Ford and his staff did not take Reagan seriously. They saw him as a person who offered simplistic solutions to complex problems. Ford's handling of the Nixon pardon, his pursuit of détente and arms control, and Kissinger's State Department furthered Reagan's conviction that Ford was not the leader the nation needed. He believed the Ford administration had allowed moderates and liberals to seize control of the Republican Party. Eastern-wing liberals such as Jacob

Javits of New York, Clifford Case of New Jersey, and Charles Mathias of Maryland made it impossible for voters to distinguish major differences between the two parties.[36] Still, Reagan held his fire by not declaring his candidacy. By 1975, he was making an estimated $800,000 through his syndicated newspaper column and speaking engagements, and he was not anxious to give up his income, which would have occurred with an official announcement.

Gerald Ford entered the White House intent on healing the nation and uniting a divided party. Although conservatives had stuck with Nixon to the bitter end, many in the party seethed with a sense of betrayal by Nixon, who had expanded the welfare and regulatory state, opened relations with mainland China, and pursued arms control with the Soviet Union through the Strategic Arms Limitation Treaty (SALT I). Ford's commitment to Nixon's foreign policy by keeping Henry Kissinger on as secretary of state and his pursuit of a second SALT agreement led to rebellion on the right. Many conservatives thought American involvement in Vietnam had been a mistake, but once involved, America should have won. When North Vietnam captured Saigon in April 1975, many on the GOP right concluded that Nixon and Kissinger had sold America's South Vietnamese allies down the river. This was followed by a Communist takeover of Cambodia by the fanatical Khmer Rouge under Pol Pot. In other parts of the world, the Soviet Union pursued an adventurist foreign policy that took advantage of America's weakness at home. Soviet involvement in leftist liberation movements in Asia, Africa, and Central America were readily apparent.

In addition, foreign policy hawks on the right, as well as some Democrats such as defense expert Paul Nitze and Senator Henry "Scoop" Jackson, a Washington State Democrat, believed that SALT I gave away too much to the Soviet Union, which had undertaken a massive arms buildup. In this charged climate, Ford met with Soviet leader Leonid Brezhnev in Vladivostok in the fall of 1974 to lay the groundwork for a new arms reduction treaty, SALT II. Hawks blasted the interim SALT II agreement once it was announced. Further outrage came when the Ford administration announced an agreement reached in Helsinki in 1975 that guaranteed de facto recognition of Soviet control of Eastern Europe. The Ford-Kissinger policy of agreeing to trade concessions to the Soviet Union further inflamed conservatives.

Reagan seized on the foreign policy issue by warning of the Soviet arms buildup, which he attributed to Kissinger. Reagan found a useful instrument for attacking Ford on the administration's ongoing negotiations with the Panamanian government headed by a military dictator to turn over the canal zone to Panama. Crowds went wild when they heard Reagan say, "We built it, we paid for it, and it's ours, and we should tell Torrijos and company we are going to keep it." At the core of Reagan's philosophy lay two tenets: a strong national defense against the Soviet threat; and decreased taxes, which he believed would reduce the size of government and stimulate the economy. These were two inviolate principles that could not be compromised. Reagan declared he was running for the Republican nomination on November 19, 1975, at the National Press Club in Washington, D.C. He stated, "A decade ago we had military superiority. Today we are in danger of being surpassed by a nation that has never made an effort to hide its hostility to everything we stand for. Through détente we have sought peace with our adversaries. We should continue to do so but must make it plain that we expect a stronger indication that they also seek a lasting peace with us."[37] While greeted with enthusiasm by many Republican conservatives, many others within the Republican establishment believed Reagan divisive.[38]

Goldwater was one of these people. Goldwater's refusal to back Reagan caused a personal rupture between the two men. As a standing Republican senator, Goldwater was naturally inclined to support the incumbent president from his own party. Goldwater and Ford had known one another in Washington for decades. Goldwater portrayed Ford as a conservative who could get things done. Furthermore, he simply could not understand why many conservatives had turned to Reagan as their leader, and he had become suspicious of him. Goldwater, with typical bluntness, asked conservative Hollywood actor Efrem Zimbalist Jr., a Reagan supporter, why conservatives had turned their backs on their one-time Arizona hero. Goldwater wrote, "I can appreciate the fact that there are strong feelings within the party, and though I have been the target of the more emotional assaults, I can understand it. What is getting tougher to understand by the minute, however, is how we can finally come so close to achieving what we set out to achieve three elections ago and risk it all now over a hair-splitting debate within the party about which of two genuine and bona fide conservatives is more conservative."[39]

Zimbalist's reply was equally blunt: as a delegate to the Republican National Convention in 1964, he wrote that he supported Goldwater, but he was perplexed by Goldwater's inability to discern differences between Reagan and Ford "in degree of quality, idealism, or intention; who can with equanimity accept, on the one hand, a Kissinger foreign policy and, on the other, the largest federal budget in our nation's history." He added, just so his point would not be missed, "I am, to be blunt, astounded that as a Republican, you can see no difference, either with respect to philosophy or the ability to implement it, between the two years of this appointed administration and the eight years of the Reagan mandate in California."[40]

Goldwater had become increasingly irate about Reagan's attacks on the Ford administration's negotiations over the Panama Canal. In a private memo to himself on May 4, 1976, Goldwater wrote that he "fully supported" Ford's negotiating position of turning the canal completely over to Panama. Reagan's positon, he thought, could lead this country into open military conflict and reflected Reagan's "lack of understanding of the facts" and "a surprisingly dangerous state of mind." In his press conference announcing his endorsement of Ford, he suggested that Reagan's foreign policy rhetoric was dangerous. Goldwater's announcement left Reagan shocked and hurt that he had not been informed beforehand about the press conference. When Reagan complained privately to him, Goldwater claimed he had tried to phone Reagan before the conference but had been unable to reach him. In another letter to Nancy Reagan, Goldwater said he had become "increasingly apprehensive about Ron's attacks on the President relative to the Panama Canal. My concern is that Ron was putting himself in a position of going to war over Panama. I tried to call you. I decided to call a press conference. The president did not know anything about it. I have put the interests of my country ahead of that because, in my opinion, he [Reagan] was treading on very dangerous water, although I will admit very popular water, and I wanted to remove the whole thing from this campaign."[41]

Reagan was not buying Goldwater's excuse. He told Goldwater that no one in his office had any record of an attempted phone call ever being received. He added for good measure, "I have never suggested going to war over Panama. . . . I should say we should not undertake negotiations if it is submitting to blackmail and is predicated upon our giving up our sovereignty right to the Canal Zone."[42]

The battle for the 1976 nomination showed a party in civil war. The Ford campaign initially dismissed the Reagan challenge. Ford considered Reagan "too slick" and "too much of a politician" without strong grassroots support.[43] Even many hard-core conservatives thought Reagan's chances to win the nomination were slim and urged him to run on a third-party ticket. Reagan's candidacy was described by the *New York Times* as a "frivolous fantasy" and by the liberal *New Republic* as a campaign headed by an "essentially mindless" and "unconvincing candy man."[44] Reagan lost the New Hampshire primary to Ford but then regained momentum when he attacked Ford on current negotiations over the Panama Canal. After the United States' defeat in Vietnam, the threatened "turnover" of the canal became a symbolic issue about American power. Reagan lost primaries to Ford in Illinois, Massachusetts, Vermont, and Florida, but his attacks concerning the canal paid off when he won the North Carolina primary. He was aided by Senator Jesse Helms's well-oiled political machine in that state. After winning in North Carolina, 52 percent to 46 percent, Reagan found himself trading punches with Ford in other primary states. Ford denounced Reagan as an extremist. By the time of the convention, Ford remained about a hundred delegates short of winning on the first ballot. Reagan was an estimated two hundred votes short. In hopes of splitting the Ford delegate vote, Reagan announced that if nominated, he would select liberal senator Richard Schweiker, a Republican from Pennsylvania, as his running mate. Reagan's announcement showed his political pragmatism, which upset some pundits as smacking of opportunism and failed ultimately to win over any Ford delegates. Ford won the nomination by a narrow margin. Eager to unite the party, Ford surprised the convention by inviting Reagan, who was sitting in a convention box with Nancy, to join him onstage.

Once onstage, Reagan gave one of the greatest speeches of his career. He began by warning of nuclear war and reaffirming his own commitment to preserve the free world before concluding, "We must go forth from here, united, determined that what a great general said a few years ago is true: 'There's no substitute for victory, Mr. President.'"[45] On hearing the speech, many delegates concluded they had nominated the wrong man. When Ford lost the election to the one-term governor of Georgia, Jimmy Carter, Republicans looked to Reagan as the next nominee.

It is doubtful that Reagan could have won the 1976 general election, even if he had secured the nomination. Carter eked out a narrow victory against an incumbent president by picking up Southern and border states, as well as the evangelical vote. Reagan's loss in 1976 would have been a setback for the conservative wing of the Republican Party and would have probably damaged his chances for winning the 1980 nomination. It took four years of a stagnant economy and the Iranian hostage crisis for voters to turn to Reagan in 1980.

Only after the election, which was narrowly won by Democrat Jimmy Carter, and when Reagan had become the clear favorite of the party for the 1980 election did Goldwater try to make amends. Under political pressure from his own state constituents and facing an uphill battle of his own for reelection to his Senate seat, Goldwater reversed himself on the Panama

Canal. He wrote Reagan, "The more I prowl around these treaties the more I smell the Trilateral Commission [a David Rockefeller–inspired organization]. I think we are going to see more and more efforts being made around the world to pay back the very stupid and foolish loans that some of the big banks of our country have made." Reagan responded by saying he was glad they were back on the same team.[46] Goldwater ended up voting against the Panama Canal treaties to return jurisdiction of the canal zone back to Panama. Still, relations between the two men were never quite the same. After the Reagan landslide in 1980, in which Goldwater barely won his last bid for the U.S. Senate, the snarky Goldwater suggested to the press that Reagan's coattails had not done too much to help him. He then added, rather ungraciously, "He'd still be chasing cows over the horizon if it hadn't been for me."[47] Politics makes for strange bedfellows, sometimes uncomfortable ones.

Winning the Presidency

Reagan began preparing for a presidential run as soon as Jimmy Carter claimed victory. His course to the presidency was by no means clear sailing, but he had fortune (or Carter's misfortune) on his side. The 1978 midterm elections showed Republicans had momentum, although their actual gains were relatively modest: three new seats in the Senate and eleven in the House. Moderate and liberal Republican losses included Edward Brooks in Massachusetts, Clifford Case in New Jersey, and James B. Pearson in Kansas, as conservatives continued the trend of moving the party to the right.

Carter faced his own problems in the Democratic Party, as the left became increasingly disenchanted with his centrist policies. This discontent manifested itself when Senator Edward "Ted" Kennedy declared he was seeking the party's presidential nomination in 1980.[48] Although Kennedy's presidential bid failed, it damaged Carter, who entered the 1980 general election with a divided party. He faced an American electorate anxious about the economy, a perceived decline in America as a world power, and cultural changes in the nation. Nonetheless, the Carter campaign remained confident that Reagan was a weak candidate who was too old and too extreme to be elected president. Just as other rivals had underestimated Reagan, so did Carter.

Reagan fought off primary challenges from George H. W. Bush and other candidates to win the nomination. During the primary, Reagan made plenty of gaffes and often got his facts wrong, and at times seemed insecure and indecisive. Yet his message for scaling back government, increasing defense spending, and restoring America compensated for any weakness on the campaign trail. In nominating Reagan, the Republican Party confirmed its shift to the right. The death of Nelson Rockefeller, the embodiment of liberal Republicanism, in 1979 marked an end of an era. After some serious talk of nominating Ford as his running mate—a kind of copresidency—Reagan scuttled this idea when he chose George H. W. Bush. Reagan's selection of Bush, a moderate, revealed Reagan's political skills in action. If Bush was willing to sign on to Reagan's agenda, Reagan had no problem with having him as a running mate. In this choice, Reagan signaled to the Republican establishment and to voters he was a pragmatist and not an ideologue.

The Reagan campaign understood that if the election turned into a replay of 1976, Carter would win. This meant that Reagan had to win Southern states that had gone Democratic in 1976 and persuade blue-collar voters that he was not a radical. When Senator Paul Laxalt of Nevada nominated Reagan at the convention, he stressed Reagan's record as governor, where he increased benefits for the truly needy, increased funding for education, protected the environment, and promoted welfare reform. At the same time, Reagan sought to win the evangelical Christian vote that had gone for Carter in 1976. This meant pushing social issues, his support of religious liberty, his antiabortion stance, and his belief in the traditional family. Reagan performed well in debates, and Carter was damaged by a crisis in Iran when radical Islamist revolutionaries took American embassy workers hostage. Few, however, predicted that Reagan would win in such a landslide, the largest in American history. He won 489 electoral votes to Carter's 49, taking forty-four states. He won the South by 5 percentage points, the Midwest by as much as 10 points in some states, and the West by nearly 20 points. Blue-collar workers swung heavily to Reagan.

Reagan won election as an avowed conservative. His campaign rhetoric expressed his conservative principles and was often heated, at times alarming the left. In office, he stuck to his core principles of lower taxes, reducing social spending, and strengthening national defense. His cabinet choices were mostly conservatives who aligned with his principles. As president, he did not succeed in every initiative. His campaign promise to overturn *Roe v. Wade* failed, as did his pledge to disband the Department of Education. Although Reagan cut staffing of regulatory agencies in the Consumer Protection Safety Commission, the Occupational Safety and Health Administration, and the Environmental Protection Agency, the regulatory state remained intact. In 1982, a national recession forced him to agree to an increase in the corporate tax rate, but this had been preceded the previous year by the largest tax cut in American history. In implementing Social Security reform, Reagan agreed to increased payroll taxes and extending age requirements for receiving benefits.

The perceived failures to fulfill his campaign promises have led to a sizable literature that the Reagan Revolution failed. Even his foreign policy, where Reagan had more leeway, brought heavy criticism from later scholars. The collapse of the Soviet Union, Reagan's liberal critics argue, would have occurred without Reagan because of its inherent weakness. Conservative defenders, politicians, and journalists tend to emphasize Reagan's ideological purity. Both critics and defenders overlook Reagan's principled pragmatism. Reagan's pragmatism was evident in his choice of George H. W. Bush as his vice president and James Baker, a Bush supporter, as his first chief of staff. Reagan summed up his entire approach to legislating when he wrote one conservative supporter, "I'm in charge and my people are helping carry out policies I set. Now we don't get everything we want and yes we have to compromise to get 75 or 80 percent of our program. We try to see that the 75 or 80 percent is more than worth the compromise we have to accept."[49]

His greatest strength as a principled and pragmatic leader, however, can be found in his willingness to learn about government and governing. As a candidate for the governor's office in 1966, he ran on stock Republican rhetoric to scale back government and reduce taxes. Once in the governor's office, adjusting to political and fiscal realities, his first major act was to accept the largest tax hike in California's history at the time. His next major piece of legislation was the signing of a liberal abortion reform act. He succeeded, however, in undertaking significant welfare reforms by working with Democrats. He left the governor's office popular with the voters. As president, his administration enacted tax cuts, only to be forced, again by fiscal and political realities, to hike corporate taxes and Social Security taxes. In his second term, however, he worked with Democrats to succeed in simplifying the tax system. His greatest success came in reaching accommodation with the Soviet Union by negotiating a verifiable arms control treaty. He set the stage for ending the Cold War, which occurred shortly after he left office. He tempered ideological principle, while maintaining core conservative values about the nature of government and the value of a free market in economic development, and that freedom is always one generation removed from extinction. He distrusted centralized government without calling for its complete dismantlement. He articulated optimism without seeking perfection in government or mankind. He expressed a deep faith in the American Dream, and he understood that dreams can become reality when acted upon.

6 | Uneasy Allies
Goldwater and Reagan Compared

Barry Goldwater and Ronald Reagan led the conservative ascendancy within the Republican Party. Sixteen years separated Goldwater's unsuccessful presidential run in 1964 and Reagan's victory in 1980. Goldwater's failed bid set the stage for Ronald Reagan's success. Reagan's televised speech for Goldwater in 1964 launched Reagan's political career, first as the two-term governor of California (1966–1974) and later as the two-term president of the United States (1980–1988). The two men generally agreed ideologically about small government, free enterprise, and strong national defense, but by the late 1970s, they proved to be uneasy political allies. They differed fundamentally on social issues and presented to the electorate distinct personalities and temperaments.

Goldwater took well-deserved pride in his image as a stubborn, principled conservative. But his career points to more political flexibility than his public image as a doctrinaire ideologue suggested. Goldwater's primary loyalty was to the Republican Party. He supported candidates who were not necessarily the most conservative but those conservatives who were the most electable. This meant supporting Nixon in 1968 and Ford in 1976, both of whom were challenged by Ronald Reagan. Reagan, too, stood as a loyal Republican, but he challenged the Republican establishment on conservative principles. Both Goldwater and Reagan were principled, charismatic, and adept politicians. If Goldwater proved more flexible by supporting candidates who differed with him ideologically, then Reagan revealed greater political skill and leadership qualities in furthering his commitment to ideological principles. As governor of California, he signed bills raising taxes and liberalizing abortion. As the Republican presidential nominee in 1980, he selected moderate rival George H. W. Bush as his running mate and Bush's campaign manager, James Baker, as his presidential chief of staff. Reagan sought party unity, while maintaining core conservative values. He did not always achieve his full objectives, but he showed a capacity for legislative compromise for meaningful incremental gain. He was a principled pragmatist in politics and brought to American conservatism a temperament that reassured voters that a conservative could be trusted in an elected executive office. In this way, he projected affability and an ability to communicate a conservative message to the larger electorate unlike previous GOP conservatives Robert Taft, William Knowland, and Barry Goldwater.

Neither Goldwater nor Reagan represented themselves as intellectuals but as politicians informed about conservative values of small government, individual rights, and economic freedom. Their private journals and letters reveal that both were well considered and reflective in their politics. Goldwater maintained a journal through memos he wrote to himself about critical issues and meetings he thought had historical importance. He kept the journal locked in a safe. His writings were not for public consumption but rather served as reminders to himself and as a legacy for posterity. Reagan's letters, often written confidentially, reveal intelligence and eloquence. Handwritten and fluid, these letters reveal a man who had thought deeply about his political values.

Born only two years apart, Goldwater and Reagan reflected the transformation of American conservatism from a small movement of intellectuals and grassroots anti-Communists in the immediate aftermath of World War II into a dominant force within the Republican Party. Goldwater's nomination to head the Republican presidential ticket in 1964 marked the first step in the conservative ascendancy within the GOP. Whatever ideological tensions existed within the conservative movement between traditionalists and libertarians, they were not evident in Goldwater's campaign. Conservatives of all stripes united around Goldwater in their opposition to liberalism. When Reagan made his first serious bid for the Republican presidential nomination in 1976 and later in 1980, the GOP right had expanded to include a coalition of religious voters, fiscal and pro-business conservatives, discontented intellectuals concerned with national defense issues, angry white Southerners, and disgruntled blue-collar workers. Reagan Republicanism was an uneasy alliance of disparate ideological and voter blocs, unified in their opposition to liberalism and their support of Reagan. Once Reagan stepped out of the White House at the end of his second term, this carefully woven tapestry of big-tent Republicans began to fray. By the late 1980s, Goldwater's politics reflected the tensions within the party when he denounced the Christian right and its focus on social issues as leading the GOP off a cliff. Reagan had unified conservatives. Once he was out of office, party factions began publicly fighting over social issues, military interventions, immigration, and party leadership.

Goldwater and Reagan represented Western conservatism. They projected in their politics and in their public images the Western American—cowboy hats, boots, and horseback riding. Each man had been elected to office for the first time in heavily Democratic states. Their Western experiences were quite different, however. Goldwater was a true-bred Westerner, Reagan a transplant from the Midwest. Born in territorial Arizona, Goldwater had deep roots in the young state's history and formation. He loved the beauty of the desert West and its native people. Like many Westerners, he was not especially religious and did not find easy accommodation with religious voters concerned with social issues such as abortion and, later, gay rights. Reagan, raised in Illinois and influenced by his religious mother, brought to his career in Hollywood and California politics values that allowed for an easier acceptance of social conservatism and individualistic libertarianism.

Goldwater, the man and the politician, prided himself on his individualism. He was direct in his speech, given to hair-trigger responses, quick to anger, and often stubborn in his views when he considered an issue a matter of principle. His career was primarily spent in Washington, D.C. His wife, Peggy, who detested politics and Washington social life, insisted that her four children be raised in Arizona. For Barry, Washington became his life. His decision to run for office a final time in 1980 was framed as a choice between an active life in the Senate or a gentle, despondent fading away in retirement. Breaking a pledge to Peggy not to run for another term and retire, and knowing that his long absences from Arizona had strained his relationship with his children, he decided nonetheless to seek one last term. He wrote in his 1988 memoir, *Goldwater,* five years after the death of his wife while he was serving his final term in office, that Peggy knew "in my heart of hearts I wanted to run. That I could not come home and die. Washington was too much a part of me. Arizona was my home, but the Senate had become my life."[1] His long absences from Arizona and maintenance of residences outside the state nearly cost him reelection in 1980.

U.S. senators have more opportunity for displays of eccentricity, public anger, and high moral stances, although other elected officials are not immune from such behavior. Executives, whether state governors or U.S. presidents, have to be more circumspect in projecting eccentricity or anger. Voters will tolerate idiosyncrasies in a senator in a way they often will not in a governor or a president. Goldwater did not make the mental transition from being the shoot-from-the hip, quick-to-anger senator to a presidential candidate able to reassure voters. His Western persona appealed to many angry conservatives who were tired of the smooth-talking moderates and liberals in their own party and in the Democratic Party, but at the height of the Cold War, the majority of Americans did not want a hair trigger–prone senator as their leader in the White House. Goldwater was not going to win the White House in 1964, but he did little to help his campaign. Throughout the primaries and the general election, he continued to shoot from the hip. However it might have appealed to die-hard conservatives, Goldwater's lack of discipline frustrated campaign staff and party leaders. His angry response to critics at the convention, manifested in his acceptance speech, ensured that party division festered. When confronted by Rockefeller's stubborn persistence in attacking extremists in the party, Goldwater reinforced the charge with his defense, "extremism in the defense of liberty is no vice."[2] Goldwater's lack of discipline and his inability to control his anger reflected a temperament easily contrasted with Reagan's personality.

Temperament is shaped by natural personality and environment. Goldwater's and Reagan's life experiences were vastly different. Goldwater's childhood was one of privilege; Reagan's was one of economic struggle. In a strange way, Goldwater's boyhood experience and his socioeconomic background were closer to Nelson Rockefeller's, while Reagan's childhood bore a general similarity to Richard Nixon's lower-middle-class background. Goldwater's wealth did not compare to Rockefeller's, but both men grew up in privileged circumstances. Nixon grew up in a more stable and rooted family than did Reagan, whose family moved frequently largely because of an alcoholic father. Childhood is not predestination. Goldwater's childhood personality, his impulsiveness and quick temper, carried into adulthood. His temperament differed greatly from his younger brother, Robert, who grew up in the same privileged family. Robert remained into adulthood moderate, quiet spoken, and deliberate. Similarly, Ronald Reagan differed from his older brother, John Neil, who was given to good times and complaint. Ronald remained steady, affable, and career driven.

Goldwater, growing up in the desert town of Phoenix, enjoyed the social status of a family-owned department store, which catered to the rich. He was indulged by his parents and grew up in a mansion with servants. Life was one of golf outings to the country club, family excursions to the desert and resorts, and the social life of the rich. Barry was a natural leader with his neighborhood pals and schoolmates. He was rambunctious, hyperactive, and a poor student. His humor, more sophomoric than malicious, showed at times an unconscious mean streak by catching people in embarrassing situations. It was a humor that carried into fraternity life in his first year in college before he was forced to drop out.

His father sought to instill in Barry the discipline necessary for adulthood by sending him to a military high school. Staunton Military Academy imparted in him discipline and a love of the military. This discipline was evident in Goldwater, the later pilot and young businessman. His open and direct personality won over friends in high school, college, and the Phoenix business community. Goldwater was an extremely private individual, but few, except his family, saw this side of him.

His conservatism and loyalty to the Republican Party were deeply felt. His party loyalty often trumped his conservative principles. As his sympathetic biographer, Lee Edwards, noted, "When it came to party politics, Goldwater was usually a Republican first, and a conservative second."[3] Goldwater's political career centered on achieving Republican victory at the polls. His gamble to run for the Senate in 1952 was premised on the assumption that the Republican Party in his state could become a majority party. Goldwater could be obstinate, though, when he felt that principle and friends were at stake. His refusal to vote for the censure of his colleague Joseph McCarthy was more than just Republicans sticking together or good politics. It reflected Goldwater's sense of loyalty to McCarthy, a friend and a fellow anti-Communist warrior. The title of Goldwater's best-selling book, *Conscience of a Conservative,* captured his sense of honor and principle. Goldwater, however steadfast he was in his conservatism, did not let ideological principle drive him to sectarianism within the Republican Party.

Two years after his crushing defeat in 1964, he was engaged in a serious discussion with Nixon to help him win the nomination. He quietly met with Nixon on June 8, 1966, to discuss defeating Romney and Rockefeller for the nomination.[4] Throughout 1967, he kept Nixon posted on the state of the Republican Party as he traveled throughout the country. Seeing Reagan as a potential threat to Nixon's nomination, Goldwater encouraged Nixon as early as late November 1967 to reach an accord with Ronald Reagan by offering him the vice-presidential slot. As the 1968 primaries heated up, Goldwater continued to urge Reagan to drop his status as a "favorite son" choice of the California convention delegation and endorse Nixon. Goldwater was willing to temper ideological principle in order to secure the most electable conservative. He took a similar tack in 1976 by endorsing incumbent president Gerald Ford.

Nixon played a pivotal role in both Goldwater's and Reagan's political careers. Nixon's loss in the 1960 election opened the way for Goldwater's presidential bid in 1964. Similarly, Reagan's entrance into California electoral politics would have been closed if Nixon had won his race for state governor in 1962. Reagan's gubernatorial election in 1966 placed him on the national stage, although it is extremely unlikely Reagan could have won the 1968 GOP nomination even if Nixon had not reentered politics. Republican leaders were not anxious to put up another conservative in 1968 after the bruising loss the party had suffered four years earlier. The Watergate scandal and Nixon's forced resignation threw the party into chaos, clearing Reagan's path to the White House in 1980.

In one of those twists of American politics, Goldwater became one of Nixon's greatest supporters, that is, until the Watergate scandal in 1974 could not be contained. Goldwater finally recommended to Nixon that he resign from the presidency rather than face an impeachment trial. Goldwater's desertion of Nixon came late, only after the court-ordered release of White House tapes provided incontrovertible evidence that Nixon had agreed to cover up an investigation into the break-in of Democratic Party headquarters during his 1972 reelection campaign. After Nixon's resignation, Goldwater met with liberal New York senator Jacob Javits for breakfast to discuss how conservatives and liberals in the GOP could join together to reconstruct a now "leaderless" Republican Party.[5] In 1980, Goldwater publically endorsed Javits in his reelection bid for senator, telling conservative William F. Buckley that "I would much rather have a man who calls himself a Republican in there on registration day, than someone who was a born-in-the-flesh Democrat."[6]

Goldwater readily aligned himself with the new Ford administration. He expressed great admiration for Henry Kissinger, Nixon's and Ford's key adviser on foreign policy. Whatever qualms Goldwater expressed in private meetings about Nixon-Ford foreign policy, Nixon's opening with China, or his détente with the Soviet Union, Goldwater supported the Nixon-Ford policies in public. Goldwater refused to join Reagan or the grassroots right in denouncing Kissinger. Reagan, however, targeted Kissinger in his stump speeches in 1976 and 1980 as a symbol of what was wrong with American foreign policy. Goldwater's support of Ford's foreign policy expressed itself in his backing of the administration's negotiations to turn the Panama Canal

Zone over to Panama. Fearing riots and guerrilla war if this was not done, Goldwater opposed Reagan's strong stand against the negotiations, which had become a rousing theme on the stump in his bid to deny the GOP nomination to Ford in 1976. Goldwater's announcement that he was supporting Ford for reelection shattered relations with Reagan. After the election, in 1977, when the final Panama Canal treaties came up for a vote in the Senate, Goldwater ended up voting no. What caused his change of mind—whether he had new information about the treaties or he saw that grassroots opposition was so intense—remains unclear. Whatever the case, by the time the treaties came up for a vote, Goldwater was denouncing them as part of a Rockefeller–Trilateral Commission project in favor of international banking interests.

Goldwater was not thrilled by Ford's selection of Nelson Rockefeller as his vice president, and as Ford's reelection campaign began to take shape, Goldwater actively worked behind the scenes to push Rockefeller off the ticket. He wrote to his longtime Arizona friend Representative John Rhodes, who had known Ford for many years, to dissuade the president from putting Rockefeller on the ticket. Goldwater feared, as he told Rhodes, that with Rockefeller as vice president, Ford is going "to wind up President in title only and Rockefeller will be the power in the country." He warned that Rockefeller can "lay his hands on more competent academic people than any man in this country. In fact, he has teams on almost any problem known to the country. If these faculties are to be used for his advantage, it is dangerous."[7] Always the good politician, after the convention, Goldwater wrote to Nelson Rockefeller, who had been pushed off the ticket in favor of Robert Dole, to tell him what a "real pleasure" it had been to see him in Miami and to be interviewed jointly by television announcer Walter Cronkite. Goldwater added in a genuine expression of warmness, "It is really amazing what has happened in twelve years and I don't attribute it to mellowing, which all of us go through as we grow older, it's just that we begin to see each other's side of the argument a little more clearly than we do when our hearts are filled with the passion of the moment."[8]

When it came to national defense, Goldwater did not mellow. The post-Vietnam cutbacks in defense spending frightened Goldwater, who thought that America was losing its position as a world power. He believed that if the United States lost its supremacy as a military power, its ability to provide leadership in foreign affairs became limited. The Soviet Union, in his eyes, was continuing to build its nuclear capacity and its ground forces in complete disregard of the spirit of détente and the Strategic Arms Limitation Treaty enacted under Nixon. Spiraling inflation and rising unemployment rates were accelerating America's decline. He began to worry about the future of the republic itself, writing Senate minority leader Howard Baker of Tennessee, "There always seems to come a time, either sooner or later, when the very trouble we are into now, end the dreams of the men [who] created [the] idea of a Republican democracy."[9]

By 1978, Goldwater had become a supporter of Reagan, but after Goldwater's support of Ford for reelection, relations between Goldwater and Reagan were never again close. Even when Reagan won the White House in 1980 in a landslide, Goldwater continued to believe that Reagan had just come along at the right time. He wrote George H. W. Bush shortly before the Republican convention not to feel badly about losing the nomination to Reagan: "Ronald Reagan has been running for this job for fifteen years, and without being at all facetious or intending to, I think if I ran for Pope for fifteen solid years, I would have a pretty good chance of getting it."[10] Goldwater continued to dismiss Reagan's skills as a politician. He wrote in his personal memoirs in 1988, "He [Reagan] came along at the right time and in just the right circumstances to a real surge in conservative thought and action."[11] There was truth in Goldwater's observation about the importance of timing in politics, but he should have acknowledged Reagan's political skills.

There was a personal side to Goldwater's tension with Ronald Reagan. Grassroots conservatives had replaced Goldwater with Ronald Reagan as the leader of the conservative movement. Conservatism had shifted in significant ways by the late 1970s to become more religious, oriented on social values, and hostile to established Republican leadership. Conservatism had become antiestablishment, and Goldwater was part of that establishment, increasingly seen as an eccentric out of touch with his times.

Goldwater lamented the role that social conservatives were playing in the Reagan coalition. In his final election race in 1980, Goldwater had swallowed hard to gain pro-life support in the state by pledging he was "pro-life." Once out of office, however, Goldwater felt unrestrained in criticizing the religious right. Never much given to organized religion in the first place, Goldwater declared, "I am concerned about clergy engaged in a heavy-handed continuing attempt to use political means to obtain moral ends. . . . It is one of the most dangerous trends in this country." He pointed to how religious influence in politics had led to divisions in Northern Ireland and the carnage in the name of religious righteousness in the radical Muslim takeover in Iran.

He expressed similar hostility to social conservatives such as New Right leaders Richard Viguerie, Paul Weyrich, and Morton Blackwell, who he described as failing to appreciate that "politics is the ordinary stuff of daily living, while the spiritual life represents eternal values and goals."[12]

In his retirement from the Senate, Goldwater actively campaigned for pro–gay rights legislation and for the open inclusion of homosexuals in the military. His opposition to social conservatives within the Republican Party led to his endorsement of Democrat Karan English over Republican Doug Wead in 1992 for the Sixth Congressional District in Arizona. Goldwater told the press that he always supported the person he considered the "best candidate." The fact was that Goldwater opposed Wead because he was a social conservative. In the 1992 election, Goldwater blasted the pro-life Arizona state initiative Proposition 110, which would have banned abortion except to save a mother's life and in reported cases of rape and incest. Following the election, Goldwater increased his activity in pro–gay rights organizations by signing on as honorary cochairman of Americans against Discrimination in its drive to pass a federal law preventing job discrimination against homosexuals. He spoke in favor of gays in the military. In a lengthy interview with the *Washington Post*, he compared those trying to exclude homosexuals from the military to those who had fought against the integration of African Americans in the military. His position on openly homosexual individuals in the military broke with Republican Senate candidate Jon Kyl, and Goldwater warned that Kyl's position might cost him the election.[13] He told the press that Jerry Falwell, a major spokesman of the religious right, should be given a "swift kick in the ass" for meddling in politics.[14]

Many saw Goldwater's "left turn" as the influence of his second wife, Susan Wechsler, his former nurse, whom he married in 1992. While his new wife encouraged Goldwater's activism, his libertarian and anti–social conservative views had become evident even before his marriage. His openly gay grandson encouraged Goldwater's stance on gay rights, but Goldwater remained as he always had been—an individualist from the West. Out of elective office, he was not restrained by party loyalty. Ideology triumphed in the end without the worry of getting elected or serving as a leader in the Senate. Goldwater's overt libertarianism in retirement expressed a fissure in the Reagan coalition between proeconomic, small-government conservatives and social conservatives. The antebellum Whig Party contained similar divisions. The party held together until the death of Henry Clay and until the slavery issue could no longer be avoided. Just as the Mexican-American War sowed the seeds of the demise of the Whig Party, so did military interventions in the twenty-first century rupture the uneasy alliance within the Republican Party.

Conservatism for Goldwater was instinctual, a reflection of his Western individualism and his experience as a businessman. Reagan's conversion to conservatism came gradually and intellectually. He read voraciously in conservative history and current conservative publications. He came to politics an ideologue and an activist. In the 1930s, his politics were those of a New Deal liberal, much like his father who admired Franklin Roosevelt and his rhetoric of defending the common man. In Hollywood, Reagan became an active liberal Democrat. Like many Hollywood liberals, he joined popular front organizations that brought together Democratic Party liberals and members of the Communist Party. Although never a fellow traveler of the Communist Party, even as late as 1946, Reagan warned of the fascist threat in America and served on the Hollywood board of the American Veterans Committee, a popular front group organized to counter the American Legion. His faith in the liberal order expressed itself in his support of Harry Truman in 1948.

Reagan often attributed his shift to conservatism the result of the Democratic Party having left him, not him leaving the Democratic Party. This made for a good sound bite meant to appeal to Democrats upset with their party's perceived turn to the left. The Democratic Party's shift came actually in the late 1960s, much later than Reagan's desertion of the party. His fight against the Communist faction within the Screen Actors Guild made Reagan into an anti-Communist, but in the early Cold War years, many Democratic liberals were staunchly anti-Communist. In itself, anti-Communism was not an inevitable path to conservatism. Reagan's conservatism was rooted in his own childhood experiences; traditional values; marriage to his second wife, Nancy Davis; and opposition to high income taxes, which he had to pay at a time when his Hollywood movie career was in decline. His conservatism reflected life experiences reinforced by his wife, his friends, and a deep reading of conservative thought. Reagan's articulation of conservative principles appealed to movement conservatives and voters disenchanted with liberalism, but more important to Reagan's success in politics was his capacity to translate ideology into governance.

Reagan's liberal politics in the earlier period derived from growing up during the Depression. Both Nixon and Reagan grew up in towns without apparent wide socioeconomic disparities. As Reagan said of his hometown, Dixon, Illinois, everyone was pretty poor, but they did not know it.[15] Both Nixon's and Reagan's fathers were boisterous, blunt in their language, and often embarrassing to their children. Both men despised the rich and big business. Reagan's father remained a Democrat, while Nixon's father shifted party loyalties, but both men shared populist sentiments and class resentments. Their mothers, whose lives were consumed with their families and church activities, exercised the greatest influence on their sons. Both mothers were fundamentalists of a sort, whose religion focused on the Bible. Hannah Nixon, a Quaker, and Nelle Reagan, a member of the Christian Church, focused their lives on serving their communities. People in their communities spoke highly of each. Many described Hannah as a saint. Quakers and the Christian Church both believed in universal redemption. The Society of Friends and the Christian Church shared deep antislavery roots, and members of these denominations espoused racial tolerance and welcomed African Americans into their homes. For the Reagan family, this racial tolerance was reinforced by Jack Reagan's political liberalism. He did not attend church regularly, but he was adamantly liberal in his views on race. The parents of both families imparted to their sons a profound sense of racial justice. Both emerged as student leaders with exceptional speaking skills.

Whatever their similar childhood experiences, Nixon and Reagan matured into completely different personalities with different leadership qualities, and those differences were just as radical as the ways Reagan differed from Rockefeller and Goldwater. From childhood through his career as an actor and later in politics, Reagan projected a sunny, amiable personality. In this regard, he was like his father, a salesman who liked people. Reagan's disposition was given to compromise, except when core principles were involved. When asked to mediate between friends and political factions, Reagan usually settled on a middle course to bring people together. When it came to core principles, however, Reagan could be quietly obstinate, albeit without displays of anger or overt stubbornness. Consistent throughout his politics, first as a liberal Democrat and later as a conservative Republican, he believed he was on the right side of history.

Even as a radio announcer and later as an actor, Reagan loved to talk about politics. He became involved in the Hollywood Democratic left early in his career. Although Reagan was active in left-wing political causes and the Screen Actors Guild, most of his closest friends in Hollywood were Republicans.

Leading Hollywood actor William Holden and his wife, Arlen, exerted a major influence on Reagan's transition from liberal to conservative. Reagan admired Holden as an actor and took acting advice from him. Both served in the Armed Services during World War II and loved horses. Although on different sides of the political fence, they both were actively involved in the Screen Actors Guild. They were aligned in their opposition to the Communist faction within the union, which blossomed into a full-blown war during the 1947 Hollywood strike.

The struggle against the Communist faction within SAG and the technical unions in Hollywood pushed Reagan to the right, but the real turning point came with the breakup of his marriage to Jane Wyman, his marriage to Nancy Davis, and a declining movie career. Reagan's career as spokesman for General Electric confirmed his conversion to conservatism. His extensive reading in classical conservative and contemporary conservative periodicals deepened his core principles. He made appearances at anti-Communist rallies and began publicly supporting Republican candidates beginning with the Eisenhower-Nixon ticket in 1952. He published in the conservative *Human Events* and became a top draw at meetings of conservative and Republican groups nationally and in California.

Reagan entered electoral politics as a conservative activist. His campaign for governor in 1966 played on the image of him as a citizen-candidate standing against the established political class. The campaign called for law and order, radically scaling back government in Sacramento, and tax relief for the middle classes. He won the governor's race in a landslide, but once in office, Reagan discovered the difference between campaign rhetoric and the actualities of governance. He learned to work with a Democratic legislature. Many Democrats were from rural districts and were fairly conservative on many issues, but Reagan learned to work with liberal Democrats as well. His first two major acts as governor were to enact the largest tax increase in state history and to sign the most liberal abortion reform bill at the time in the country. Abortions in California soared in his subsequent two terms from a little over five hundred legal abortions in 1966 to an annual average of a hundred thousand. For a conservative Republican at another time, such measures would have rung a death knell. The abortion issue in 1967 had not yet become a rallying cry among conservative activists, but within the next couple of years, where a candidate stood on abortion became a litmus test for endorsement. The same could be said about raising taxes. Reagan convinced California Republicans and the state's general electorate that raising taxes was necessary and that he had not betrayed his principles as a conservative in signing prochoice abortion legislation. This revealed his ability to communicate his ideas to the larger public.

Working with Democrats, he achieved welfare reform, deinstitutionalization of mental institutions, and tax reform. His welfare reform legislation became a model across the country. These policies imparted to Reagan a reputation as a reform-minded and competent governor, equally given to fulfilling an ideological agenda and the practicalities of government. His policies were not without unintended consequences. Deinstitutionalization of mental patients, a measure supported by the left and the right in the 1960s, contributed to the homeless problem that emerged in the country in subsequent decades. The Reagan administration supported the measure as cost cutting, while many liberals expressed an anti-institutional perspective prevalent in the 1960s. Later, as president, Reagan came under heated attack by the left for having created a national homelessness problem through his economic policies. His critics did not point to Reagan's closing of state mental hospitals while he was governor as contributing to the problem because they had supported Reagan's reform legislation. Nor did they point out that the major cause of homelessness in America at the time was not due to government doing too little but doing too much. An increase in federal housing subsidies gave the poor more discretionary income to be spent on alcohol and drugs, the major contributors of homelessness in America.[16]

Although Reagan made an ill-fated attempt to win the Republican presidential nomination in 1968, once Nixon was in the White House, he accommodated himself to Nixon's presidency. Reagan defended Nixon's Vietnam War policies. Reagan was a hawk when it came to Vietnam and assailed the peacenik antiwar movement. On a deeper level, Reagan as a conservative was fundamentally at odds with Nixon ideologically. Reagan did not support détente or arms control with the Soviet Union. Reagan expressed criticism of Nixon's expansion of the welfare and regulatory state, although as governor he avoided direct attacks on the president.

On the personal level, Nixon and Reagan were not close, if only because they were political rivals. Nixon resented and would not forgive Reagan's bid to win the GOP nomination in 1968. Reagan had never been wild about Nixon, the man, the politician, or the rival. Although most Hollywood Republicans in 1952 (and there were many then), supported the Eisenhower-Nixon ticket, Reagan was not one of them. A lifelong Democrat who campaigned for Truman in 1948, Reagan in 1952 declared himself a Democrat for Eisenhower. He believed that Nixon was corrupt and backed by California oil interests.

Reagan did not appear to be prominent on Nixon's political radar until the 1964 presidential campaign, which launched Reagan into the governor's mansion two years later, in 1966. For his part, Nixon found Reagan an especially odd personality. This was captured in a White House conversation, recorded on tape, between Nixon and his chief of staff H. R. Haldeman in August 1972, at the height of the presidential election campaign. After a telephone conversation with Reagan, Nixon turned to his aide to describe his impressions of Rockefeller and Reagan. He described Rockefeller as "sort of bouncy and upbeat," while Reagan "just isn't pleasant to be around."

"No, he [Reagan] isn't," Haldeman said.
"I don't know. Maybe he's different with others," Nixon said.
"No, no, I don't think so," Haldeman said.
"He's just an uncomfortable man to be around—strange," Nixon said.[17]

The truth was that Reagan simply was not comfortable around Nixon and did not trust him. Reagan's amiable personality and his penchant for telling jokes and Hollywood stories, which he used to put people at ease, were not devices he could employ with Nixon. As an added factor, in 1972, President Nixon occupied the spot Reagan coveted.

After leaving the governorship in 1974, Reagan reverted to his ideological activism. His syndicated newspaper column and radio show provided a venue to voice his conservative critique of the Ford administration. At the outset of his campaign for the nomination, Reagan focused on streamlining government by transferring programs to the states. He never fully explained how states were going to take over these programs without raising taxes. When his campaign failed to gain traction, Reagan turned to attacking the administration's foreign policy, specifically détente and arms control with the Soviet Union. He discovered that crowds cheered when he denounced the proposed turnover of the Panama Canal to a left-wing Panamanian regime. For all of his red-meat, right-wing rhetoric, there remained the pragmatic Reagan. Realizing that he did not have enough delegates to defeat Ford at the convention, Reagan floated placing liberal Republican senator Richard Schweiker of Pennsylvania on the ticket as his running mate. The ploy was a lure to the Pennsylvania delegation to desert Ford. It did not work and Ford won the nomination, but Reagan's pragmatic side was apparent. Grassroots conservatives found something attractive in Reagan's pragmatism, a trait they would not have forgiven in another candidate.

Reagan's campaign for the presidency in 1980 showed the ideological pragmatist Reagan at his best. Carter was an easy foil for Reagan's appeal to rebuild the American economy and restore America's position as a world power. Voter distrust of government ran high and patriotic fervor even higher. Reagan tapped into voter discontent. The fact of the matter was that Reagan's rhetoric against federal welfare and regulatory policies was aimed at overturning Nixon's policies. Carter was by no means the great liberal that Reagan made him out to be on the campaign trail. Reagan won in a landslide.

In the White House, Reagan turned to governance. His administration was exceptionally well organized. Reagan showed his skills in public and government relations. He became well known for conducting personal telephone conversations with critical members of the House and the Senate, Republicans and Democrats alike. He formed personal relationships with leading Democrats, such as House Speaker Thomas P. "Tip" O'Neill. He won over budget-hawk conservatives in the Senate and the House who were reluctant to cut taxes for fear of runaway deficits. The core of his domestic and foreign policy views during his presidency was a belief that centralized government posed a threat to individual liberty. This imparted a consistency in his domestic policy not found in the Nixon administration. Nixon's interest in domestic policy often seemed framed within political calculation as how best to win election. At the core of Reagan's political philosophy rested an espousal of individual liberty against state collectivism. He remained consistent in this philosophy. In 1962, he declared, "I don't equate Liberalism and Socialism and Socialism and Communism, but this doesn't preclude my pointing out that they do have in common one characteristic—collectivism. All three of these philosophies seek to answer all human needs through more and more government."[18]

Reagan's skills as a politician were evident in securing Social Security reform, economic deregulation, tax cuts in his first administration, and, remarkably, tax reform in his second term. His core ideological principles about strengthening American defense and ensuring American nuclear superiority were evident in his foreign policy. The culmination of his foreign policy came in his second term with the signing of a major and verifiable arms reduction treaty with the Soviet Union. Reagan's foreign policy set the stage for the end of the Cold War that came in George H. W. Bush's administration.

These were remarkable successes for any president. The Reagan presidency, while called the Reagan Revolution by his supporters, came with costs, sometimes the result of ideological adherence. The belief that tax cuts would spark enough economic growth to enhance revenues proved only partially true. Economic growth did create more revenue but not enough to compensate for the costs of defense spending. The administration's anti-Communist opposition to the pro-Soviet Sandinista regime in Nicaragua created an environment for what became known as the Iran-Contra scandal. The episode involved officials in the National Security Council becoming involved in a byzantine program of selling missiles to an anti-American Iranian government and using the cash from these deals to supply anti-Sandinista forces in Nicaragua. The policy skirted congressional legislation that prevented arming the Nicaraguan anti-Sandinistas and was in clear violation of the intent of the law. The scandal marred Reagan's second term, although he left the White House in 1988 one of the most popular presidents in modern history.

By the time Goldwater died in 1998 and Reagan in 2001, the Republican Party had become the voice of conservatism. The election of George W. Bush in 2000 proved to be the high-water mark of a powerful, yet fragile coalition that had been put together beginning in the 1960s. Goldwater's nomination launched the conservative takeover of the Republican Party. The Goldwater movement, however, was far different than the Reagan coalition. The Goldwater movement consisted of conservatives who rallied against the New Deal and Communism. Reagan represented a winning coalition of social conservatives, Northern blue-collar workers, and white Southern voters. Reagan's election ruptured the New Deal coalition, which had remained intact until the late 1960s. Nixon's election in 1968 and 1972 showed the first signs of this liberal crack-up, amid a deteriorating economy, an oil crisis, and the perceived decline of America as a world power. The Reagan coalition endured from 1980 through 2008, despite Bill Clinton's two terms as president.

Whatever their differences in temperament, Goldwater and Reagan were skilled and charismatic politicians able to tap into deep feelings among many voters who believed in the exceptional nature of the nation's experiment in constitutional, republican government. Neither man was able to turn back the clock of the progressive state that had first emerged in the Progressive movement at the turn of the century, accelerated in the New Deal, and cemented during the Great Society. Goldwater and Reagan offered a voice counter to the progressive state. In effect, they cast themselves in American form as the ancient Romans Cato and Cicero, who warned of the decline of the republic. The Roman republic fell to Caesar. For American conservatives in the late twentieth and early twenty-first centuries, Caesar came in the form of the leviathan state ruled by an imperial president and despotic government bureaucrats. Like Cato and Cicero before them, Goldwater and Reagan believed that a republic need not necessarily decline. Political liberty and economic freedom rested on the virtuous leaders and a virtuous citizenry. Goldwater and Reagan shared a belief, as had the nation's founders, that republics are by their nature fragile. Goldwater and Reagan stood as politicians fighting for principles and ideals rooted in the nation's history. They were noble in their cause. Whether history judges them as Cato and Cicero in their struggle to preserve the republic, or more like Caligula's imperial soldiers fighting the oceanic tides, remains to be seen. Whatever the case, both men changed the course of American politics.

Epilogue
Voters and Leaders in Disarray

Ideological polarization, political alienation, and general distrust in government and its elected representatives have created a general anxiety that the American system is not working today. American politics in the twenty-first century combines an odd phenomenon of hyperpartisan activism and voter apathy. For those 50 percent or so of eligible voters who turn out to vote in presidential elections, many cast their ballots along ideological lines. Firm in their convictions, they vote as confirmed liberals or conservatives who will not brook deviation in their candidates. At the same time, a growing number of voters refuse to register for either of the two major parties and declare themselves Independents. Most Independent voters continue to vote consistently along party lines, even as they claim to vote for the best candidate available, not the party. To these groups can be added a large number of Americans who express complete alienation from the political system by not voting at all. Their noninvolvement suggests a belief that voting does not matter, all the candidates are the same, the system is rigged and corrupt, or they just do not care about politics one way or the other.

Americans seem to be repulsed by the rough-and-tumble of politics. Legislative compromise, political horse trading, and deal making suggest to many that politics and politicians are corrupt, self-serving, and without principle or conviction. At the same time, many of these same people who are also critical of self-serving politicians without principle are critical of politicians who appear too ideological in their positions and who are unwilling to compromise over principle. The concepts of principled pragmatism and legislative compromise in American politics seem to have become a lost ideal for many U.S. voters, who continue to express concern with the moral character and temperament of those seeking the presidency. Too often, though, these qualities are framed largely by voters as a matter of party loyalty and ideological alignment. A liberal voter will find it impossible for a conservative candidate to be morally suited for the presidency. How can any conservative be of high character if their major concern is *not* economic, racial, gender, and environmental justice? For a conservative voter, a liberal candidate, by the very nature of her or his politics, betrays the founding principles of the Constitution by enlarging government at the expense of those inalienable rights of life, liberty, and property.

American voters and political parties have become so ideological that memories of political horse trading and legislative compromise that characterized most of nineteenth-century politics are largely forgotten. Similarly, many scholars and journalists looking at politics and political leaders in the post–World War II period also view events through an ideological lens. Too often, these scholars forget that politics in a democracy is about gaining power and winning elections. Nixon, Rockefeller, Goldwater, and Reagan held political beliefs, which can be described as politically left or right, liberal or conservative, but when it came to the actual political arena, these men showed in varying ways a remarkable capacity to adjust their ideological orientations to the reality of politics. It tells us much—and belies politics as a pursuit only of ideology—that Nixon sought to make deals with Rockefeller; Rockefeller, in turn, proposed at different times alliances with Goldwater and Reagan; and Goldwater and Reagan, both ideological conservatives, became political rivals. Viewing political history only through the lens of ideological warfare makes for drama, but it neglects the nuances and twists and turns of actual politics. This is not to deny the importance of ideology in modern American politics; it is to say, however, that American politics is more than just ideological warfare. Nixon, Rockefeller, Goldwater, and Reagan were not pure political ideologues; they were politicians seeking power for their own advancement, often at the expense of party loyalty and their espoused political beliefs. Their political careers can be weighed on a scale ranging from opportunism to principle. All of these men were partisan Republicans, and all understood the importance of ideology as a force in modern American politics; but they were politicians above all else.

Neither partisan nor ideological divide is new to American politics. In the early nineteenth century, party leaders expressed deep ideological differences over a range of issues including the creation of a national bank, the tariff, internal improvements, western expansion, and slavery. These issues inflamed party leaders and voters. But because national parties throughout this period were coalitions of ethnoreligious voters and regional alliances, Congress reached legislative compromises on most of these issues. The slave problem, as it was called in the antebellum era, proved to be one incommensurable moral issue that could not be compromised. The 1860 election of Abraham Lincoln, who won election only with Northern votes, confirmed that the sectional divide had become insurmountable. Following the Civil War, the two dominant parties, Democrat and Republican, presented sharply different political and policy programs over taxes, tariffs, immigration, and the money question—and as the century drew to a close, they differed on imperialism and corporate trusts. Nonetheless, parties continued to be built around uneasy coalitions of often divergent economic and cultural interests. The result was a general tempering of ideological polarization within the electorate.

This began to change following World War II. The struggle within the Republican Party in the late twentieth century reflected both an ideological fight between a moderate-liberal wing, represented by Nelson Rockefeller, and a conservative wing, represented by Barry Goldwater and Ronald Reagan. The struggle between the East and the Sunbelt West over control of the party was handled in different ways by the candidates. For example, Richard Nixon presented himself as a unity candidate who could reconcile regional and ideological differences. In 1976, Reagan sought to reassure the Eastern wing of the party by announcing before the GOP convention that he would select Senator Richard Schweiker as his running mate. Reagan sought to win Pennsylvania delegates' vote at the convention, but he was also signaling that the Eastern wing of the party would continue to have a voice.

Ideological division within the Republican Party continued throughout this period. This divide had reached a crescendo in 1964 in the contest between Rockefeller and Goldwater. Whatever the ideological differences within the party, Republicans understood that in order to win the White House, they needed to win crossover Democrats. Self-identified Republicans were a minority of voters. For this reason, after winning the 1964 nomination, Goldwater campaign strategists tried unsuccessfully to move more to the center. Richard Nixon unified the party in winning the 1968 nomination by reassuring conservatives that as president he would pursue a strong national defense policy and appoint conservatives to the Supreme Court. Moderates within the party did not need to be told that Nixon was not a far-right extremist. Nixon offered party leaders and voters a chance to win the White House after eight years of liberal Democratic rule. The debacle of Vietnam and the perceived failure of the Great Society gave resonance to his message. His resignation from the presidency in 1974 left the Republican Party a minority party once again. Many wondered if the Republican Party would survive the Watergate disaster. Nixon's successor to the White House, Gerald Ford, sought to unify the Republican Party and the American people, anxious about the status of the nation following the Vietnam War and an economy wracked by rising unemployment and inflation. The malaise of the Carter years and increasing worry about America's perceived decline in world affairs enabled Reagan to rally his conservative base to win the nomination and then win the White House in 1980 by playing on the theme of restoring America's economy and greatness as a country. At the height of the Cold War, he convinced voters that he would reestablish American military superiority. Critical to this argument was persuading voters that he was not a trigger-happy right winger who would get America into a nuclear war with the Soviet Union. He convinced the electorate that he had the temperament to be president. Republican success in turning the South into a stronghold during the Reagan years reinforced conservative ideological dominance within the party. Republican moderates within Congress continued to maintain powerful control within the party throughout the Reagan and Bush years, while Democrats retained control of both houses of Congress.

A revolt by conservative House members in 1994, led by Newt Gingrich, congressman from Georgia, marked the strength of conservatives within the party and the decline of liberal-moderate Republicans. This was paralleled by the gradual decline of Southern conservatives, so-called Blue Dogs, within the Democratic Party. Congress, especially in the House, became an ideological battleground. The Democratic loss of the South to the Republican Party, combined with the breakup of the New Deal coalition, helped intensify growing polarization within the electorate. Although some political scientists, such as Morris P. Fiorina, argue that polarization was found only in the halls of Congress and among media pundits, and not in the electorate, a closer look at voting behavior suggests that this trend extended beyond the hallways of Congress and the Washington beltway.[1] Political polarization among the elites in Washington and the general electorate coincided.[2] Republican congressional leaders were not the catalyst for ideological polarization in American politics but reflected a trend already well established within the general voting population. By 2004, 75 percent of Americans believed that profound and not easily reconciled differences characterized the two parties.

Ideologically driven voting has become prominent within the American electorate. About 40 percent of the general electorate vote ideologically.

Politically engaged Democrats call themselves liberals (82 percent); these voters are mirrored within the Republican Party, in which 91 percent self-identify as conservatives. Moderates remain the largest grouping within the electorate, but hard-core ideological voters dominate each of their parties, especially in presidential primary contests and midterm congressional elections. One of the major results of this ideological polarization is blaming the other party for gridlock in Washington, D.C. This has resulted in greater frustration among the general public and a view that things have failed in the nation's capital.

The decline in trust in government can be traced back to the 1960s, starting with the Vietnam War and accelerated by Nixon's Watergate scandal in the 1970s. Today, after the Great Recession, distrust in government is as pronounced as ever.[3] Thus, the remarkable feature of postwar American politics during the period in which Nixon, Rockefeller, Goldwater, and Reagan vied for the presidency was a climate of growing distrust in government. This phenomenon occurred paradoxically at a time when governmental powers and obligations to its citizens increased, and democratic rights and civil protections were extended to new groups. This decline in trust occurred at a time when the United States elevated its involvement in democratic state building abroad. Thus, while the United States undertook efforts to bring democracy to other nations, and at the same time insisted on the implementation of human rights, the American public appeared less ready to participate in the democratic process at home.

This general distrust in government itself coincides with a loss of confidence in political leaders in both parties. Although Americans have manifested periodic anxiety about political corruption, today Americans express an unprecedented loss of confidence in their leaders and established institutions. Surveys conducted over the last decade or so reveal dwindling confidence in fundamental political institutions—the presidency, the Supreme Court, and Congress. Not a single one of these institutions garners more than 33 percent support in confidence from the American public.[4] Confidence in many other institutions was not any higher, including the church and organized religion, the medical system, public schools, banks, organized labor, newspapers, television news, and big business—all which elicited less than majority confidence by the public. Overall confidence in all institutions fell continually from 1993 to 2015. On average, a little over one-third of Americans have confidence in government or public and private institutions.[5]

Paradoxically, Americans remain highly patriotic, even though they express distrust in the political institutions and leaders essential to maintaining democratic governance. Surveys show that Americans remain among the most patriotic people in advanced industrial countries; therefore, it seems contradictory that they express so little confidence in their political institutions, political leadership, and social institutions.[6] Approximately 52 percent of Americans say they are proud to be an American, while another 32 percent say they are very proud to be an American. Only 8 percent declare that they have little or no pride in being an American. The majority of whites are extremely proud to be an American, and 36 percent of African Americans say they are extremely proud to be an American.

In this paradox of patriotism and distrust of government, there exists a certain conceit of the American people in democratic government. Americans take tremendous pride in their democracy. They believe it is the best form of government devised by humankind. Books on the founding fathers and presidents such as Thomas Jefferson, John Adams, Alexander Hamilton, and Abraham Lincoln continue to make the list of the best-sellers. Americans express extraordinary confidence in the virtues of American democracy; yet behind these expressions of patriotism, they appear to be anxious about democratic institutions and leadership at home. If their lack of participation is any indication, large numbers of Americans believe that involvement in the democratic process, a necessary first step in regaining control of government, does not matter very much.

Why? Liberal journalist E. J. Dionne Jr. offered one explanation in his book *Why Americans Hate Politics* (1991). He traced American disillusionment with its leaders (and by implication, its institutions) to political polarization that emerged in the late 1960s and early 1970s. During these decades, he argued, the Democratic Party had swung too far left, while the Republican Party moved to the right. He maintained that Republicans, divided over libertarian rights and moral conservatism, experienced difficulties in coming up with a coherent program of government. With liberalism discredited and conservatives unable to present a real policy alternative to the nation's economic, social, and cultural problems, he concluded, Americans lost confidence in politics; even more, many hated politics. What Americans wanted, Dionne maintained, were practical solutions to problems, not ideological warfare.

Much like Daniel Boorstin argued earlier in his classic *The Americans*, the American people were pragmatic and interested in utilitarian problem solving, not in utopian ideologies. Dionne called for the creation of a new political center, a coalition for social reform that could command broad support in the middle class and could, by implication, allow Americans to rediscover a commitment to politics, public life, and government.

Dionne's analysis of the malaise, if you will, of the people rested on the assumption that bifurcated political ideologies had alienated the American people from government and led implicitly to a distrust in government. A new kind of politics, therefore, would restore peoples' faith in democratic politics. Only a year after the book appeared, Americans elected a centrist Democrat, Bill Clinton, who, after an initial probe to the left with a proposal for a national health care system, followed centrist policies for his two terms in office. Although conservatives decried his politics as leftism in sheep's clothing, Clinton pursued a generally moderate policy agenda, albeit with the prompting of a Republican-controlled House. Scandals, principally related to personal matters—although not solely—tarnished Clinton's presidency, but even after eight years of centrist politics, Americans continued to distrust their institutions and were not very interested in politics if voting participation was any indication. Dionne's solution did not seem to have the result he had proposed; polarized ideological partisanship continued to characterize politics in the decade of the 1990s. Still, something else seemed to be going on among Americans, not explained simply by a repulsion to ideological warfare.

Writing nearly a half-century earlier, Walter Lippmann, in his *Essays in the Public Philosophy* (1955), offered another, arguably deeper explanation as to what he described as "a functional derangement of the relationship between the mass of people and the government. The people have acquired power which they are incapable of exercising, and the governments they elect have lost powers which they must recover if they are to govern." In his jeremiad against the decline of the public philosophy, he declared that "this devitalization of the government power is the malady of democratic states. . . . That is the central and critical condition of Western society: that the democracies are ceasing to receive the traditions of civility in which the good society, the liberal, democratic way of life at its best, originated and developed."[7]

Lippmann offered a surprising explanation as to the crisis of democratic government: the United States suffered from an excess of democracy. Informing his readers that he was not arguing for the disenfranchisement of the masses, he maintained that the public good was not served when the "public good" is determined by the passions of the masses. He warned that

American society was losing its ability to engage in a public discourse about the goods or goals of society; a society that no longer concerns itself with binding principles and no longer held beliefs in common about what constitutes the good society eventually will fail. He further argued that when a society relegates morals to the inner sanctum of private choice, it has no means of maintaining itself. As time went on, he said, "There fell out of fashion the public philosophy of the founders of Western institutions. . . . It became the rule that ideas and principles are private—with only subjective relevance and significance." The consequence was that "all that has to do with what man is and should be, or how he should hold himself in the scheme of things, what are his rightful ends and the legitimate means, became private and subjective and publicly unaccountable."

Lippmann did not offer an easy remedy as to how to restore public discourse, or public philosophy, in a mass democracy. He wrote that the problem is nearly intractable as to "how to educate rapidly and sufficiently the ever-expanding masses who are losing contact with the traditions of Western society. The explosive increase of the population in the past hundred and fifty years, its recent enfranchisement during the past fifty years, the dissolution, or at least the radical weakening, of the bonds of the family, the churches, and of the local community" have combined to create a crisis for American democracy. The problem lay in the absence of core values that provided the foundation for any liberal democracy. "There is, moreover, no body of public knowledge and no public philosophy" that is being transmitted by political, education, or public institutions. Lippmann's analysis that the erosion of fundamental beliefs—as opposed to popular sentiment that democracy is "a good thing"—suggested that ultimately the people themselves would lose faith in their political and social institutions.

If social egalitarianism subverted the public philosophy by creating "a plurality of incompatible faiths," other factors need to be explored to explain the intensity of political alienation and distrust of civic institutions since the 1960s. When Lippmann wrote *Public Philosophy* in 1955, confidence in government and political leaders, as well as in leaders in business, the media, religion, and education, remained high. The seeds of alienation arguably might have been sown earlier in the century, but the severity of distrust in government today needs a fuller explanation about what transpired politically and culturally in American history since the 1960s. Perhaps Lippmann's perception was correct that the public was not being taught and no longer adhered to the public philosophy upon which the foundations of democratic government stood, but the loss of trust in government—although not in patriotism and nationalism—came about through specific political events.

However one explains today's loss of confidence in democratic institutions, the fear of decline and anxiety about political corruption is by no means a new phenomenon in the history of the United States. It is more severely felt today and by a larger number of Americans, but such anxieties have found periodic expression in American politics. In the late eighteenth century, Federalist clergy worried that republican principles were being undermined by the loss of religious faith in the cities and on the western frontier. They also blamed the influence of French radicalism and the flood of immigrants coming to the new nation. In antebellum America, evangelical Christians warned of the decline of public morality, as evidenced in intemperance, dueling, disregard for the Sabbath, and signs of moral corruption. The election of Andrew Jackson in 1828 and his reelection four years later symbolized the decay of the Christian republic. Jackson, a slaveholder, duelist, and alleged adulterer, showed the decline of republican principles in his removal of the Indians, his use of patronage, and his veto of the national bank. Abolitionist William Lloyd Garrison went so far in his opposition to slavery that he charged that the U.S. Constitution itself was corrupt for having allowed slavery in the first place. The decades following the Civil War heightened many peoples' fear that American political institutions had been corrupted by special interests, political scandal, partisan factionalism, party bosses, city political machines, and self-serving politicians.

What makes the early twenty-first century unique is the intensity of these anxieties and the pervasive distrust that permeates all layers of society. In 2016, Donald Trump tapped into voter distrust in government and politicians by running as a populist without clear ideological principle. His opponents within the Democratic Party and some conservative pundits viewed his rhetoric as morally offensive and his appeals to voters demagogic. Many average voters, however, were attracted to his denunciation of elites and his promise to "drain the swamp" in Washington. These voters welcomed his exaggerated rhetoric and saw it as a display of courage and strong leadership. They voted for him in the belief that once in office he would show the capacity to govern as a strong leader given to pragmatism and principle. His attraction as a candidate was that he appealed to the passions of the people and declared himself as a candidate who reflects their anxieties. He translated moral character into the self-interest of the people. This conflation of the people's emotions and the public interest was not new to American politics by any means, but Trump's unrestrained appeal to voter passions was quite unlike anything ever seen in American politics. He made Andrew Jackson, who projected himself as the representative common man, look, in hindsight, even-tempered.

This appeal only to voter passion is far from what the founders envisioned from good leaders within a republic. Their ideals of virtue and a sense of honor as necessary qualities to a well-ordered republic seem especially hollow and antiquated in today's politics. The founders' commitment to virtue was unique to the eighteenth century before the rise of popular democracy. Still, it is worth reminding ourselves that the founders of the American republic saw politics as a higher calling by associating moral character and temperament as matters of disinterest. Virtuous leadership meant standing above party faction, local or regional interest, passionate self-interest, and personal ambition, and working for the larger common good. These aspirations were derived from their reading of the ancients and contemporary political thinkers but also from lessons they had learned from what they saw as the corruption of the British Parliament and the subversion of the "ancient constitution" derived from their Anglo-Saxon ancestors. This ideal of disinterest in politics was quickly belied by the actual practice of partisan politics in the early nation. Candidates seeking election in a democratic culture must show passion and make it clear they stand with the common folks. Once elected to office, they pledge to represent the will of the people. Expression of disinterested leadership is not the path to election in an egalitarian democracy. The language of the "common good" is translated into an appeal to win ideological voters with their own narrow concepts of what the common good means.

In a political culture in which large numbers of voters do not share common values, defining the common good or the public interest becomes nearly impossible. Moreover, given the widespread cynicism toward politicians—that most are corrupt, pawns of special-interest groups, and without moral character—voters see rhetoric about serving the common good as just that, mere political rhetoric. Disinterested political engagement, standing above faction, and defining the common good as something not necessarily defined by partisan interest become remote concepts in a polarized and alienated political environment. In such an environment, candidates tend to be judged by their ideological proclivities rather than their moral character or possession of the temperament necessary for governance. Governance often means compromise, and ideological voters will deem compromise as betrayal. If the ability to govern is given less prominence by voters than ideological alignment, or if the public sees all politicians as corrupt, opportunities for demagoguery in the political culture are heightened.

Political campaigns often provide inaccurate instruments for measuring a candidate's temperament, character, or ability to govern. Obviously, the purpose of a serious campaign is to win election, and a candidate will appeal to those voters most likely to be won on Election Day. Campaigns are about persuading voters that one candidate is worth voting for and the opposing candidate is not worthy. As a result, political campaigns combine both positive and negative messages, which can distort the realities of a candidate's temperament and ability to govern. Campaign rhetoric is often so vituperative that it provides little evidence of what a candidate's leadership qualities will be once in office. The appeal to voters' base passions is arguably unavoidable within a democracy. Demagoguery is not peculiar to democracies, but it is democracy's mortal enemy because it subverts trust in government within the electorate, does little to educate voters as to the complexity of problems, and offers little in the way of offering an agenda for future governance.

Hyperbolic speech is part and parcel of political campaigns and can be an effective tool for a president in office. During their presidencies, John Adams, Thomas Jefferson, and James Madison employed heated rhetoric against political opponents and foreign enemies, even though they were leaders of great virtue strongly committed to republican values. The observation that hyperbolic speech is inherent in democratic politics neither denies the importance of judicious temperament in presidential leadership nor does it assign a Machiavellian utility to the projection of virtue as a disingenuous ploy to rally supporters. The point is that emphatic language is endemic to democratic politics. In the end, heated rhetoric and demagoguery are separated by a thin line that depends on the inner character and values of the candidate and president that often are not fully apparent at the moment and can be judged only over time. This presents a conundrum for the voter and one that later historians cannot easily resolve. Nonetheless, the insistence on judicious temperament and prudent character as fundamental to good leadership remains essential to the preservation of what our forebears envisioned.

The most important lesson the founders learned from their reading of the ancients is that popular democracy may be vulnerable to demagogues who subvert liberty for tyranny. The founders called for leadership founded on enlightened disinterest, best preserved in a mixed government; adherence to the rule of law and constitutional tradition; and a culture that cultivates virtue in leaders and the citizenry. By their nature, republics are fragile, given to decay and ultimate collapse. The founders believed that virtuous leaders were essential to a republic. They studied Plutarch to reaffirm the importance of character in politics.

Few American voters and probably fewer politicians have read *Plutarch's Lives* to discern what the necessary political character is for a leader. American voters believe that most, if not all, politicians are self-interested people of singular ambition. That cynical perception translates into a vote of whether a candidate's self-interest coincides with the voter's interest. Yet good character and even temperament remain essential qualities of leadership when it comes to actual governing. If political campaigns are not necessarily the best instrument for judging fully a presidential candidate's temperament for leadership, the final test for a president is found unavoidably once in the White House. Here, a president's qualities of leadership and the ability to govern effectively are inescapably on public display.

In the last half of the twentieth century, only two of the leading contenders for the Republican presidential nomination after Eisenhower were elected to the White House: Nixon and Reagan. Nixon won the 1968 election running as the "New Nixon," which projected a softer image to the voters. He avoided taking tough stands on issues until the last month of the campaign when polls showed his opponent Hubert Humphrey closing the gap; at this point, Nixon began to hammer Democrats on the law-and-order issue. The image of the New Nixon was a way of countering opponents who had portrayed him since he first entered Congress in 1946 as a man with deep character flaws. Whether this picture as "Tricky Dick" was fair or accurate about the young Nixon, his presidency revealed that he had become a flawed character by the time he entered the White House. Nixon accomplished much in his administration, but his secretive, nearly paranoid response to political enemies and his unlawful attempt to cover up the Watergate break-in during his reelection campaign in 1972 forced him to resign from office.

Goldwater and Rockefeller failed in their attempts to win the White House, and so it is impossible to reach a firm conclusion as to what kind of leaders they might have been. Goldwater's behavior during the 1964 campaign suggests he was too quick to anger, was given to shooting from the hip, and was thin skinned. Such qualities usually do not make for successful presidencies. Goldwater as president would probably have resisted the Great Society program promoted by Lyndon Johnson. In addition, a Goldwater presidency would have confronted a civil rights movement that was becoming increasingly militant. Goldwater's refusal to vote for the Civil Rights Act of

1964 undermined his credibility among black and many white voters. His Southern base would have hampered Goldwater from promoting further civil rights legislation to ensure black voting rights in the South. Further, Goldwater's response to the war in Vietnam presents an intriguing case for counterfactual history. He might have avoided a land war in Vietnam, having seen the stalemate in the Korean War, but he might have unleashed an air campaign in North Vietnam that would have encountered fierce opposition from the Soviet Union and an antiwar movement at home.

A Rockefeller presidency in 1968 also would have faced strong sentiment to expand the welfare-entitlement and regulatory state espoused by liberals in the Democratic Party. Rockefeller presented himself as a reformer who supported more federal funding to address urban problems and income inequality. Johnson's Great Society under a Rockefeller presidency might have become the even Greater Society. As governor, Rockefeller had shown little inclination for cutting government spending. A Rockefeller foreign policy, surely, would have been crafted by his chief adviser, Henry Kissinger. In 1964, Kissinger believed that unless America made a full commitment to win the war in Vietnam, the United States should pursue a restrained policy of negotiation with North Vietnam and the Soviet Union. Foreign policy under a Rockefeller presidency, acting upon Kissinger's advice, would have looked in all likelihood much like Nixon's foreign policy: détente with the Soviet Union, opening of relations with China, strategic arms control, and selected covert military operations against hostile governments.

Rockefeller brought to his presidential bids qualifications showing he could manage large bureaucracies. Few doubted his managerial skills. The more fundamental issue for voters, his rivals, and even some of his supporters was his flawed character. This was not just a matter of his propensity for personal indulgence but a temperament that it was his way or no way. Much like Nixon, Rockefeller was not driven by ideology but by a will to power. He was a builder, no matter the costs of runaway government. He insisted on being surrounded by yes-men on his staff, which left his ambitions unrestrained. His bids for the Republican presidential nomination reveal an obstinate unwillingness to unify the Republican Party, except for the desperate attempt he made in 1968 to entice Reagan to sign on to a Rockefeller ticket. Reagan's refusal to run as vice president suggests that a Rockefeller presidency would have continued to face a conservative faction within the party. A Rockefeller presidency would have left a deeply divided Republican Party.

Reagan, an avowed ideological conservative, showed the temperament and leadership qualities necessary to governance. Historians of his political career and his presidency will differ as to the merits of the Reagan Revolution. His ability to bring to office a principled pragmatism, however, illustrates the necessity of tempering purist ideology with the importance of achieving ideological goals through principled compromise and an understanding that well-ordered governance is essential to the preservation of democracy. Reagan ran for elected office, both for the governorship in California and then for the presidency, espousing conservative principles. His campaign rhetoric was often exaggerated and belied a temperament to govern. In the White House, he could employ heated language. This was apparent in his foreign policy as president as well. After denouncing the Soviet Union as the "evil empire," he had success at the negotiating table with Mikhail Gorbachev on Reagan's terms. It was a remarkable achievement for Reagan, an anti-Communist, Cold Warrior, and hard-right conservative.

These four men, rivals for the presidency, were neither completely saint nor sinner. They were men with flaws. Whatever their motivations to run for the highest office in the land, they sought to serve their country. Their ambitions might have been directed to other avenues rather than presidential politics. Instead, they offered themselves to the voters because they believed they could lead the nation to a better future. History will judge them accordingly, as it will future presidents.

Notes

Introduction

1. Michael Bowen, *The Roots of Modern Conservatism: Dewey, Taft, and the Battle for the Soul of the Republican Party* (Chapel Hill, 2014).

2. L. B. Namier, *Personalities and Powers* (London, 1955), 3; Quentin Skinner, "The Principles and Practice of Opposition: The Case of Bolingbroke Versus Walpole," in *Historical Perspectives: Studies in English Thought and Society*, edited by Neil McKendrick (London, 1974), 93–128; and Isaac Kramnick, *Bolingbroke and His Circle: The Politics of Nostalgia in the Age of Walpole* (Cambridge, MA, 1968).

3. Quoted in E. Vernon Armold, *Roman Stoicism* (London, 1940), 46.

4. Ronald Syme, *The Roman Revolution* (Oxford, 1960 rev. ed.), 55, 155.

5. John Locke, *Treatise on Human Understanding* (1690), 27.

6. Charles-Louis Montesquieu, *The Spirit of Laws* (1748), esp. vol. 1, book 3, chapters 3–4, "On the Principles of Democracy."

7. Donald Winch, *Adam Smith's Politics: An Essay in Historiographic Revision* (Cambridge, 1978). In the vast literature on the concept of virtue in political thought, of particular value is J. G. A. Pocock, *Virtue, Commerce, and History: Essays on Political Thought and History, Chiefly in the Eighteenth Century* (Cambridge, 1985).

8. Alexis de Tocqueville, *Democracy in America*, book 4, chapter 16 (1840).

9. John Adams to Thomas Jefferson, November 13, 1815, in Adrienne Koch, ed., *The American Enlightenment* (New York, 1965), 225–26.

10. Woodrow Wilson, "Democracy and Efficiency," *Atlantic Monthly*, March 1901, in *Selected Literary and Political Papers and Addresses of Woodrow Wilson* (New York, 1925), I: 112.

11. For example, see John Adams to Lord Kames, May 2, 1760; and Thomas Jefferson to John Adams, October 28, 1813, in Koch, ed., *American Enlightenment*, 85–86, 356–57.

Chapter 1

1. Jonathan Aitken, *Nixon: A Life* (London, 1993), 5. The most fully developed psychological portraits of Nixon's "disturbed" childhood are found in Fawn Brodie, *Nixon: The Shaping of His Character* (New York, 1981), Garry Wills, *Nixon Agonistes: The Crisis of*

the Self-Made Man (New York, 1969); Vamik D. Volkan et al., *Richard Nixon: A Psycho-biography* (New York, 1997); Bruce Mazlish, *In Search of Nixon: A Psychohistorical Inquiry* (New York, 1972).

2. For an excellent study of Quakerism in this period, see Thomas D. Hamm, *The Transformation of American Quakerism: Orthodox Friends, 1800–1907* (Bloomington, IN, 1988). For the seeds of Unitarianism-Universalism within Eastern Quakerism, see H. Larry Ingle, *Quakers in Conflict: The Hicksite Reformation* (Knoxville, TN, 1986).

3. Larry Ingle, "Richard Nixon's First Cover-Up," *Friends Journal* (May 2013), and "Richard Nixon, Whittaker Chambers, Alger Hiss, and Quakerism," *Quaker History* (Spring 2012), 1–11.

4. Richard Nixon, *RN: The Memoirs of Richard Nixon* (New York, 1978), 6–8.

5. Ibid., 9.

6. Herbert S. Parmet, *Richard M. Nixon: An America Enigma* (New York, 2008), 1.

7. Julie Nixon Eisenhower, *Pat Nixon: The Untold Story* (New York, 1986), 62–63.

8. Aitken, *Nixon*; Nixon Eisenhower, *Pat Nixon*, 62–63.

9. Aitken, *Nixon*, 48.

10. Los Angeles Almanac, http://www.laalmanac.com/population/po26.php.

11. Aitken, *Nixon*, 46. "Mary Skidmore," in *The Young Nixon: An Oral Inquiry*, edited by Renée K. Schulte (Fullerton, CA, 1978), 78.

12. "Jane Milhous Beeson," in Schulte, ed., *Young Nixon*, 55–56.

13. "James Grieves," in Schulte, ed., *Young Nixon*, 100.

14. Nixon, *RN*, 20.

15. Charles W. Cooper, *Whittier: Independent College in California, Founded by Quakers, 1887* (Los Angeles, 1967).

16. "Paul Smith," in Schulte, ed., *Young Nixon*, 142.

17. Nixon, *RN*, 18–19.

18. Aitken, *Nixon*, 76–77.

19. Opponents later charged that Nixon's campaign was backed by large oil interests and real estate tycoons. Historian Irwin Gellman challenges these charges in his well-researched *The Contender: Richard Nixon—The Congressional Years, 1946–52* (New York, 1952).

20. Nixon Eisenhower, *Pat Nixon*, 86–87, 106.

21. Aitken, *Nixon*, 113–32.

22. For the Nixon, Knowland, and Warren rivalry, see James Worthen, *The Young Nixon and His Rivals: Four California Republicans Eye the White House, 1946–1958* (Jefferson City, NC, 2010); and Donald T. Critchlow, *When Hollywood Was Right: How Movie Stars, Studio Moguls, and Big Business Remade American Politics* (New York, 2013).

23. Herbert G. Klein, *Making It Perfectly Clear* (Garden City, NY, 1980), 77.

24. Sinclair's poor relation with the Communists is discussed in detail in Critchlow, *When Hollywood Was Right*.

25. Nixon Eisenhower, *Pat Nixon*, 98.

26. Quoted in Earl Mazo and Stephen Hess, *Nixon: A Political Portrait* (New York, 1968), 42; Christopher Matthews, *Kennedy and Nixon: The Rivalry That Shaped Postwar America* (New York, 1996), 61.

27. Nixon, *RN,* 59–61.

28. Ibid., 61.

29. Ibid., 58.

30. U.S. Congress, *Hearings Before the Committee on Un-American Activities* (Washington, D.C., 1947), 47; Critchlow, *When Hollywood Was Right,* 76–108.

31. The most engaging recounting of Chambers's testimony and life other than his memoir *Witness* (New York, 1952) is Sam Tanenhaus, *Whittaker Chambers, A Biography* (New York, 1998).

32. Nixon Eisenhower, *Pat Nixon,* 102.

33. Democrats regained control of the Senate and gained more seats in the House than in any year since the 1932 election. In the 1948 campaign, Nixon at first backed Harold Stassen, a moderate Republican former governor of Minnesota, against conservative senator Robert Taft and Thomas Dewey, governor of New York. Dewey won the nomination only to go down in defeat to Truman's "Give 'em Hell" campaign. For an insightful study of the Republican presidential contest in 1948, see Michael Bowen, *The Roots of Modern Conservatism: Dewey, Taft, and the Battle for the Soul of the Republican Party* (Chapel Hill, 2014), and, a popular take on the general election, David Pietrusze, *1948: Truman's Improbable Victory and the Year That Transformed America* (New York, 2011).

34. Kurt Schuparra, *Triumph of the Right: The Rise of the California Conservative Movement, 1945-1966* (Armonk, NY, 1998), 13–15.

35. Quoted in Matthews, *Kennedy and Nixon,* 69.

36. For Nixon's and Kennedy's relationship, see Lance Morrow, *The Best Year of Their Lives: Kennedy, Johnson, and Nixon in 1948* (New York, 2006).

37. The best book on the 1950 Nixon-Douglas race remains Gellman's *The Contender,* 296–343. See also Klein, *Making It Perfectly Clear,* 185; and Mazo and Hess, *Nixon,* 75.

38. Worthen, *Young Nixon and His Rivals.*

39. James T. Patterson, *Mr. Republican: A Biography of Robert A. Taft* (Boston, 1972), 499–568; Stephen E. Ambrose, *Eisenhower: Soldier, General of the Army, President-Elect* (New York, 1983), 529–72. Irwin Gellman challenges the "Great Train Robbery" accusation in *The President and the Apprentice: Eisenhower and Nixon, 1952-1960* (New Haven, CT, 2015).

40. Mazo and Hess, *Nixon,* 85.

41. Gellman, *The President and the Apprentice,* 33–54. Stevenson, it should be noted, was quiet about the Alger Hiss affair as well, although he and his campaign assailed Nixon as Eisenhower's attack dog. In Hiss's first perjury trial, Stevenson served as a character witness for Hiss. Gellman, 23, 35.

42. Nixon, *RN,* 116–17.

43. Ibid., 121.

44. Mazo and Hess, *Nixon,* 108–9.

45. Klein, *Making It Perfectly Clear,* 138.

46. Richard Nixon, *Six Crises* (New York, 1962), 128.

47. Gellman, *The President and the Apprentice.* Eisenhower's presidency is explored in Fred L. Greenstein, *The Hidden-Hand Presidency: Eisenhower as Leader* (New York,

1982); Gary W. Reichard, *The Reaffirmation of Republicanism: Eisenhower and the Eighty-Third Congress* (Knoxville, TN, 1975); Herbert S. Parmet, *Richard Nixon and His America* (Boston, 1990); and Elmo Richardson, *The Presidency of Dwight Eisenhower* (Lawrence, KS, 1979).

48. For Nixon's important role in crafting the Civil Rights Act of 1957 and the Democratic Senate weakening of the bill, see David A. Nichols, *A Matter of Justice: Eisenhower and the Beginnings of the Civil Rights Revolution* (New York, 2008). Robert A. Caro, in *The Passage of Power: The Years of Lyndon Johnson* (New York, 2013), presents another take on this civil rights legislation, giving Johnson a major role in its enactment.

49. Gellman, *The President and the Apprentice,* 291; and Worthen, *Young Nixon and His Rivals.*

50. Quoted in Aitken, *Nixon,* 232.

51. M. Stanton Evans, *Blacklisted by History: The Untold Story of Senator Joe McCarthy* (New York, 2007); and David M. Oshinsky, *A Conspiracy So Immense: The World of Joe McCarthy* (New York, 1983).

52. Worthen, *Young Nixon and His Rivals*; Gellman, *The President and the Apprentice,* 200.

53. Gellman, *The President and the Apprentice,* 311.

54. Monica Crowley, *Nixon: Off the Record* (New York, 1996), 16.

55. Nixon, *RN*; Aitken, *Nixon,* 233.

56. Mark Feldstein, "Fighting Quakers," *Journalism History* (Summer 2004), 76–90, examines in full Pearson's obsession with Nixon.

57. Theodore White, *The Making of the President, 1960* (New York, 1961); also W. J. Rorabaugh, *The Real Making of the President: Kennedy, Nixon, and the 1960 Election* (Lawrence, KS, 2009). Matthews, in *Kennedy and Nixon,* offers some astute insights into the ruptured relationship between Nixon and Kennedy, who entered Congress together in 1946. For other discussions of the West Virginia primary and the Kennedy machine, see Seymour Hersh, *The Dark Side of Camelot* (Boston, 1997), and James Hilty, *Robert Kennedy: Brother Protector* (Philadelphia, 2001), 144–45.

58. This charge of the break-in as a prelude to Watergate in 1972 is made by historian Robert Dallek, in *An Unfinished Life: John F. Kennedy, 1917-1963* (New York, 2003). For charges of collusion in promoting anti-Catholicism, see Shaun Casey, *The Making of a Catholic President: Kennedy vs. Nixon 1960* (New York, 2009).

59. The John Birch Society had come under widespread attack in the early 1960s in dozens of books and magazine articles. The campaign often linked regular Goldwater Republicans and mainstream conservatives such as William Buckley Jr. with white supremacist and armed militia organizations such as the Ku Klux Klan and Robert De Pugh's Minutemen. The most notable attack appeared in Arnold Forster and Benjamin R. Epstein, *Danger on the Right* (New York, 1964), one of the most widely read books among many published at this time. This book came out after the 1962 election, but it had been preceded by Richard Dudman, *Men of the Far Right* (New York, 1961); Murray Havens, *The American Ultras: The Extreme Right and the Military Industrial Complex* (New York, 1962); and Fred J. Cook, "The Ultras: Aims, Affiliations, and Finances of the Radical Right," *Nation,* June 23, 1961.

60. Gladwin Hill, *Dancing Bear: An Inside Look at California Politics* (Cleveland, OH, 1968); Schuparra, *Triumph of the Right*, 141–42.

Chapter 2

1. Richard Norton Smith, *On His Own Terms: A Life of Nelson Rockefeller* (New York, 2014), 619.

2. For Rockefeller's life, see Smith, *On His Own Terms*, on which I relied heavily for information about his political career; Cary Reich, *The Life of Nelson A. Rockefeller* (New York, 1996); James Desmond, *Nelson Rockefeller: A Political Biography* (New York, 1964); and Michael Kramer and Sam Roberts, *"I Never Wanted to Be Vice-President of Anything!" An Investigative Biography* (New York, 1976).

3. Reich, *Life of Nelson Rockefeller*, 47.

4. Quoted in ibid., 106.

5. The best studies of infighting within the American United Nations delegates are Ruth B. Russell, *A History of the United Nations: The Role of the United States, 1940-1945*, (Washington, DC, 1958); and Irwin Gellman, *Secret Affairs: FDR, Cordell Hull, and Sumner Welles* (Baltimore, 1995).

6. Darlene Rivas, *Missionary Capitalist: Nelson Rockefeller in Venezuela* (Chapel Hill, 2002).

7. Insight into the Eisenhower administration and Eisenhower-Rockefeller relations can be found in Emmet John Hughes, *The Ordeal of Power: A Political Memoir of the Eisenhower Years* (New York, 1975); and Robert J. Donovan, *Confidential Secretary: Ann Whitman's 20 Years with Eisenhower and Rockefeller* (New York, 1968).

8. See note 2.

9. Smith, *On His Own Terms*, 276–302.

10. Ibid., 310.

11. L. Judson Morhouse to Rockefeller, September 15, 1959, Nelson Rockefeller Papers, Rockefeller Archive Center, Sleepy Hollow, NY (hereafter Rockefeller Papers), Box 51, Folder 217.

12. Smith, *On His Own Terms*, 314–15.

13. Quoted in ibid., 387; and Desmond, *Nelson Rockefeller*, 212–59.

14. Smith, *On His Own Terms*, 330–40.

15. Quoted in Niall Ferguson, *Kissinger, 1923-1968: The Idealist* (New York, 2015), 446.

16. Quoted in Smith, *On His Own Terms*, 344.

17. Richard Nixon, *The Memoirs of Richard Nixon* (New York, 1979), 266.

18. "Transcript of the Vice President's Press Conference, July 23, 1960," Rockefeller Papers, Box 51, Folder 217; Smith, *On His Own Terms*, 345–47.

19. Quoted in Donald T. Critchlow, *The Conservative Ascendancy: How the Republican Right Rose to Power in Modern America* (Lawrence, KS, 2011), 52.

20. An excellent history of the 1960 campaign can be found in William Rorabaugh, *The Real Making of the President: Kennedy, Nixon and the 1960 Election* (Lawrence, KS, 2009).

21. Smith, *On His Own Terms*, 319, and for staff assessment of Rockefeller, 315.

22. Ibid., 322–23.

23. The Rockefeller-Murphy relationship is discussed in Smith, *On His Own Terms,* 328–29, 358–60, 375–79, 406–7.

24. Rockefeller's letter to Javits is quoted verbatim in George L. Hinman to Governor Nelson A. Rockefeller, August 10, 1962, Rockefeller Papers, Series J. 2, Box 20, Folder 118.

25. Quoted in Kramer and Roberts, *"I Never Wanted to Be Vice President of Anything!"* 145.

26. Gregory L Schneider, *Cadres of Conservatism* (New York, 1999), 46–47.

27. Kramer and Roberts, *"I Never Wanted to Be Vice President of Anything!"* 167.

28. Barry Goldwater to Nelson Rockefeller, November 17, 1961. Rockefeller Papers, Series J. 2, Box 20, Folder 118; and Smith, *On His Own Terms,* 357.

29. Quoted in Kramer and Roberts, *"I Never Wanted to Be Vice President of Anything!"* 267.

30. Barry Goldwater, *With No Apologies* (New York, 1980), 152.

31. Barry Goldwater to Nelson A. Rockefeller, February 5, 1963, Rockefeller Papers, Series J. 2, Box 20, Folder 114.

32. "A Bulletin from 1010Wins," June 8, 1963, Rockefeller Papers, Series J.2, Box 20, Folder 113.

33. For example, see Kent and Phoebe Courtney, *The Socialist Views of Nelson Rockefeller* (New Orleans, 1964).

34. Bob Douglass to Charles F. Moore Jr., January 16, 1964, Rockefeller Papers, Series J. 2, Box 20, Folder 114.

35. Quoted in Ferguson, *Kissinger,* 597.

36. George Hinman, Memorandum, April 27, 1962, Rockefeller Papers, Series J. 2, Box 20, Folder 118; and Peter O'Donnell Jr. to Goldwater State Chairmen, September 10, 1963, Rockefeller Papers, Series J.2, Box 20, Folder 114. The abundant material collected by the Rockefeller campaign about Goldwater is extensive. They collected transcripts of Goldwater interviews, press conferences, updates on campaign visits, and inside reports of confidential meetings. See, for example, G. L. Hinman, "Barry Goldwater—Chicago Group," January 25, 1963; and "Informant Advised GLH," January 14, 1963; "Memo—Barry Goldwater," September 17, 1962; Rockefeller Papers, Series J.2, Box 20, Folder 117; "Memo for the Files—Tennessee, December 23, 1962, Rockefeller Papers, Series J.2, Box 20, Folder 118.

37. G. L. Hinman to Governor Rockefeller, September 10, 1961, Rockefeller Papers, Series J.2, Box 20L, Folder 8; and G. L. Hinman, "Files," May 29, 1962, Rockefeller Papers, Series J.2., Box 20, Folder 118.

38. "Note for Files," Rockefeller Papers, Series J.2, Box 20, Folder 118.

39. Arthur M. Richardson, "Report on California," March 5, 1962, Rockefeller Papers, Series J.2, Box 20, Folder 266.

40. George Hinman, "California—No.2," February 26, 1962, Rockefeller Papers, Series J.2, Box 43, Folder 266.

41. George Hinman, "California," November 5, 1962, Rockefeller Papers, Series J. 2, Box 43, Folder 266.

42. Unknown author, "Memo for Nixon File," April 15, 1963, Rockefeller Papers, Series J.2, Box 43, Folder 266.

43. Bernard E. Chernin, Handwritten notes on news clipping, "Knight Ends Rockefeller '64 Nomination Drive," March 30, 1963; and Goodwin Knight to George Hinman, September 28, 1967, Rockefeller Papers, Series J.2, Box 31 Folder 186.

44. Quoted in Ferguson, *Kissinger,* 600–602.

45. Smith, *On His Own Terms,* 393.

46. Theodore H. White, *The Making of the President 1964* (New York, 2010); and J. William Middendorf II, *A Glorious Disaster: Barry Goldwater's Presidential Campaign and the Origins of the Conservative Movement* (New York, 2000).

47. Goldwater, *With No Apologies,* 175.

48. Ferguson, *Kissinger,* 603.

49. Goldwater, *With No Apologies,* 179.

50. Robert L. McManus, "Text of Remarks by Governor Nelson A. Rockefeller Prepared for Delivery Before Third Session of the 1964 Republican Convention, July 14, 1964." For full text, see "In Their Own Words," Rockefeller Archive Center, http://www.rockarch.org/inownwords/nar1964text.php.

51. Quoted in Ferguson, *Kissinger,* 605, 606.

52. Graham Molitor to Oscar Ruebhausen, June 27, 1968, Rockefeller Papers, Series J.3, Box 3, Folder 34.

53. Emmet Hughes to Nelson Rockefeller, May 19, 1968, Rockefeller Papers, Series J.3, Box 3, Folder 33; and "The Rockefeller Strategy: A Comprehensive Plan for Winning the 1968 Republican Nomination," April 16, 1968, Rockefeller Papers, Series J.3, Box 8, Folder 69.

54. "The Rockefeller Strategy: A Comprehensive Plan for Winning the 1968 Republican Nomination," April 16, 1968, Rockefeller Papers, Series J.3, Box 8, Folder 69.

55. For further insights into the Nixon campaign aside from standard memoirs and journalistic accounts, see Richard J. Whalen, *Catch the Fallen Flag: A Republican's Challenge to His Party* (New York, 1972); and Patrick Buchanan, *The Greatest Comeback: How Richard Nixon Rose from Defeat to Create the New Majority* (New York, 2014).

56. Carl Solberg, *Hubert Humphrey: A Biography* (New York, 1984), 351. See also Sheldon D. Englemayer and Robert J. Wagman, *Hubert Humphrey: The Man and His Dream* (New York, 1979).

57. Quoted in Ferguson, *Kissinger,* 245.

58. Tom Wicker, *A Time to Die: The Attica Prison Revolt* (New York, 2011).

59. Smith, *In His Own Terms,* 643.

60. Quoted in Kramer and Roberts, *"I Never Wanted to be Vice-President of Anything!"* 71.

61. An inside account of troubles within the Ford administration, told from a pro-Rockefeller and anti-Nixon point of view, is found in Robert T. Hartmann, *Palace Politics: An Inside Account of the Ford Years* (New York, 1980). See also Gerald R. Ford, *A Time to Heal: The Autobiography of Gerald R. Ford* (New York, 1970).

Chapter 3

1. Henry Kissinger, *Years of Renewal* (New York, 1999), 43.

2. Christopher Marlowe, *Doctor Faustus* (New York, 1968 ed.), 108.

3. William Shakespeare, *Henry IV, Part II,* Act 4, Scene 3.

4. David A. Nichols, *A Matter of Justice: Eisenhower and the Beginnings of the Civil Rights Revolution* (New York, 2007); and Robert F. Burk, *The Eisenhower Administration and Black Civil Rights* (Knoxville, TN, 1984). For a favorable view of Johnson's role in the passage of the Civil Rights Act of 1957, see Robert A. Caro, *The Passage of Power: The Years of Lyndon Johnson* (New York, 2013).

5. Byron E. Shafer and Richard Johnston, *The End of Southern Exceptionalism: Class, Race and Partisan Change in the Postwar South* (Cambridge, MA, 2009); Sean P. Cunningham, *American Politics in the Postwar Sunbelt: Conservative Growth in a Battleground Region* (New York, 2014); Carol Abbott, *The New Urban America: Growth and Politics in Sunbelt Cities* (Chapel Hill, NC, 1987); and Elizabeth Tandy Shermer, *Sunbelt Capitalism: Phoenix and the Transformation of American Politics* (Philadelphia, 2015).

6. Alan Petigny, *The Permissive Society: America, 1941-1965* (New York, 2009).

7. Richard Norton Smith, *On His Own Terms: A Life of Nelson Rockefeller* (New York, 2016). For an interesting essay on Rockefeller as a Social Gospel Christian, see Mark Tooley, "Nelson Rockefeller as a Social Gospel Christian," *First Things* (May 20, 2015).

8. Donald T. Critchlow, *Intended Consequences: Birth Control, Abortion, and the Federal Government in Modern America* (New York, 1999).

9. Cary Reich, *The Life of Nelson A. Rockefeller* (New York, 1996), 114.

10. For a differing view that Nixon appealed to the fears of voters, especially in 1968, see Rick Perlstein, *Nixonland: The Rise of a President and the Fracturing of America* (New York, 2009).

11. Herb Block, "Here He Comes Now," *Washington Post,* October 29, 1954.

Chapter 4

1. This point is made by Lee Edwards, *Goldwater: The Man Who Made a Revolution* (Washington, DC, 1995), 43. Historian Robert Alan Goldberg captures the man and the politician in *Barry Goldwater* (New Haven, CT, 1995), but for further insights see Barry M. Goldwater, *With No Apologies: The Personal and Political Memoirs of a United States Senator* (New York, 1979).

2. Dean Smith, *The Goldwaters of Arizona* (Flagstaff, AZ, 1986), 11. The following discussion of the Goldwater history and Barry Goldwater's childhood draws heavily from this informative family history. The history of the Goldwater family is detailed further in Goldberg, *Barry Goldwater.* Another useful source on the Goldwater family as well as Goldwater's political career before 1964 is Edwin McDowell, *Barry Goldwater: Portrait of an Arizonan* (Chicago, 1964).

3. Mark E. Pry, "Arizona and the Politics of Statehood, 1889–1912" (PhD dissertation, Arizona State University, 1995); and David R. Berman, *Politics, Labor and the War on Big Business: The Path of Reform in Arizona, 1890-1920* (Boulder, CO, 2012).

4. Goldberg, *Barry Goldwater,* 23–44, esp. 23.

5. Ibid., 54–55.

6. "Margaret "Peggy" Johnson Goldwater," *Arizona Women's Heritage Trail,* http:// www.womensheritagetrail.org/women/PeggyGoldwater.php; and Paul M. Steiner to Twin-

kle Thompson, January 29, January 28, 1976, Barry Goldwater Papers, Arizona State University, Tempe, Alpha Files.

7. "Comments of Jim O'Shea, President of Planned Parenthood of Central and Northern Arizona, 'An Evening with Peggy Goldwater and Friends,'" October 22, 1982, Planned Parenthood Collection, Arizona Historical Society Archives (hereafter AHSA), Box 16; "Margaret Sanger to Mrs. Heard," March 16, 1937, Planned Parenthood Collection, AHSA, Box 46.

8. Planned Parenthood Committee of Phoenix, "Fundraising Letter," February 1, 1960, Planned Parenthood Collection, AHSA, Box 17.

9. Planned Parenthood Association of Phoenix, "Annual Meeting," April 1966, Planned Parenthood Collection, AHSA, Box 17; Mrs. Elisabeth Gatov, "Organization Outline for Statewide Public Affairs Committee," n.d., Planned Parenthood Collection, AHSA, Box 16.

10. Mrs. Barry Goldwater and Rt. Rev. Joseph W. Hart, "1965 Campaign Letter," n.d., Planned Parenthood Collection, AHSA, Box 17.

11. Charles H. Percy to Mrs. Barry Goldwater, May 1, 1967, Planned Parenthood Collection, AHSA, Box 17.

12. "Population Awareness Week Proclamation," 1974, Planned Parenthood Collection, AHSA, Box 46.

13. "Abortion Resolution," October 30, 1969, Planned Parenthood Collection, AHSA, Box 17.

14. David R. Berman, *Parties and Elections in Arizona: 1863–1984* (Tempe, AZ, 1985); and Berman, *Arizona Politics and Government* (Lincoln, NE, 1998).

15. Stephen C. Shadegg, *Arizona Politics: The Struggle to End One-Party Rule* (Tempe, AZ, 1986).

16. Elizabeth Tandy Shermer, *Sunbelt Capitalism: Phoenix and the Transformation of American Politics* (Philadelphia, 2015).

17. Ferenc Morton Szasz, *Religion in the Modern American West* (Tucson, AZ, 2000), 169.

18. Phillip VanderMeer, *Desert Visions and the Making of Phoenix, 1860–2009* (Albuquerque, NM, 2010); and Shermer, *Sunbelt Capitalism*.

19. This discussion of the takeover of the Republican Party beginning with the Saratoga breakfast group is drawn from Shadegg, *Arizona Politics*.

20. Shadegg, *Arizona Politics*, 32.

21. James Elton McMillan Jr., *Ernest W. McFarland: Southwestern Progress—The United States Senate Years, 1940–52* (PhD dissertation, Arizona State University, 1990), 432.

22. Quoted in McDowell, *Barry Goldwater*, 95.

23. McMillan, "Ernest W. McFarland," 181.

24. Stephen Shadegg to Carl Hayden, December 10, 1950, Stephen Shadegg Papers, ASUL, Box 35, Folder 3.

25. The 1952 election is discussed in McMillan, "Ernest W. McFarland," 412–32; and Shadegg, *Arizona Politics*.

26. Goldwater, *With No Apologies,* 56.

27. Shadegg, *Arizona Politics,* 78–79.

28. Goldwater's relationship with McCarthy is explored by Goldberg, *Barry Goldwater,* 197–98.

29. Quoted in Irwin F. Gellman, *The President and the Apprentice: Eisenhower and Nixon, 1952-1961* (New Haven, CT, 2015), 112.

30. Eric Johnston to Ernest McFarland, November 6, 1952, in James E. McMillan, ed., *The Ernest W. McFarland Papers* (Prescott, AZ, 1995), 437–42.

31. Stephen Shadegg to Carl Hayden, January 5, 1953, Stephen Shadegg Papers, ASUL, Box 35, Folder 3.

32. Barry Goldwater to Dwight D. Eisenhower, March 23, 1956, Barry Goldwater Papers, ASUL, Alpha Files.

33. Shadegg, *Arizona Politics,* 113.

34. Goldberg, *Barry Goldwater,* 129–33; and Shadegg, *Arizona Politics,* 89–105.

35. Goldwater, *With No Apologies,* 23.

36. Historian Gregory L. Schneider, in *The Conservative Century: From Reaction to Revolution* (Latham, MD, 2009), accurately describes the early conservative movement as protean, contrary to many scholars who give greater ideological coherence and organized strategy to the movement. For the role of business in shaping the conservative movement, see Kim Phillips-Fein, *Invisible Hands: The Businessman's Crusade Against the New Deal* (New York, 2010); and Angus Burgin, *The Great Persuasion: Reinventing Free Markets Since the Great Depression* (Cambridge, MA, 2015). For an overstated case of right-wing nut involvement in the Republican Party, see Edward H. Miller, *Nut Country: Right-Wing Dallas and the Birth of the Southern Strategy* (Chicago, 2015). For an overview of the rise of conservatism in the Republican Party, see Donald T. Critchlow, *The Conservative Ascendancy: How the Republican Right Rose to Power in Modern America* (Lawrence, KS, 2011).

37. Clarence Manion's career is discussed in Robert A. Burns, *Being Catholic, Being American: The Notre Dame Story, 1934-52* (Notre Dame, IN, 2000). The Draft Goldwater Committee is discussed in detail in Donald T. Critchlow, *Conservative Ascendancy,* 39–56; Rick Perlstein, *Before the Storm: Barry Goldwater and the End of American Consensus* (New York, 2011); Goldberg, *Barry Goldwater*; and Lee Edwards, *Goldwater: The Man Who Made a Revolution* (Washington, DC, 1995).

38. Goldberg, *Goldwater,* 142.

39. Quoted in McDowell, *Barry Goldwater,* 24–25. John A. Andrew, *The Other Side of the Sixties: Young Americans for Freedom and the Rise of Conservative Politics* (New Brunswick, NJ, 1997), 48; and Perlstein, *Before the Storm,* 79.

40. Edwards, *Goldwater,* 134.

41. Goldwater, *With No Apologies,* 113.

42. Quoted in McDowell, *Barry Goldwater,* 26–27.

43. "Mr. Goldwater," *Congressional Record-Senate,* 110:II (Washington DC, 1964), 14,319.

44. Critchlow, *Conservative Ascendancy,* 69–75.

45. "Text of Scranton Letter to Goldwater," *Chicago Tribune,* July 14, 1964.

46. Goldwater, *With No Apologies,* 190.

47. Richard Nixon, *RN: The Memoirs of Richard Nixon* (New York, 1979), 323–24.

48. Goldwater, *With No Apologies,* 192–93.

49. Donald T. Critchlow, *When Hollywood Was Right: How Movie Stars, Studio Moguls, and Big Business Remade American Politics* (New York, 2013), 178–79.

50. Critchlow, *Conservative Ascendancy,* 145–46.

51. Edwards, *Goldwater,* 429.

Chapter 5

1. Anne Edwards, *Early Reagan: The Rise to Power* (New York, 1987).

2. Quoted in Edwards, *Early Reagan,* 57–58.

3. Donald T. Critchlow, *When Hollywood Was Right: How Movie Stars, Studio Moguls, and Big Business Remade American Politics* (New York, 2013); Kathryn Cramer Brownell, *Showbiz Politics: Hollywood in American Political Life* (Chapel Hill, 2014); and Steven Ross, *Hollywood Left and Right: How Movie Stats Shaped American Politics* (New York, 2012).

4. Critchlow, *When Hollywood Was Right,* 81–85. For a Marxist interpretation of the conflict, see Gerald Horne, *Class Struggle in Hollywood, 1930-1950* (Austin, TX, 2005).

5. Stephen Vaughn, "Ronald Reagan and the Struggle for Black Dignity in Cinema, 1937–1953," *Journal of African American History* (Winter 2002), 83–97, esp. 83.

6. Michael Nelson, *Resilient America: Electing Nixon in 1968, Channeling Dissent and Divided Government* (Lawrence, KS, 2014), 39.

7. H. A. Smith, Memorandum, Interview with Ronald Reagan, September 2, 1947, Records of the House Un-American Activities Committee, Executive Sessions, RG 253, Box 6, National Archives, Washington, DC.

8. U.S. Congress, *Hearing Before the Committee on Un-American Activities* (Washington, DC, 1947), 150, 207; and "Few Reds in Industry, Say Stars," *Hollywood Reporter,* October 24, 1947.

9. Quoted in Nelson, *Resilient America,* 48.

10. Critchlow, *When Hollywood Was Right,* 176–80.

11. Especially useful on Reagan involvement with General Electric is Thomas W. Evans, *The Education of Ronald Reagan: The General Electric Years and the Untold Story of His Conversion to Conservatism* (New York, 2006).

12. Quoted in F. Clifton White, *Why Reagan Won: A Narrative History of the Conservative Movement* (Chicago, 1981), 14–16; Matthew Dallek, *The Right Moment: Ronald Reagan's First Victory and the Decisive Turning Point in American Politics* (New York, 2000); and Critchlow, *When Hollywood Was Right,* 178.

13. Dallek, *Right Moment,* 66–67.

14. Ibid., 67.

15. Lou Cannon, *Governor Reagan: His Rise to Power* (New York, 2003), 133–48. Among other useful biographies of Reagan, see Iwan Morgan, *Reagan: America's Icon* (London, 2016); and Steven F. Hayward's two-volume *The Age of Reagan: The Fall of the Old Liberal Order, 1964-1980* (Roseville, CA, 2001).

16. For information on the 1966 governor's race, see Dallek, *Right Moment*; Critchlow, *When Hollywood Was Right,* 184–215; Cannon, *Governor Reagan,* 133–48.

17. Quoted in Cannon, *Governor Reagan*, 153.

18. Totton J. Anderson and Eugene C. Lee, "The 1966 Election in California," *Western Political Quarterly* (June 1967), 535–54; Kurt Schuparra, *Triumph of the Right: The Rise of the California Conservative Movement, 1945-66* (Cleveland, OH, 1968), 205–11.

19. Cannon, *Governor Reagan*, 184,

20. Ibid., 186.

21. Ibid., 194.

22. Quoted in ibid., 352–53.

23. Nelson, *Resilient America*, 29.

24. The 1968 campaign is astutely explored by Nelson, *Resilient America*.

25. Quoted in Nelson, *Resilient America*, 38

26. Quoted in Patrick Buchanan, *The Greatest Comeback: How Richard Nixon Rose from Defeat to Create the New Majority* (New York, 2016), 122–23.

27. Ibid., 60–66, 138–39.

28. Memorandum, June 8, 1966, "Nixon," Alpha File, Barry Goldwater Papers, Arizona State University Libraries (hereafter ASUL), Box 15.

29. Barry Goldwater to Richard Nixon, November 7, 1967; Goldwater to Nixon, January 5, 1968; and Goldwater to Thomas Reed, May 20, 1968, "Nixon," Alpha File, Barry Goldwater Papers, ASUL, Box 15.

30. Cannon, *Governor Reagan*, 265.

31. Quoted in Nelson, *Resilient America*, 144.

32. Quoted in ibid., 145; see also Lewis Gould, *1968: The Election That Changed America* (Chicago, 1993). The best book on the 1968 election remains Lewis Chester, Godfrey Hodgson, and Bruce Page, *An American Melodrama: The Presidential Campaign of 1968* (New York, 1969).

33. Buchanan, *Greatest Comeback*, 304–5.

34. Quoted in Nelson, *Resilient America*, 128.

35. Donald T. Critchlow, *Phyllis Schlafly and Grassroots Conservatism: A Woman's Crusade* (Princeton, 2005), 192.

36. Barry M. Goldwater, *With No Apologies: The Personal and Political Memoirs of a United States Senator* (New York, 1979), 278.

37. "Ronald Reagan Announcement for Presidential Candidacy, November 20, 1975," Ronald Reagan Presidential Library Archives, https://www.reagan.utexas.edu/archives /reference/11.20.75.html.

38. Craig Shirley, *Reagan's Revolution: The Untold Story of the Campaign That Started It All* (Nashville, TN, 2005).

39. Barry Goldwater to Efrem Zimbalist Jr., June 29, 1976, Ronald Reagan Series, Rosalind Kress Haley Collection, Eagle Forum Educational Foundation Archives, Clayton, Missouri.

40. Efrem Zimbalist Jr. to Barry Goldwater, July 15, 1976, Ronald Reagan Series, Rosalind Kress Haley Collection, Eagle Forum Educational Foundation Archives, Clayton, Missouri.

41. Barry Goldwater, Memo, May 4, 1976; Barry Goldwater to Nancy and Ron Reagan, May 13, 1976, "Reagan," Barry Goldwater Papers, ASUL, Alpha File, Box 15.

42. Barry Goldwater to Nancy and Ron Reagan, May 13, 1976; Ronald Reagan to Barry Goldwater, June 3, 1976, "Reagan," Barry Goldwater Papers, ASUL, Alpha File, Box 15.

43. Richard Cheney, Memorandum, November 13, 1975, Box 1, Richard Cheney Papers; and Foster Chanock, "Key Issue Differences," June 1976, Box 1, Foster Chanock Papers, Ford Presidential Library, Ann Arbor, Michigan.

44. Quoted in Hayward, *Age of Reagan*, 455.

45. Quoted in ibid., 503.

46. Barry Goldwater to Ronald Reagan, December 15, 1977; Ronald Reagan to Barry Goldwater, December 30, 1977; Barry Goldwater to Ronald Reagan, January 4, 1978; Ronald Reagan to Barry Goldwater, February 3, 1979; Barry Goldwater to Nancy Reagan, August 1, 1979; Barry Goldwater to Ronald Reagan, August 14, 1978; and Barry Goldwater to Ronald Reagan, August 17, 1978, "Reagan," Barry Goldwater Papers, ASUL, Alpha File, Box 15.

47. Goldwater, *With No Apologies,* 448.

48. Laura Kalman, *Right Star Rising: A New Politics, 1974–1980* (New York, 2010).

49. Ronald Reagan to Clymer L. Wright Jr., May 18, 1982, in *Reagan: A Life in Letters,* edited by Kiron Skinner et al. (New York, 2001), 555.

Chapter 6

1. Barry M. Goldwater with Jack Cassidy, *Goldwater* (New York, 1988), 375.

2. "Acceptance Address by Barry Goldwater, 1964 Republican National Convention, July 16, 1964," in Gerhard Peters and John T. Wooley, *American History Project*, http://presidency.ucsb.edu.

3. Lee Edwards, *Goldwater: The Man Who Made a Revolution* (Washington, DC, 1995), 368.

4. Barry Goldwater, "Memo," 1966, Barry Goldwater Papers, Arizona State University Libraries (hereafter ASUL), Alpha File.

5. Barry Goldwater, Memo, July 23, 1973, Barry Goldwater Papers, ASUL, Alpha Files, Box 15.

6. Barry Goldwater to William F. Buckley Jr., August 22, 1980, Barry Goldwater Papers, ASUL, Alpha Files, Box 2.

7. Barry Goldwater to John J. Rhodes, August 28, 1974, Barry Goldwater Papers, ASUL, Alpha Files, Box 19.

8. Barry Goldwater to Nelson Rockefeller, August 23, 1976, Barry Goldwater Papers, ASUL, Alpha Files, Box 12.

9. Barry Goldwater to Howard Baker, February 1, 1977, Barry Goldwater Papers, ASUL, Alpha Files, Box 2.

10. Barry Goldwater to George H. W. Bush, June 20, 1980, Barry Goldwater Papers, ASUL, Alpha Files, Box 2.

11. Goldwater, *Goldwater*, 388.

12. Ibid., 386–87.

13. Barry Goldwater to Pat Murphy, March 12, 1993, Barry Goldwater Papers, Alpha File, Box 11.

14. Discussion of Goldwater's prolife and progay activism can be found in Lloyd Grove, "Barry Goldwater's Left Turn," *Washington Post,* July 28, 1994; Barry Goldwater, "Ban on Gays Is Senseless Attempt to Stall the Inevitable," *Washington Post,* October 21 1992; "Right to Life Accuses Goldwater of Switching Position on Abortion," *Arizona Daily Star,* November 1, 1992; Glen Creno, "Goldwater: Abortion Stand May Hurt GOP," *Phoenix Gazette,* October 1, 1992; and Pat Murphy, "Arch-Conservatives Sore at Old Mr. Conservative," *Buffalo News,* December 28, 1992.

15. Ronald Reagan, *Where's the Rest of Me?* (New York, 1963), 36.

16. Christopher Jencks, *Rethinking Social Policy: Race, Poverty, and the Underclass* (New York, 1992), and *The Homeless* (New York, 1994).

17. Camp David Hard Wire 204-1, August 17, 1972, White House Tapes, Richard Nixon Presidential Library and Museum, Yorba Linda, California.

18. Ronald Reagan, "Address Before the San Antonio Chamber of Commerce and the Downtown Lions Club," February 21, 1962, in Bourke B. Hickenlooper Papers, Herbert Hoover Presidential Papers, Herbert Hoover Presidential Library and Museum, West Branch, Iowa, Box 50. Quoted in Donald T. Critchlow, *When Hollywood Was Right* (New York, 2013), 177.

Epilogue

1. Morris P. Fiorina et al., *Culture War? The Myth of a Polarized America* (New York, 2006); and Ronald Brownstein, *The Second Civil War: How Extreme Partisanship Has Paralyzed Washington and Polarized America* (New York, 2007). For a counterargument, see Alan I. Abramowitz, *The Disappearing Center: Engaged Citizens, Polarization and American Democracy* (New Haven, CT, 2010).

2. The one exception to ideologically driven voting is among African Americans who continue to vote overwhelmingly Democratic whether they identify themselves ideologically as liberal, moderate, or conservative.

3. See Adam Nekola, "Public Trust in Government: 1958–2014," *Pew Research Center,* November 13, 2014; and "75% See Widespread Government Corruption," *Gallup,* September [2014].

4. The figures themselves are startling. In a recent Gallup survey, confidence in the presidency—either "a great deal" or "quite a bit"—stood at 33 percent of those interviewed; the Supreme Court stood at 32 percent; and Congress, below 10 percent. "Confidence in Institutions," *Gallup Historical Trends* (2015).

5. Jeffrey Jones, "Confidence in U.S. Institutions Still Below Historical Norms," *Gallup,* June 15, 2015.

6. Tom Rosentiel, "Proud Patriots—Harsh Critics of Government," *Pew Research Center,* June 14, 2016.

7. Walter Lippmann, *Essays in the Public Philosophy* (1955; reprinted New Brunswick, NJ, 1989), 14, 96–97.

Index

Act of Chapultepec, 43
Agnew, Spiro, 59–60, 120–122
Aid to Families with Dependent Children
  (AFDC), 84–85, 90
Aiken, George, 30
Ailes, Roger, 117
Alger, Bruce, 97
American Veterans Committee, 140
Armed Forces Services Committee, 91
Attica State Prison riot, 61

Baker, Howard, 138
Baker, James, 5, 129, 131
Baroody, William, 101, 112
Bentley, Elizabeth, 26
Blackwell, Morton, 139
Bliss, Ray, 116
Bricker Amendment, 32, 92
Bricker, John W., 32
Brooks, Edward, 127
Brophy, Frank, 96
Brown, Edmund "Pat," 37, 98, 113–115
Buchanan, Patrick, 117, 120
Buckley, William F., 52, 94, 95, 111, 118, 120,
  136
Burch, Dean, 116
Bush, George H.W., 5, 127–129, 131, 138,
  145–146, 151
Bush, Prescott, 53, 69

California Citizens for Goldwater, 80, 111
California elections, 2, 13, 27–28, 34–37, 51,
  54–57, 75, 94–99, 111–115, 118–121
California Welfare Reform Act, 115
Carter, Jimmy, 10, 126–128, 145, 151
Case, Clifford, 123, 127
Chambers, Whittaker, 26
Cheney, Richard "Dick," 61
Chotiner, Murray, 23, 30–31

Christopher, George, 99, 113
Civil Rights Act, 32, 64, 98–99, 159
Cleveland, Grover, 45
Clinton, Bill, 146, 154
Cold War, 44, 63–64, 75, 95–96, 129, 134, 140,
  145, 151
Cold Warriors, 63–64
Compact of Fifth Avenue, 5, 50, 71, 97
Congress of Industrial Organizations Political
  Action Committee (CIO–PAC), 23
Consumer Protection Safety Commission, 128
crisis of democratic government, 154
Cronkite, Walter, 120, 137

Davis, Phil, 111
DeConcini, Dennis, 102
Dewey, John, 41
Dewey, Thomas, 2, 25, 27, 29–31, 45, 53, 121;
  Eastern wing, 29
Dole, Robert, 137
Donovan, Colonel William, 69
Douglas, Helen Gahagan, 27–28, 75, 109
Downey, Sheridan, 27–28
Draft Goldwater Committee, 95–96
"drain the swamp," 156
Dulles, John Foster, 44

Eisenhower–Khrushchev summit, 96
Eisenhower–Nixon ticket, 142–143
Eisenhower, Dwight D., 2, 10, 13, 29–34, 44,
  46, 48, 64, 70, 75–76, 89, 90–93, 100–101,
  103, 111, 142, 159
End Poverty in California (EPIC), 23, 27
English, Karan, 139
English Whig, 24
Environmental Protection Agency, 129

Falwell, Jerry, 102, 139
Federal Housing Administration, 90

Firestone, Leonard, 112
Ford, Gerald R., 2, 5, 61, 80, 102, 122–128, 131, 136–138, 144, 151
foreign policy hawks, 123
founders, 6–11, 157–158; view of character, 6–10; view of popular democracy, 157–158; view of principled pragmatism, 10–11
Frohmiller, Ana, 89

Gardner, John, 120
Goldwater, Barry, 1–5, 10–11, 37, 39, 50–59, 63, 65–67, 71–72, 79–103, 111–112, 116–120, 122, 124–127, 131–147, 149–152, 159–160; Americans Against Discrimination, 139; character, 103; compared to Reagan, 131–147; *Conscience of a Conservative*, 95, 112; Labor Relations Committee service, 91; Peggy Johnson, 83–84, 133; pro–gay rights, 139; pro-life, 138–139; "Suggested Declaration of Republican Principles," 96–97; Susan Wechsler, 139
Goldwater, Morris, 81, 93
Goldwater Department Store, 81–83
Grassroots conservatism, 2, 32, 36, 47, 53, 64–65, 76, 79, 95–96, 111, 116–117, 125, 132, 136–138, 144
Gregg, Hugh, 56

Haldeman, H. R., 144
"Ham and Eggs," 27
Harriman, W. Averell, 45–46, 55, 70
Hatfield, Mark, 118
Hayden, Carl, 86, 90, 91, 93, 102
Helms, Jesse, 126
Herter Committee, 24
Hinman, George, 45, 54–55
Hiss, Alger, 26, 44, 76
Hobby, Oveta Culp, 44
Hoover, Herbert, 27, 30
Hoover, J. Edgar, 26
Houck, L.R., 97
House Un–American Activities Committee (HUAC), 25, 26, 28, 109, 110
Hughes, Emmet, 49, 60
Hume, Jaquelin, 112
Humphrey, George, 44
Humphrey, Hubert, 35, 59, 109, 121, 159
Hunt, George W., 86
Hunt, H. L., 91 94

ideological polarization, 11, 105, 148–153

Jackson, Henry "Scoop," 123
Javits, Jacob, 52, 123, 136
John Birch Society, 36–37, 53–54, 57, 94, 113
Johnson, Lyndon B., 2, 15, 35, 49, 56, 64, 101, 117, 159

Kaiser, Leland, 112
Kennedy, Bobby, 117
Kennedy, Edward "Ted," 127
Kennedy, John F., 15, 24, 28, 35–36, 49–50, 56, 60, 71, 73, 98–99
Kennedy, Joseph, 28
Kissinger, Henry, 55, 57–62, 64, 77, 122–124, 136, 160
Kitchel, Denison, 84, 87, 101, 112
Knight, Goodwin "Goodie," 33, 35, 37, 55
Knott, Walter, 101, 112
Knowland, William, 27, 29, 32, 35, 94, 132
Kyl, Jon, 139

Labor Relations Committee, 91
Laxalt, Paul, 128
legislative compromise, 1, 132, 148–150
Lincoln School, 41
Lodge, Henry Cabot, Jr., 29, 49, 56, 97–99

Manion, Clarence, 95–96
Mathias, Charles, 123
McCarthy, Joseph, 33, 79, 90, 92, 135; censure, 92
McClellan, John, 91
McFarland, Ernest, 89, 90–94
McIntyre, Cardinal James Francis, 57
Miller, William E., 52, 100
Molitor, Graham, 59
Monson, Arch, Jr., 112
Moretti, Bob, 115
Morhouse, L. Judson, 47
Mundt, Karl, 26, 30

Namier, Lewis, 5–6
National Association for the Advancement of Colored People (NAACP), 98
National Review, 51–53, 94, 118
New Deal, 23, 65–66, 77, 79–80, 86, 94–95, 107, 140, 146, 151; coalition, 65, 146, 151; liberalism, 65, 79, 140; political order, 65
New Deal–Fair Deal, 28
Nixon–Agnew campaign, 121
Nixon, Richard, 13–37, 39, 46–52, 55–78, 80, 95–105, 109, 111, 113, 115–123, 131, 134–136, 138, 141–146, 149–152, 159–160; assessment of Reagan, 144; compared to

Rockefeller, 62–78; Family Assistance Plan, 115; "Great Train Robbery," 29; Pat Ryan, 21–23, 29, 31, 34, 74; *Six Crises*, 36
Northeastern Republicanism, 65

Occupational Safety and Health Administration, 128
Office of the Coordinator of Inter–American Affairs, 43

Panama Canal, 125–127, 136–137
Pearson, James B., 127
Percy, Charles, 49, 84–85
Phelps Dodge Corporation, 87
Planned Parenthood Federation of America, 83–85, 183
presidential elections, 9, 29, 148
Price, Raymond, 117
principled pragmatism, 10–11, 129, 148, 161
Pulliam, Eugene C., 91, 96
Pyle, J. Howard, 84, 89–93

Rand, Ayn, 95
RCA Building commission, 42
Reagan, Ronald, 1–5, 10–11, 25, 59, 65, 67, 77, 79–80, 101–130, 131–147, 149–152, 159–161; assessment of Goldwater, 119; character, 129–130, 141; compared to Goldwater, 131–147; Jane Wyman, 107–108, 110, 142; Nancy Davis, 110, 125–126, 140, 142; Social Security reform, 129, 145; "A Time for Choosing" speech, 111–112, 114
Republican in name only (RINO), 79, 104
Reuther, Walter, 91
Rhodes, John, 87, 91, 137
Rivera, Diego: RCA building mural controversy, 42–43
Rockefeller, Nelson, 1–5, 10–11, 35, 38–61, 62–78, 79, 80, 95–103, 105, 112, 116–122, 128, 134–137, 141, 144, 149–150, 152, 159–160; assessment of Nixon, 47, 117–118; character, 77; compared to Nixon, 62–78; Eastern wing, 94; Happy Murphy, 51, 53, 56–57, 69, 99; liberals, 97; Mary Todhunter Clark, 42
Rockefeller–Nixon agreement, 97
Rockefeller–Trilateral Commission, 127, 137
Roe v. Wade, 85, 128
Romney, George, 55–56, 100, 105, 116–117, 135
Roosevelt, Franklin D., 9, 35, 43–45, 69, 140
Rubel, A. C., 112
Ruebhausen, Oscar, 60

Rumsfeld, Donald, 61, 71
Rusher, William, 51–52

Safire, William, 117
Salvatori, Henry, 101, 111, 112
Schlafly, Phyllis, 118
Schreiber, Taft, 112
Schweiker, Richard, 126, 144, 150
Scranton, William, 56 100
Screen Actors Guild, 105–109, 140–142
Senate Select Committee on Improper Activities in Labor and Management, 91
Shadegg, Stephen C., 54, 90–91, 93, 96, 103
Shell, Joseph, 37, 111
Shorey, Greg, 97
Smith, Al, 45
Smith, Margaret Chase, 56
Smith, William French, 112
social egalitarianism, 73, 155
Spencer–Roberts firm, 112–113
Stassen, Harold, 27, 31, 33
Stettinius, Edward, 43, 70
Stevenson, Adlai, 30–31
Strategic Arms Limitation Treaty (SALT I and II), 64, 123, 138, 160
Sunbelt conservatism, 47, 65–66, 95, 150

Taft, Robert A., 2, 24, 29, 32, 64, 79, 90–91, 132; isolationists, 24, 29
Tammany Hall Democrats, 71
Tennessee Valley Authority (TVA), 96, 101
Thurmond, Strom, 120
Trilateral Commission, 127, 137
Truman, Harry, 27, 31, 44, 109, 140, 143; "The Truman Fair Deal," 89–90
Trump, Donald, 3, 156–157
Tuttle, Homes P., 111–114

Udall, Morris, 102
United Automobile Workers, 91
United Nations Organization, 44, 70, 91; Article 51, 44
Unruh, Jesse, 115

Vietnam War, 55, 56, 60, 64, 77, 101, 117, 118, 121, 123, 126, 137, 143, 150–152, 160
Viguerie, Richard, 139
Voorhis, Horace Jeremiah "Jerry," 22–23, 26

Wallace, George, 120–121
Wallace, Henry, 28
Warren, Earl, 27, 29, 33, 35

Watergate scandal, 2, 10, 35, 122, 136, 151–152, 159
Wead, Doug, 139
Weinberger, Caspar, 55, 114
Welch, Robert, 36, 94
Western conservatism, 4, 133
Weyrich, Paul, 139

White, F. Clifton, 53, 111, 116
Williams, Jack, 85

Young Americans for Freedom, 52, 111

Zimbalist Jr., Efrem, 124–125

Acknowledgments

With a little help from my friends, this book was made better than it would have been without their contributions. In particular, I thank William Rorabaugh, Irwin Gellman, and Greg Schneider, who read an early draft of the manuscript, and the anonymous reader for the press—who later revealed himself as Vincent Cannato—who read the penultimate and final manuscript. My wife, Patricia Critchlow, proofread many drafts of the entire manuscript, a task well beyond the duties of a partner.

Robert Lockhart, my editor at the press, contributed immensely to the final product, reading and rereading drafts. His eye for narrative, word usage, and argument revealed his well-deserved reputation as one of the best editors in the business.

A number of people helped with research on this book. Cody Bendix and Johnny Cornell helped with research in the Barry Goldwater Papers at Arizona State University, while Mikaela Colby undertook research in the Phoenix Planned Parenthood Collection located at the Arizona Historical Society in Phoenix. Patricia Critchlow and her sister Rosemary Powers took a ten-day trip to conduct research in the Nelson Rockefeller Papers at the Rockefeller Archive Center in Pocantico Hills, New York, where they found an excellent and helpful archives staff.

The American academy is far different today than when I began my career too many decades ago to count. Humanities were the soul and the pride of most universities and colleges when I got my first tenure-track job at the University of Notre Dame. Since then the humanities field has fallen on hard times, as higher education has become increasingly corporatized and many students less interested in the arts and letters. Arizona State University is at the forefront of the New American University. As the university looks to the future, my colleagues in History keep the rich fabric of our human past alive for our students, fellow scholars, and the larger public. This commitment expressed itself in a willingness to discuss and offer varying degrees of advice on this project; my appreciation in this regard goes to Jonathan Barth, Daniel Strand, Mauricio Suchowlansky, Kent Wright, Catherine O'Donnell, Calvin Schermerhorn, Matt Garcia, and Roxane Barwick (who also indexed the book). These colleagues represent what the academy and a learned community of scholars and staff should be in the ideal and in actuality.